Understanding Multimodal Discourses in English Language Teaching Textbooks

Also Available from Bloomsbury

Interpersonal Meaning in Multimodal English Textbooks, *Yumin Chen*
Identity, Motivation, and Multilingual Education in Asian Contexts,
Mark Feng Teng and Wang Lixun
Language Learning Strategies and Individual Learner Characteristics, *edited by*
Rebecca L. Oxford and Carmen M. Amerstorfer
What Makes Writing Academic, *Julia Molinari*
Researching Language Learning Motivation, *edited by*
Ali H. Al-Hoorie and Fruzsina Szabó
The Value of English in Global Mobility and Higher Education,
Manuela Vida-Mannl
Teaching Pragmatics and Instructed Second Language Learning,
Nicola Halenko
Social Networks in Language Learning and Language Teaching, *edited by*
Avary Carhill-Poza and Naomi Kurata
The Sociopolitics of English Language Testing, *edited by*
Seyyed-Abdolhamid Mirhosseini and Peter I. De Costa
Content Knowledge in English Language Teacher Education, *edited by*
Darío Luis Banegas

Understanding Multimodal Discourses in English Language Teaching Textbooks

Implications for Students and Practitioners

Christopher A. Smith

BLOOMSBURY ACADEMIC
LONDON • NEW YORK • OXFORD • NEW DELHI • SYDNEY

BLOOMSBURY ACADEMIC
Bloomsbury Publishing Plc
50 Bedford Square, London, WC1B 3DP, UK
1385 Broadway, New York, NY 10018, USA
29 Earlsfort Terrace, Dublin 2, Ireland

BLOOMSBURY, BLOOMSBURY ACADEMIC and the Diana logo are
trademarks of Bloomsbury Publishing Plc

First published in Great Britain 2022
Paperback edition published 2024

A catalogue record for this book is available from the British Library.

A catalog record for this book is available from the Library of Congress.

ISBN: HB: 978-1-3502-5695-8
PB: 978-1-3502-5699-6
ePDF: 978-1-3502-5696-5
eBook: 978-1-3502-5697-2

Typeset by Deanta Global Publishing Services, Chennai, India

To find out more about our authors and books visit www.bloomsbury.com and
sign up for our newsletters.

For Keumhwa, Alexander, Claire,
Doris, Wesley, Se-jin and Bok-gi

Contents

Illustrations

Figures

Tables

Preface

When I was a kid, growing up in the 1970s and 1980s and going to school in Ontario, Canada, I was always fascinated by the textbooks that I would receive at the beginning of each school year. Those (sometimes) weighty, glossy, unmarred tomes with uncracked bindings promised all sorts of insights just waiting to be discovered. In Grade 5, I remember, quite vividly, receiving my science textbook for that year. Our teacher reverentially pulled each one from a freshly opened box at the front of the class, then walked up and down the aisles as he placed each one on our desks. I recall, noting with great pleasure, a detailed illustration of the earth floating in space but sliced in such a way to make it appear as if a one-quarter chunk of its bulk were removed, so that the reader could see all the successive layers that composed the earth, right down to the fiery, orange, magma core. Above the illustration, in blockbuster font, the featured title 'NATURAL SCIENCES' promised epic revelations of understanding. From that innocent time in my life, I've always been fascinated with school textbooks because I wondered who were deemed masterful enough in knowledge to compose such compendiums? Furthermore, I wondered who the illustrators and photographers were? And who chose them to contribute their craft to these masterfully designed volumes of knowledge for students young and old?

At that time, I did not understand or know or have any inkling about 'multimodal discourses'. To be honest, I didn't really know what multimodal discourses were even ten years ago. However, I recall Gunther Kress (1940–2019), the much-admired semiotician, speaking about changes in perceptions of discourses, noting that 'the world once read is now the world seen'. At risk of appearing to rhyme, I believe *the world seen* has always *been*. In fact, I have been seeing it for an exceptionally long time – most of my life, to be precise. I just didn't know that *what I was seeing* I was also *reading*. Speech and text have always been the providence of meaning-making, but now *the world seen* is included. Rooted in the imagination of that little boy, fascinated with his Grade 5 textbook of Natural Sciences, this book not only shares insights and methods for *reading* English language learning textbooks but presents an exploration of how those multimodal discourses are presented, negotiated and valued by students and practitioners.

– Christopher A. Smith, PhD

Foreword

Textbooks belong to our experiences of formal education as much as grades, sitting at desks or counting down the minutes to recess. Despite the digitalization of all domains of life over the last twenty years, students in most parts of the world still learn from textbooks – though they may be glossier than fifty years ago, and learners may access them on their computers or tablets rather than hold them in physical form. Guided by national and increasingly global curricular trends, textbooks represent a curated selection of what counts as legitimate knowledge within a particular subject field. Yet precisely because of this element of selection, textbooks can never be simply seen as neutral repositories of universally agreed-upon knowledge, skills or competencies; they are the result of values-based decision-making.

The selective and ideological nature of textbooks' content as legitimate knowledge is pushed into public consciousness every time a controversy emerges surrounding how textbooks deal with a particular topic. History and social studies textbooks are notorious for being the subject of such controversies. News reports just in the last few years from the United States, Japan, Korea or Hungary have drawn attention to how political as well as commercial interests shape the version of history students' encounter in textbooks, resulting in often blatantly false and biased accounts of events. Yet the same biases and selective vision are applied to other school subjects as well, though the result and thus the significance of this selective vision may not be as easily discernible as in the case of history.

It is precisely for this reason that applied linguists have for decades now critically examined language textbooks, generating a rich body of work on the imprint and impact of curricular selections in language textbooks on language learning and learners. These studies have questioned the possibility of ideologically neutral language learning, which presumes that languages are simply a tool of communication, and mastery involves the co-deployment of grammatically correct form for a pragmatically appropriate function. Instead, scholars and educators now recognize that language cannot be separated from its context of use, that social and cultural considerations underscore the very options available to speakers in grammar and vocabulary, and that this has implications for what and how is presented to learners in a textbook and in lessons.

These insights are perhaps most acutely felt in the case of English, given its salient place in the global communication landscape and in the global language education marketplace. Yet precisely because English has become a global lingua franca, spoken by and among people who might never have physically visited countries where English is the dominant language, some crucial questions arise for language educators in general and textbooks in particular. Provided that textbooks curate a version of English, and the English-speaking world, for learners' engagement, whose world(s) should EFL textbooks portray? If we accept that learning a language is a process of socialization into accepted/ acceptable ways of thinking, seeing and feeling and being, what or whose values and standards should guide the selection of forms and functions of language that learners encounter in their textbook? At its most basic, for instance, what kind of English(es) does the textbook introduce and endorse? The 'accent-free', monolingual, scholastic kind which is still the basis for national or international gatekeeping language exams, or the kind that one hears practically everywhere else?

These questions naturally evoke further considerations which stem from textbooks' didactic character and attend to its pedagogical aim: What should language learners do with the portrayed world of English and the variety being presented as legitimate? How should they engage with it? Is the pedagogical focus on the acquisition of linguistic form, perhaps with additional 'cultural vignettes', as explicit knowledge to absorb? Are learners invited to learn English along with a critical-reflexive stance which questions the very world being opened up through their developing linguistic mastery? Of course, the answers to these questions depend largely on exactly what considerations have guided the selection of textbook material and design. And as research has shown and as scholars have argued, in the case of global commercial EFL publishing, the primacy of profit dictates that linguistic-visual content and pedagogical approach remain conservative, eschewing social problems or controversial-critical perspectives in favour of safe topics and a visually appealing, consumer-friendly world.

This is precisely the starting point and point of contention for the present book. Situating his work within the field of critical applied linguistics and drawing on an impressive array of contemporary theories of language, curriculum and pedagogy, the author sets out with an ambitious agenda: to develop a framework that locates and examines the EFL textbook within a complex web of relations.

As the author rightfully argues, the world offered up by textbooks must be investigated critically, but the results of that investigation must be placed within the ecology of English education characterizing the teaching context. While the textbook may be the centre around which teaching and learning pivot, broader questions of culture and curriculum shape how EFL textbooks are selected and how they will be used in the classroom. Critical studies must therefore not only target the text, because the ideological impact of text is mediated (as the author puts it) 'in mind' as well as 'in class'; in other words, it is shaped by how teachers and students perceive English education and how they negotiate the visual and textual discourses of the textbook during actual instances of classroom learning. In fact, as the data and analyses in this book aptly illustrate, despite the deeply inner-circle dominant linguistic-cultural perspective of the textbook under scrutiny, its users are not merely passive consumers; students voice *dis*trust and cultural irrelevance, and teachers exercise autonomy in mixing and matching the textbook with their own supplements and materials, and deviate from and critique its content when it does not align with their professional beliefs. In short, and in line with the central theme of the book, textbooks remain crucial components of EFL education in many parts of the world, but we need to account for the complex ways in which textbooks interact with those who use them and how that interaction in turn is shaped by larger contextual factors concerning the what, why and how of foreign language education.

Understanding Multimodal Discourses in English Language Teaching Textbooks fills important gaps in our understanding of the place of language teaching materials within ecologies of language learning. First and foremost, it is one of perhaps only a handful of studies that combines critical analysis of textbooks with an explicit exploration of their in-situ use as well as users' perceptions and attitudes towards the textbook. Second, its incorporation of multimodality as a key conceptual and analytic component underscores the need for researchers to account for language learning as meaning-making (both as text and in situ) through multiple semiotic modalities. Third, the book has a strong pedagogic angle and offers practical heuristics for language educators, who wish to research and understand textbooks and their use in classrooms in a systematic way. Textbooks, especially EFL textbooks, are here to stay – and this book takes important steps towards empowering teachers to be critical users of textbooks.

Csilla Weninger
National Institute of Education
Nanyang Technological University
Singapore

Acknowledgements

The author would like to acknowledge the support from colleagues in the field of critical discourse studies, curriculum studies and studies of language learning textbooks, especially Dr Jaffer Sheyholislami, Dr Janna Fox and Dr Csilla Weninger for her generosity in writing the foreword for this book.

Thanks to friends and colleagues in Korea (Dale Marcelle and Audwin Wilkinson), who graciously permitted my participation in their university classes for research towards the completion of this book. Thank you for years of friendship and support on this journey.

Many thanks to the commissioning editors and staff at Bloomsbury (Academic) Publishing for this opportunity and for helping see this project come to fruition.

Finally, I am ever thankful to my wife, Keumhwa Jung, without whose spark I would not have risen from ashes in a faraway land nor rekindled my love of reading and writing. Thank you for your limitless patience and unwavering commitment to our life together.

Introduction

Global Perspectives of English Language Learning

All languages are rooted in their cultures and social realities, so we can assume that English as a second language (ESL) (English is the L1 where the instruction occurs) or English as a foreign language (EFL) (English is not the L1 where the instruction occurs) is taught along with cultural values primarily sourced in inner-circle[1] nations, such as the United States or the United Kingdom. In this book, we highlight *the textbook* as a perennially unchallenged vehicle in the consumption of certain cultural values in English education. Furthermore, the phrase 'English language teaching (ELT) textbook' serves as a broad-sweeping label for books widely published by British or American institutions for global ESL/EFL markets.

While much research attention has been given to ELT textbooks, which we will explore, few studies investigate their multimodal discourses and what power relations and ideologies they project, how the various modes of meaning-making in colour, iconography, size and shape, to name only a few semiotic resources, are delivered and what, exactly, is being interpreted by teachers in the classroom or in the process of a course of English study and the ways it is negotiated with or received/interpreted by students. This book investigates a triangulation of these observations: What are the power relations and ideologies in the multimodal discourses of an ELT textbook? How are the English lessons taught in expanding-circle classrooms? How do students and practitioners value the multimodal discourses and that negotiated process? While this book features vignettes that explore the analysis, use and perceived value of an ELT textbook in Korean EFL contexts, it has implications, both academic and practical, for the larger, expanded-circle category of nations and regions, such as China, Japan, Russian, the Middle East, Africa, and South and Latin America. As noted in the forthcoming discussion, the learning of English, for which globally published ELT textbooks are often a compulsory investiture, is connected to upward socio-economic mobility in many of these nations. Therefore, we assume that Korean contexts resonate with many others.

Although this book underscores a methodological exploration about English language teaching textbooks and the negotiation of their multimodal discourses, it is important to set the stage by taking a closer look at global eventualities that shaped the current state of English language learning. There is little doubt that English continues to be the preferred *additional, second* and/or *foreign* (depending on one's geopolitical or socio-economic positioning) language to learn in the world today. That worldly preference is tightly connected with English's status as a global language. For Crystal (2003), the status of a 'global language' is achieved when it becomes socially, politically or economically consequential to every nation around the world. In the case of the English language, for some countries, it has become a symbol of upward socio-economic mobility (Pennycook & Candlin, 2017) and a recognizable commodity as a prestigious medium for communication and trade (Rubdy & Tan, 2008). For others, English has been and continues to be a vehicle for domination (i.e. Phillipson, 2012).

A global language doesn't just *sorta kinda happen*, as some might argue – it is not a natural process. Some have tried to summarize the process of how the English language achieved the status of a global language in the last few hundred years by noting the combined effects of British naval might of the nineteenth century, allowing for British Imperial colonization and the consolidation of international trade, followed by the rise of the American military–industrial complex of the twentieth century as key reasons (i.e. Burchfield, 1994; Crystal, 2003; Bailey et al., 1986).

While Crystal (2003) has argued that the growth and popularity of English was and continues to be an unplanned phenomenon without any intervention, Graddol et al. (2020) invoke contradictory views that contend that simplification. Although colonization may have sown the seeds for the global spread of English, the latter part of the twentieth century witnessed technological and communicative innovation, and evolution weaved among very specific geo-historical and sociocultural eventualities that spawned multiple English variations. In other words, it is not so simple as it has been theorized to label English as a *global language* as a result of a series of unplanned or coincidental phenomena. A global language may not be achieved solely through its characteristics or as a medium for great literature, or its association with cultural communities, rather it becomes global because of the political and military power of its people and that society's stable economic robustness to maintain it (Crystal, 2003). However, McCrum (2011) believes the maintenance to which Crystal (2003) refers is diachronic and argues that languages have evolved much like we have, changing slowly over many generations in a process that may currently be (linguistically) infantile. Furthermore, while the spread of English may have been born from imperialist engagements, it is also an adaptable language, welcoming to change from its Anglo-Saxon roots on up (McCrum, 2011).

Whatever the case may be, one-fifth of the world's population are English speakers, categorized as native, second language or foreign language speakers (Pennycook & Candlin, 2017) and that percentage continues to rise. While the debates on the beneficial and negative consequences (i.e. Phillipson, 2012) of English as a global language continue, there is no doubt that English education relates to upward socio-economic mobility in many developing countries around the world. It is not an abstract entity (Kuteeva, 2020) nor is it separated, as some believe, from its users and uses (Hall et al., 2017). It is a medium through which one tunes and raises their voice to participate in the discourse of the powerful (Pennycook & Candlin, 2017). Resonance with power and domination marks English as worthy of rigorous attention by applied linguists to ask where, when, why and how it is used, and by whom. By extension, in English language education, whether ESL or EFL, we should be equally compelled to ask where, when, why and how it is taught, and by whom.

Kuteeva (2020) reminds us that many of Pennycook's (1994) questions about social unfairness and language learning require continued investigation because they were re-explored in a 2017 edition. A critical stance should be maintained by contemporary scholars raising concerns about teaching practices, institutional politics, etc. because English language learning is used as a medium for the promotion of diversity and cosmopolitan ideologies (Kuteeva, 2020). A measure of vigilance is necessary for identifying how power manifests in such apparently progressive veneers because the complex constructions surrounding English as a global language, a lingua franca, a cultural commodity or as an academic subject create fluid, insidious affordances for dominant discourses.

The Call of English Language Teaching – The Author's Personal Reflection

In 1994, after a sojourn with the Ontario College of Art and Design University (Toronto, Canada) in their Florence (Italy) campus to complete undergraduate studies in fine arts, I became an English teacher. If you need a moment to read the previous sentence again, I'll wait. The point is that not all English teachers are born and ready to do so – for some, it just happens. In my case, after failed attempts to get regular work in Toronto, I got an ESL certificate and headed to Korea. At the time, common advertisements for teaching in Asia filled classified sections of many newspapers (yes, they existed back then), such as: 'All you need is a degree to teach English abroad! Come, work and Play!' I feel compelled to note that the Teaching English as a Second Language (TESL) certificate that I got from a local college in Toronto at that time was being offered alongside CPR training and cooking classes. Some people took all three.

In Korea, the private academy that hired me specialized in children's English classes. The pedagogical theory informing that academy's curriculum was quite simple: put a native English speaker in the same room as some children and hope that English learning/acquisition *happens.* After a week of jet lag and some career confusion, I met with the academy director to ask for guidance. As a classically trained artist, I felt, perhaps, that I was not the right fit for teaching English to children. The language academy's director, whose qualification for the position was a degree in economics, noted that all I had to do was follow the textbook. Step by step, much like the ominous litany that one so often hears about contemporary air travel – *the planes practically fly themselves* – he advised that I let the textbook lessons do all work. 'Just conversations with them!' He advised, cheerfully ignoring the 'be' verb. At that moment, my interest in the power and institutional endorsement of English language teaching textbooks was sparked.

A few years later, I was teaching university courses in Korea. Twice each year, between 1999 and 2014, a new cohort of fresh, nervous, excited, exhausted, apprehensive but overall friendly, young Korean faces greeted my entrance into their university EFL classrooms. For my courses, all students were required (not by me) to purchase costly, *high-quality* English language learning textbooks, carefully chosen for each course by non-specialist, institutional stakeholders for their recognizable prestige and appearance. As a native-English-speaking English instructor, I was expected to masterfully negotiate the contents of those shiny, new textbooks that they may be regarded as a necessary investiture at the end of every semester. Today, this scenario continues to unfold in the first week of freshmen classes because all university students across Korea must complete a basic *English communication* course to meet the requirements of any undergraduate degree programme (Haggerty & Fox, 2016; KICE, 2001).

Looking back at my sojourn as an English instructor in Asia, I recall feeling fortunate to be counted among the 'qualified', native-English-speaking foreigners banking on the need for English education in Asia and only moderately guilty that my major was Fine Art. To underpin that curious misalignment of expertise, over many years of friendship, a Korean colleague frequently noted how fortunate I was to be a native English speaker because that minimum qualification appeared adequate for a fine arts university major to teach English. At that time in Korea, many insufficiencies in an English teaching candidate's background and qualifications were often overlooked because the need for *any* kind of English education was in such demand that perplexed fine artists (such as I) found themselves instructing children 'ABC's' in Seoul. To that point, a common joke among expatriates in Korea at that time considered sufficient qualification to teach English as (a) being a native English speaker with any BA degree, (b) standing upright (most of the time) and (c) having a pulse. Fortunately, by the time I was teaching at university programmes in 1999, *sensible* English education policies were beginning to see implementation nationwide and strictly enforced (such as actual training in foreign language education pedagogy).

The Importance of Research in ELT Textbooks – Korean and Global Perspectives

Despite the Korean government's efforts to reform English education, course textbooks remained unchanged and ever-more costly necessities for each student to bear (literally and financially). Year after year, new editions of globally published EFL textbooks, with online components and supplemental multimedia packages, all wrapped in newly designed covers, promise new levels of academic excellence with every purchase (Bell & Gower, 2011). The author shamefully admits to once ordering 450 copies of *New Interchange 3: Student Book* (Richards et al., 1994) for their university bookstore because it came with several free *teacher's samples* of ELT student books available in the Cambridge University Press catalogue that year.

Trained instructors in Korea at that time were in high demand because they knew some of the curricular commonplaces (Null, 2016) of EFL in Korean contexts and listened to their own beliefs, assumptions and knowledge (BAK) about teaching (Woods, 1996; Smith, 2021). Therefore, it is not surprising that a culture of textbook reliance increased among poorly trained instructors, who placed too much emphasis on textbooks that were likely chosen for them by uninformed administrative staff. In other words, by blindly following globally published ELT publication packages, students and teachers may have contributed to a *McDonaldized* culture of trust in their textbooks (Littlejohn, 2012), where the hallmarks of that fast-food brand, such as predictability, efficiency, calculability and control (Franklin, 2003, 2005), are evident in their contents. *McDonaldization* (i.e. Ritzer, 1993) and its connection with ELT textbook consumption (i.e. Littlejohn, 2012) will be explored in more depth in the following chapter.

Generally, a textbook in the hand of a student or a teacher is a tactile promise of knowledge. Some measure of trust, solicited from the student in reflection of the trust afforded their teacher, extends to the textbook (Gray, 2010; Harwood, 2014). ELT textbooks, therefore, while likely representing a physical link between the student and their teacher, may also be a kind of educational tender for linguistic services, simultaneously manifested as a guide to the course curriculum and a vehicle for an instructor's pedagogical vision (Apple & Apple, 2018). However, textbooks can also convey content that is given legitimacy because of its promissory nature tendered by the teacher or the institution (Pennycook & Candlin, 2017; Shin & Crookes, 2005; Xiong, 2012). Sometimes textbooks are the only sources of reading for EFL students, especially in Korea (Choi, 2008; KICE, 2001; Lee, 2011). Considering the lack of choices, Curdt-Christiansen and Weninger (2015) remind us textbooks proffered to students in those situations are afforded the distinction of 'authorized official texts' (p. 4) promoting or diminishing certain cultural values and ideologies (p. 4). Hence, the haphazard delivery of textbook content inspires questioning because that can reveal their ideological systems as they relate 'to the broader social order and structure' (Curdt-Christiansen & Weninger, 2015, p. 3). Those social structures can emerge in an EFL textbook's multimodal content as constructed legitimations of *us* and *them* (or *others*) (Curdt-Christiansen & Weninger, 2015) and appear to associate the intended audiences of these textbooks with the latter (Lee, 2011; Song, 2013).

In the term 'multimodality', which we will explore in more depth in the next few chapters, mode refers to a means for making meaning, such as speech, writing, image, sound or colour, so multimodality refers to people using multiple means of meaning-making (Jewitt et al., 2016; Kress & Van Leeuwen, 2006; Norris, 2019). For now, it is important to keep in mind that multimodality is a semiotic and diachronic system of meaning-making beyond the limitations of text that reflect the changing world of communication, drastically elevated with the birth of digital formats and tuned to the vibrations of technological innovation (Machin & Mayr, 2012; Kress, 2010).

In the context of this book, globalization has contributed to new multicultural ecologies (Curdt-Christiansen & Weninger, 2015), so the continuous examination of textbooks is required to keep abreast of sociolinguistic evolvements in English education. Considering the influx of untrained educators in Korea, for example, more common in the past, textbooks likely replaced their instructor's inadequacies and continue to do so because the *culture of trust* in textbooks appears firmly planted in that pedagogical culture. For many EFL students, their textbook represents a key component providing them and their teachers with the necessary, material reference for linguistic inquiry while encouraging learner practice and communicative interaction (Lee, 2011; Richards, 2014; Song, 2013; Tomlinson, 2011). Perhaps this is the reason why so many of those textbooks, marketed to EFL students thirsty for useful lessons, continue to outsell the most wildly popular bestsellers of fiction (Littlejohn, 2012).

To understand how trust in textbook contents might impact ELT, attention is especially given to materials that the author has used and, perhaps more importantly, trusted over many years. Also, we keep in mind that while many of the most popular ELT textbooks are published in the form of multimedia packages, including supplemental online components of audio/visual materials, workbooks and associated websites with instructor guidebooks and downloadable documents for classroom activities (Brown, 2011; Gray, 2010; Harwood, 2014; Littlejohn, 2012), most still underscore and promote the core student book that is most referenced in English language learning classrooms because 'very little seems to have changed in the way that languages are typically taught and learned' (Tomlinson & Masuhara, 2017, p. 8).

In this book, the term 'ELT textbook' refers to those texts widely published by British or American institutions and organizations for global EFL markets. While current studies of ideology in the discourse of ELT textbooks continue to draw critical research attention (i.e. Liu, 2020; Xiang & Yenika-Agbaw, 2021), research looking at their multimodal discourses remains somewhat limited (Curdt-Christiansen & Weninger, 2015), even if it has received a marginal increase in research attention over the last few years (Smith, 2021). For this reason, this book seeks clarification of what pedagogical implications arise from the negotiation of the multimodal discourse in a popular ELT publication. To accomplish this, the book offers frameworks for (a) a multimodal critical discourse study (MCDS) because it appears to be the most viable tool for dissecting dominant visual and textual narratives in content, (b) observing how the textbook's multimodal content is negotiated by instructors and students during classroom consumption and (c) establishing how students and instructors account for the content. Hopefully, this book will give credence to the perspectives of three different ELT textbook consumers – the researcher(s) (the author is a former instructor), current instructors and students. Triangulating critical data in this way may provide a more a rigorous accounting of the multimodal content in a popular textbook publication than in previous explorations and from that richer harvest of data, pedagogical implications may become more evident.

This book is expected to contribute to a broadening field of critical discourse studies (van Dijk, 2011; Wodak & Meyer, 2016) in EFL education, where teachers and students are no longer positioned as senders/receivers of carefully constructed linguistic components via textbooks but as social actors endeavouring to translate, deliver, negotiate and consume meanings beyond those linguistic forms. Embracing the presumption that all texts (including EFL textbooks) are ideological in nature (Fairclough, 1992, 2013; van Dijk, 1993, 2011; Wodak & Meyer, 2016), those meanings can manifest as dominant and culturally marginalizing narratives that EFL students consume without questioning (Canagarajah, 1993, 2006; Song, 2013; Smith, 2021). By engaging in a novel approach to multimodal critical discourse studies and multimodal interactional analysis to expose those narratives as they appear in isolation and in situ, this book hopefully inspires more considered delivery and consumption of its multimodal discourse in EFL education.

Design and Structure of the Book

The design and structure of this book are rooted in the following questions: What are the power relations and ideologies in the multimodal discourse of a globally published ELT textbook? How do instructors and students negotiate and account for the multimodal discourses of a globally published ELT textbook in class? What pedagogical implications emerge from the triangulated findings of a multimodal critical discourse study of an ELT textbook, on the one hand, and its negotiated discourses and values by the consumers, on the other, about EFL learning and textbook consumption?

The first question underpins a multimodal critical discourse study of the multimodal content in an ELT textbook. By revealing how the world of English (Cortez, 2008) is presented to non-English-speaking students in a global publication, we may begin to see a picture of the power relations and ideologies in the content and anticipate what pedagogical consequences they predicate for classroom negotiations. The second question draws attention to the findings in the first question by asking how such content may be negotiated in action (Littlejohn, 1992) or in situ (Smith, 2021; Wohlwend, 2011). In other words, how do students relate to the multimodal content? Does the content inspire them to achieve greater English proficiency or demotivate learning? Do the students appear to resist or subscribe to the content? As for the instructors: How are they presenting the power relations and ideologies in the multimodal content? Are they resisting, transforming, appropriating or neutralizing (Cortez, 2008) any of the multimodal content in classroom negotiations? Finally, after a critical accounting of the power relations and ideologies in an ELT textbook and assessing how they are negotiated in classrooms, the third question highlights what pedagogical implications emerge from the revelations of the first two questions. In other words, it asks if a student's investment in language learning has been sufficiently brokered by the instructor and the textbook content. Are the instructors forced to resist, transform, appropriate or modify (Cortez, 2008) the content in the language learning process?

Based on the questions noted here, the research design featured in Figure 0.1 outlines a triangulation of analyses: (i) multimodal critical discourse study of an ELT textbook, (ii) multimodal interactional analysis of the ELT textbook usage in situ, (iii) values coding of interviews with students and practitioners. Duff (2007) maintains that a triangulation of 'insider perspectives' (p. 4) can be an extremely informative endeavour for classroom research (Zappa-Hollman & Duff, 2019). Discussions in upcoming chapters will explore multimodality, criticality and discourse studies (the pluralization of discourse analysis), and how they serve to inform the analyses in this book.

The convergence of data harvested from the analyses may yield a clearer picture (pun intended) of the multimodal content in EFL textbooks and their pedagogical significance in ELL. Each of these analyses will be featured in Chapters 2, 3 and 4, where vignettes highlighting their use in expanding-circle contexts give details regarding locations where the studies occurred, participants, operational procedures, instruments and justifications for choosing those data and the methods for analysing them.

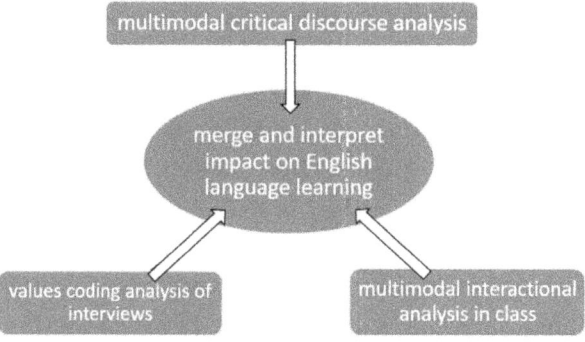

Figure 0.1 Triangulated analysis design.

Why This Book?

Understanding Multimodal Discourses in English Language Teaching Textbooks: Implications for Students and Practitioners presents guidance that addresses the concerns surrounding multimodal discourses in ELT textbooks. On crossroads where ELT classroom pedagogy meets the need for triangulation in critical analysis, this book recognizes that the primary consumers of ELT textbooks, students and practitioners, may not revere them as much as they may project. Perhaps outwardly, they uncritically digest the contents of textbooks because they are regarded as extensions of the teacher's or institution's pedagogical vision. However, evidence in the forthcoming analyses suggests that some students and practitioners do not value their ELT textbooks because they are often chosen for them and are pressured to use them by institutional milieu as one of the necessary components for language learning in global, expanding-circle communities (Tomlinson, 2011; Tomlinson & Masuhara, 2017). The aim is to create a critical awareness among teachers and practitioners: that they may not be just teaching a language but a culture and a value system that may or may not be desirable in the target context. Where some studies look at socio-historical beginnings of ELT, underscoring consumption and production for expanding-circle markets, and noting the importance of studying their role in the pedagogical culture of language learning, others include ideological discussions of textbook use in class, noting the need for research into multimodal discourse of textbooks (Gray, 2010; Harwood) (2014). These works, along with Curdt-Christiansen and Weninger (2015), who dive deeply into the ideologies of textbook content and use in language learning, Tomlinson (2011), and Tomlinson and Masuhara (2017), serve as heuristic anchors that students and practitioners using this book may consider: *Now that we know the socio-historical connection of language learning and textbooks, how they are produced and consumed, and what ideological politics in content are woven into the binary engines of production and consumption, what do we do now that we have to use them in our classes?* These questions seeded the design of this book because they anticipate that students and practitioners may further ask: *How do I critically measure the effectiveness of the lessons in the book that I have to use for my course? How can I understand and negotiate with the ideological standards of my textbook in a way that diminishes social unfairness while increasing the value of my course of study?* In other words, few studies specifically discuss how to analyse their language learning materials, how to engage in 'course-correction' while navigating perceived social unfairness or culturally marginalizing content in textbooks and how to measure the perceived value of those materials from the perspectives of their primary consumers.

Numerous studies, explored in more depth in Chapter 1, recommend or imply the need for live research of textbook use 'in situ', attention to multimodal discourse and emphasis of research or focus on the primary consumers of ELT textbooks (students and teachers). The frameworks operationalized in this book answer those calls because it constructs a malleable framework, applicable in any language learning context, to look at multimodal discourse and interaction of textbook lessons. Therefore, this book can assist educators, institutional milieu and students to engage in evaluation and pedagogical judgement of the materials they use in their language learning investments to inform their pedagogical needs. No books or research articles have accomplished the triangulated framework that this book proposes to help students and practitioners make the best of the textbooks that they may (at times) be forced to use.

The primary market for this book is student-teachers (where teacher training hopefully includes a survey of learning materials at their disposal) and existing practitioners in English language education because there are no guides to help them understand and negotiate the multimodal discourses in globally published ELT textbooks. While many publications usually have a 'Teacher's/Instructor's Guide' for delivering a specific textbook's content, in addition to larger, teacher-focused compendiums, such as Tomlinson and Masuhara's (2017) *Research for Materials Development in Language Learning: Evidence for Best Practice*, which specifically discuss textbook production and classroom use, there do not appear to be any books that address how to employ critical analysis for ELT textbooks in specific English language learning contexts. Online learning has risen with the increased capabilities of communication over recent years. That shift (1) increased language learning because people had more time for self-development in online formats, (2) led to a commensurate increase in sales of digital copies of ELT textbooks and (3) decreased language educator–student ratio. In other words, more books are being sold but fewer teachers are available per student to help them negotiate the contents. This book endeavours to partially fill the gap by helping students and practitioners critically understand, evaluate and negotiate the multimodal discourses in globally published ELT textbooks.

Structure of the Book

Chapter 1 explores the social politics behind ELT textbooks, their production and consumption, followed by a review of critical research into ELT textbooks and their use in expanding-circle cultures. The need for critical analyses and evaluation is underscored by the lack of research featuring power and ideologies in the multimodal discourse of globally published textbook content.

Chapter 2 begins with a brief discussion of the multimodal discourses typically found in globally published ELT textbooks. An overview of theoretical foundations of critical discourse studies set the stage for building a framework that can analyse the multimodal discourse in textbook contents. The critical multimodal analysis template (CMAT) emerges from those discussions and is given illustrative detail about each component of the procedure. A vignette, featuring the findings of CMAT by an EFL professor using a popular ELT textbook at a university in Korea, highlights the usefulness of the framework. The chapter concludes with a summary of potential uses for CMAT and preludes Chapter 3 by suggesting the findings can be corroborated by looking closer at live, classroom negotiations of the analysed content.

Chapter 3 begins with an illustration of a typical classroom *ecology* (i.e. Van Lier, 2015) that one might expect to find in university EFL programmes and features textbooks as a common focal point in that pedagogical culture. The illustration underscores the importance of understanding critical pedagogy and the complex relationships that form between teachers and students and their textbook in ELT, and how lesson contents are negotiated in classrooms. Building from theoretical principles of critical pedagogy, a question is premised on how to operationalize an analytical framework for seeing textbooks negotiated in live classrooms. Starting with theoretical discussions of multimodal discourse and multimodal interactional analysis, a basic framework is constructed to prioritize conceptual focus on ELT textbook content during class time, where the multimodal discourse in lessons is actively negotiated between teachers and students. A multimodal analysis of visually recorded English classrooms (MAVREC) emerges from the discussion as a solution to interactional analysis, given detailed illustration and explanation for each component of the analysis. A detailed description of MAVREC in a sample vignette features interactions in an English language learning classroom at a Korean university with the same course professor featured in Chapter 2. Chapter 3 concludes with a summary of the design of MAVREC, the vignette results, a discussion of how those findings corroborate with those in Chapter 2, then preludes Chapter 4 by suggesting CMAT and MAVREC can find salient corroboration in the mind, values and stances that students and practitioners give the multimodal discourses in their respective textbooks.

Chapter 4 begins by reminding us that the opinions and concerns of the most earnest consumers of globally published textbook content – students and teachers – rarely outweigh the sociopolitical interests of academic publishing institutions associated with textbook production. In this chapter, building from theoretical foundations of critical applied linguistics, a third step is taken towards understanding negotiated ideologies in the multimodal discourse of globally published ELT textbooks and features a semi-structured interview coding (SSInC) framework that encourages students and teachers (consumers) to freely evaluate their textbooks in a private interview. The interview includes students and teachers in a sample vignette, featuring participants from the same course featured in Chapter 3. The chapter concludes with a summary of highlights of findings from the sample SSInC analysis, how those findings corroborate with previous frameworks (CMAT and MAVREC) and a prelude to how students and practitioners can begin to synthesize them.

Chapter 5 begins with a discussion of criticisms directed at studies involving discourse analysis and a reminder of a call for 'triangulation' by proponents of that research. The discussion underscores the importance of triangulation in discourse analysis and corroborates findings from the sampled vignettes featured in Chapter 2 (CMAT), Chapter 3 (MAVREC) and Chapter 4 (SSInC) to support that assertion. After illustrating a synopsis for operationalizing a triangulated framework that can be tailored to the researcher's interests, the findings of the vignettes are synthesized and discussed. A summary of chapter highlights draws focused attention to the implications that the book can have in ELT education and serves to foreshadow the final chapter.

Chapter 6 attempts to bring the discussions in the book full circle and features the researcher's personal experiences using the frameworks from Chapters 2, 3 and 4 with colleagues in expanding-circle EFL programmes. The discussion addresses the logistical or cultural challenges that some educators must overcome, regarding the use of ELT textbooks. A summary of chapters and conclusions reached in the vignettes tapers towards implications of this book's possible use in EFL programmes and what future developments for textbook evaluation they may have, moving forward. A conclusive statement brings the discussion of the chapter and the book to an optimistic completion that encourages students and teachers to see themselves as interchangeable actors in the pedagogical culture of English language learning, whose voices partially construct the rhetorical accomplishment of a curriculum.

Finally, *Discussion Questions* are included at the end of Chapters 1–5. The questions are meant to further stimulate classroom discussion and/or personal, critical reflection and research. Additionally, the questions serve to sharpening the reader's understanding of some of the terms and concepts discussed throughout each chapter, which prove helpful engaging with the analyses, findings and discussions that follow.

Note

1 Referring to Kachru's (1992) theory of *World Englishes*, 'inner circle' refers to nations where English is a first language, 'outer circle' identifies an historical or colonial connection and 'expanding circle' refers to countries where English is a second or foreign language.

The Production and Consumption of ELT Textbooks

When *textbook* is preceded by the adjective *school*, it is afforded more legitimacy because of the implication of an institutional endorsement (Dendrinos, 2015). That legitimacy gives a measure of value to content that helps construct realities to which students anchor their own (Curdt-Christiansen & Weninger, 2015). In this way, textbooks are empowered to mould and influence the perspectives of their primary consumers because they represent a tactile promise of investment in knowledge, which is often rooted in certain ideologies (Fuchs & Bock, 2018; Macgilchrist, 2017; Smith, 2021; van Dijk, 2011). In the contexts of language learning, those realities have the power to *other* economically disadvantaged students or portray non-English-speaking global citizens as members of less important communities (Canagarajah, 1993, 2016; Dendrinos, 2015; Fitzgibbon, 2013; Lee, 2011a; Song, 2013; Smith, 2020; 2021). In so doing, these publications fail to nurture an appreciation for cultural difference and foster a greater sense of *otherness* (van Dijk, 2011) that may harm an L2 learner's educational experience (Pennycook & Candlin, 2017). For these reasons, the focus of this initial discussion will draw attention to globally published ELT textbooks for global EFL learning programmes. Attention is given, in a general sense, to textbooks published by British or American institutions for a global EFL market (Harwood, 2014). Popular global ELT textbook examples are the *New Interchange* series (Richards et al., 1994) by Cambridge University Press, the *American Headway* series (Soars et al., 2015) by Oxford University Press and the *Top Notch* series (i.e. Saslow & Ascher, 2006) from Pearson-Longman Publishing.

Kramsch and Vinall (2015) build on the arguments of Curdt-Christiansen and Weninger (2015) that textbooks require scrutiny because they can masquerade as ideological vehicles for certain social orders. Textbooks are not static devices but complex artefacts of an ever-changing pedagogical field (Weninger & Kiss, 2013). Despite their diachronic nature and the various roles that they have in language learning, ELT textbooks are persistently connected to globalization (Kramsch & Vinall, 2015). That connection underscores the political nature of their publication and use in expanding-circle ELL programmes (Dendrinos, 2015; Gray, 2010; Harwood, 2014).

Education may be one facet of political culture and identity, so language policy and planning are likely vehicles for the power and prestige afforded to English education in a particular society (Dendrinos, 2015). However, according to a limited amount of research, attention is given to language curriculum and textbooks because they have been masquerading as a-political devices. On the contrary, English is a language of international scope and influence, as we have already discussed in the Introduction, defining the linguistic and cultural *standard* of social institutions (Canagarajah, 1997). The *standard* was developed in no small part by ELT textbooks as vehicles for the empowerment of US and UK economic interests (Pennycook & Candlin, 2017; Fitzgibbon, 2013). Canagarajah's (1997) assertion aligns with Gray (2010) because ELT textbook publishers actively include discourses of feminism, multiculturalism and globalization to embellish English education with 'a range of values and associations that include individualism, egalitarianism, cosmopolitanism, mobility and affluence, in which students are increasingly addressed as consumers' (p. 3). In other words, the production of ELT textbook content has a direct influence on consumption. According to Littlejohn (2012), forces behind the production of ELT textbooks are fuelled by a massive industry. For example, as of 2011, a student book of a moderately successful publication may sell 100,000 copies per year, while a successful one easily exceeds one million copies – a far greater achievement than even the most successful bestsellers of fiction (Littlejohn, 2012). Therefore, the platform for the advancement of social orders helping inner-circle interests is far broader than any other within the publishing industry. To further expand such a platform, global ELT textbook publishers likely strive for universal appeal.

Gray (2010) criticizes the representation of English discourse in ELT textbooks for lacking variety and one book looking much like any other. From a Korean perspective (Yim, 2007; Song, 2013), much of ELT textbook content has aggrandized, inner-circle exaggerations meant to inspire L2 English students to try to become a kind of non-existent, ideal English speaker. This is a dangerous standardization because the English content carries an implication that only one mode of English exists for students of all worldly locales (Smith, 2020). Such standardization of representation in ELT textbook content is one of commercial, rather than pedagogic, interest because they serve to *train* consumers to accept their standardized products, achieving a standard of content to publish which leads to cheaper publishing costs, wider distribution and higher sales (Canagarajah, 2016; Littlejohn, 2012; Gray, 2010; Harwood, 2014; Bell and Gower, 2011; Yim, 2007). The strategy of standardization must be good for business because in the 2011 fiscal year, collective sales of ELT textbooks among the top publishers (Cambridge University Press, Oxford University Press and Pearson-Longman) grossed more than one billion British pounds worldwide.

ELT textbooks remain a key component in foreign or second language programmes because they provide teachers and students with the necessary, material reference for linguistic inquiry while encouraging learner practice and communicative interaction (Cunningsworth, 1995; Richards, 2014; Song, 2013; Tomlinson, 2011; Tomlinson & Masuhara, 2017). However, some research argues that they are also *cultural artefacts* produced in a system of institutional power, where highly specific social contexts, norms and values are *learned* under the banner of education (Canagarajah, 2016; Curdt-Christiansen & Weninger, 2015; Dendrinos, 2015; Gray, 2010; Harwood, 2014; Littlejohn, 2012; Song, 2013). It is not surprising, then, that the banner of education has nurtured a culture of EFL education in expanding-circle contexts, composed of multiple stakeholders in the educational milieu who exert significant sociopolitical pressure on language educational policies and planning (Curdt-Christiansen & Weninger, 2015). Those pressures are, not surprisingly, evident in ELT textbooks and language learning materials, where political ideologies are mediated in their multimodal contents (Weninger & Kiss, 2013). Therefore, it seems no language learning textbook, in any curriculum, is neutral in expressing, either implicitly or explicitly, a particular social order (Apple, 1985; Auerbach & Burgess, 1985; Weninger, 2018). Some critical discourse studies (CDS) revealed that ELT textbooks' stereotypical representations of non-English-speaking discourse communities have inspired revisions of certain publications (Kramsch & Vinall, 2015). However, the ideological leanings found all too frequently in ELT textbooks 'remain hostage to the commercial interests of publishers and to the demands of the decentralized educational system of an American liberal democracy' (Kramsch & Vinall, 2015, p. 14). Hence, critical studies of ELT textbooks reveal consistent biases, often favouring inner-circle countries (Kachru, 1992), where white, male, Anglo-centric cultures dominate all others (Ahn, 2014; Choi, 2008; Lee, 2009; Lee, 2011; Lee, 2014; Matsuda, 2002; Sherman, 2010; Shin et al., 2011; Smith, 2021, Song, 2013; Taylor-Mendes, 2009; Yim, 2014). In other words, ELT textbooks, like pedagogical icebergs, have so much more lurking beneath their fetching covers and associated multimedia packages. Considering the social, political and economic *gravitas* textbooks represent in ELT education, and the importance such artefacts may have influencing student–teacher relationships, their consumption and production have rightly earned the attention of investigative research.

ELT Textbook Production

The production and consumption of ELT textbooks are shown to be binary engines driving the global ELT industry forward. An exploration of this drive reveals some evidence of interdependency between the production and consumption and an impactful dynamic on ELT culture (Gray, 2010; Harwood, 2014, Littlejohn, 2012). In fact, Harwood (2014) argues that consumption and production are two *essential* angles of approach towards an understanding of a textbook's educational impact on ELT culture. Studies on production can reveal why ELT textbooks 'are the way they are' (Littlejohn, 1992, p. 1) while providing a greater understanding of stakeholder influences nurturing the culture and commerce of ELT marketplaces (Apple, 1985; Harwood, 2014). Production, it is important to point out, refers to how texts are designed, written and published, with a bead on how such processes are connected within the ELT industry (Harwood, 2014). However, like many contemporary intellectual commodities, ELT textbooks find origins in sociopolitical and economic expansion.

The way that language textbooks have been produced and consumed over the last 100 years has changed due to some historically relevant phases (Curdt-Christiansen & Weninger, 2015). Those phases in textbook production were likely reflective of socio-economic politics of the times. The nineteenth century saw an imperialist spread of capitalism (Marx & Engels, 1967) on a global scale, driven by corporate interest seeking continued expansion for trading markets (Phillipson, 2012). Included in such markets, corporate stakeholders held vested interest in intellectual and material production because they augment a uniformity in corporate identity that ensures global participation, expansion and, most importantly, continued profit (Fitzgibbon, 2013). Not surprisingly, English language manifested as one of many intellectual commodities ensuring global corporate identity for publishing houses (Harwood, 2014), particularly in the United States and the United Kingdom. With it came the vehicles of corporate identity material in the form of English publications (Harwood, 2014), specifically, English language teaching materials. Hence, the early forms of language learning materials served nation states for nurturing intercontinental or intercultural communications (Curdt-Christiansen & Weninger, 2015).

However, by the time grammar-translation methods were used, textbooks became sources of standardized forms of languages, legitimized in their content by showcasing contrastive comparisons with other languages and cultures (Curdt-Christiansen & Weninger, 2015). In other words, the direct or implied insistence in their contents that *this is French* and *that is English* presented textbooks as linguistically authentic arenas of communication (Kramsch & Vinall, 2015). Those standardizations served to encourage a cultural awareness in language learning that was quickly changed to a more military-inspired pedagogical approach in the Second World War because there was a sudden need to be able to speak with allies and foes (Curdt-Christiansen & Weninger, 2015).

In the 1970s and 1980s, communicative language teaching (i.e. Canale & Swain, 1980; Littlewood & William, 1981; Nunan, 1987; Savignon, 1987) caused textbooks to change in resonance with more individualistic needs, so the content became more functional for contemporary communication, rather than translative (Biggs & Tang, 2007; Curdt-Christiansen & Weninger, 2015; Stoller, 2015). In this way, the culturally sensitive standards that formed language learning textbook content in the past became somewhat antiquated or stereotypical in the face of contemporary content that reflected a certain version of social reality (Curdt-Christiansen & Weninger, 2015).

The global spread of English created the need for English language education and by extension a social commodity in English language and its associated learning materials (Cameron, 2012; Canagarajah, 2016; Gray, 2010; Harwood, 2014; Kubota, 2011; Littlejohn, 1992, 2012; Rubdy & Tan, 2008; Tomlinson & Masuhara, 2017). The direction of the ELT textbook industry has been driven by a pedagogy that promotes an atmosphere of *only English*, or English as the preferred lingua franca worldwide, to ensure continued profits while promoting the superiority of inner-circle social norms for an English-speaking world (Auerbach, 1995; Dendrinos, 2015; Fitzgibbon, 2013; Kachru, 1992; Weninger & Kiss, 2013). The results of the production–consumption dynamic have led to a standardization of ELT textbooks that likely pressure students and teachers from diverse backgrounds into a template of standardized consumption (Gray, 2010; Harwood, 2014; Littlejohn, 1992; Tomlinson, 2011). Logically, the growing relationship between consumers and producers led to the growth of contemporary ELT textbooks as tremendously lucrative products, but the scales of profit do not appear to lean in favour of the consumer (Gray, 2010). In the contexts of inner-circle EFL education, attitudes towards American and British English, for example, are more favourable and recognized as a standard against all other varieties, embodying a notion of correctness and prestige (Ahn, 2014; Canagarajah, 1993; Choi, 2008; Fitzgibbon, 2013; Gray, 2010; Harwood, 2014; Lee, 2011; Ramanathan, 1999; Smith, 2020; Song, 2013). Therefore, it is not surprising that publishing giants in England and the United States, such as Cambridge, Oxford University Press and Pearson-Longman, having earned *brand* recognition (Littlejohn, 2012), see a consistent surplus of EFL students as rich demographics from which to profit in a global market.

The production of ELT textbooks involves the work of many people engaged interdependently at various stages and can take more than five years from conception to publication (Littlejohn, 1992; 2012). Unfortunately, most publishers must answer to stakeholders concerned more with profits than the provision of strong theoretical pedagogy in textbook content (Littlejohn, 1992). The following priorities are considered before all else: (1) minimal financial risk; (2) content must reflect what will sell, not what may sell; (3) market perceptions must align with EFL consumer needs; (4) content must be conservative rather than radical, evolutionary rather than revolutionary; (5) market timing; (6) secrecy in content development (Littlejohn, 1992). Given such pressures, it is not surprising that most ELT textbook authors who are commissioned by publishers are chosen for their known capacity to be compromising and reliable (Littlejohn, 2012; Gray, 2010). Overall, publishers want to publish what they think will sell based on conservative estimations. Authors, Littlejohn (1992) admits, are agents of the publisher, commissioned to deliver the culture of ELT textbook publishing. In this way, the publishing industry plays an influential role on the realization and design of content in EFL textbooks so that they continue to sell in considerable numbers (Littlejohn, 1992).

In short, fiscal considerations of production appear to receive the lion's share of attention in the process before pedagogically sound content is even considered. Tomlinson's (2011) five-step process in ELT material development has the writers, researchers and educators coalesce at step five. While Tomlinson and Masuhara (2017) contend that it is inevitable that a textbook will project the social realities surrounding the target language and its associated cultures – a potentially dangerous position of power because of their revered status in many expanding-circle communities – it is the teacher's responsibility to *make it work*. This seemingly positive perspective of a billion-dollar industry echoes the arguments of gun manufacturers that claim users should bear the responsibility of the misuse of their products. In other words, the argument appears somewhat idealistic considering the EFL market will always be the final arbiter of ELT textbook content (Littlejohn, 1992; 2012; Gray, 2010; Harwood, 2014).

Furthermore, arbiters of the textbook industry (i.e. Richards, 2014; Tomlinson, 2011; Tomlinson & Masuhara, 2017) admit material production is a *practical undertaking* – perhaps a less arresting way of saying *it is all about money.*

Harwood (2014), in a chapter devoted to the production of ELT materials, lists the number of individuals involved with the authors in content and design as reviewers, acquisitions editors, development editors, copy editors, graphic designers, all overseen by senior managers. It is not much wonder, therefore, that English has become a *McDonaldized* product (Franklin, 2003, 2005; Littlejohn, 2012) – a term given brief attention later in this discussion – where an expected product is made for standardized consumption habits (Gray, 2010). In this way, ELT textbooks are an effective delivery system for English as an internationally recognized commodity (Cameron, 2012; Gray, 2010; Harwood, 2014; Kubota, 2011; Rubdy & Tan, 2008), *traded* in a global marketplace.

In a revealing article drawing attention to the compromises authors must make in ELT materials development, Bell and Gower (2011) noted that the production of textbooks led to the birth of the *global ELT textbook* – a one-size-fits-all, expensive, multimedia package 'with a dedicated website of extras, usually produced in a native-speaker situation' (p. 170). Publishing companies, seeking continued brand recognition on a global scale, produce endless series of new editions, effectively choking the market from producing any other kind of product. For this reason, the consumption habits of EFL students and practitioners in expanding-circle communities have been standardized. In a study of Spanish as a foreign language textbooks, Kramsch and Vinall (2015) note they are enhanced by interactive, online, digital media alternatives and increasingly perceived as *authentic* platforms of Spanish communication. These supplemental sources are attractive to publishers for their increasing revenue generation (Bell & Gower, 2011; Harwood, 2014; Littlejohn, 2012).

Textbook writers or authors, like ELT textbook consumers, are the last to be considered in production (Littlejohn, 1992; Gray, 2010). However, Bell and Gower (2011) note that a writer's role in production may be one of collaboration rather than composition. Admittedly, Harwood (2014) implies such collaboration can be quite profitable, so the culture and commerce of ELT textbooks spring partially from the common interests of publishers and authors. Gray (2010) describes the writing process as one where publishing editors *help* their writers get started by giving them guidelines to which they must adhere (Gray, 2010). Most fall into two categories: inclusive language (referring mainly to designing non-sexist representation of men and women, both linguistically and visually) and inappropriate topics (Gray, 2010). While inclusive language in second or foreign language education contexts has received some attention (i.e. Kormos & Nijakowska, 2017; Krulatz & Iversen, 2020; Paiz, 2019) in recent years and has been relatedly connected to gender-biased content for some years (Curdt-Christiansen & Weninger, 2015), few critical studies, under the umbrella of language learning materials production, feature current discussions on inclusive or sensitive use of pronouns, for example, according to individuals' gender identification. Inappropriate topics in this second guideline have been amusingly categorized within an acronym: 'PARSNIP (politics, alcohol, religion, sex, narcotics, -isms, and pork)' (Gray, 2010, p. 119). Perhaps PARSNIP has two roles in guiding the writers of ELT textbook content as an easy reference for recall and to remind them that content should be reflective of the vegetable to which the acronym refers – remarkably uninteresting.

ELT Textbook Consumption

While arguments can be made that the consumers of ELT textbooks should include parents and institutional milieu, for the purposes of this discussion, consumption will refer to the use and interpretation of textbooks in classrooms by students and practitioners. As for *how* a textbook is consumed or negotiated (Smith, 2021), it differs depending on the alignments between the textbook's content, the teacher, the students, the class environment and the school or institution (Harwood, 2014; Tomlinson & Masuhara, 2017). Furthermore, for investigating their consumption, ELT textbooks should be considered *materials-in-action* (Littlejohn, 1992) or textbooks *in situ* (Smith, 2021), referring to how teachers and students reflexively negotiate textbook content and tasks.

Harwood (2014) points out a peculiar consistency in studies of the consumption of ELT textbooks, drawing attention to teachers' uses of them in EFL classrooms but rarely involving or including the perspectives of considerations of the students. Gray (2010) and Auerbach and Burgess (1985) appear to fall into this category, seeing teachers as the primary consumers, while Tomlinson (2011) appears to echo Harwood (2014), who claims that student perceptions are lacking scholarly research attention, corroborated by Smith (2021) and Littlejohn (1992), and further maintains that the greatest gap in research may be ethnographic observations of ELT textbooks in use.

Teaching and Training the Consumers

Brown (2011) describes ELT textbooks as useful tools for teacher training, but teachers are not the only participants who are training to consume the content. As mentioned earlier, although teachers may be the vehicles through which standardized EFL learning content travels and is received, students are also trained to accept such content as the standard of English to learn (Canagarajah, 1993; Curdt-Christiansen & Weninger, 2015; Littlejohn, 1992; Harwood, 2014; Bell & Gower, 2011; Tomlinson; 2011). As noted earlier, globally published ELT textbooks often come in the form of multimedia packages (Bell & Gower, 2011). Sometimes such packages can include audio/visual supplemental materials, multiple types of student books and workbooks, an associated website, teacher guidebooks and other forms of auxiliary publication (Bell & Gower, 2011, p. 171). Littlejohn (1992), Brown (2011), and Bell and Gower (2011) likely agree with Grossman and Thompson (2008), who note that EFL textbooks, packaged in this fashion, can be a valuable resource for freshman teachers to achieve their respective pedagogical visions.

Richards (2014) gives some attention to materials consumption in EFL learning, devoting an entire chapter to illustrating how institutions, the individual teacher, teaching practice and learner factors can facilitate successful language learning programmes. While informative, Richards (2014) omits any critical observations of ELT textbook content but underscores *consumer preparedness*, telling his readers how ELT textbooks should be used. As Brown (2011) points out, Richards's (2014) guidance in EFL textbook usage may be due to the lack of any well-established or well-accepted resource pool of classroom activities, with universal appeal, from which teachers can draw and create useful exercises. Masuhara (2011) draws specific attention to EFL teacher opinions of *global* ELT textbooks, echoing Bell and Gower (2011), Brown (2011), Canagarajah (2006, 2016), Curdt-Christiansen and Weninger (2015), Dendrinos (2015), Gray (2010), Littlejohn (2012), Masuhara (2011), Richards (2001), Tomlinson (2011), and Tomlinson and Masuhara (2017), to name only a few significant scholars, who argue that teachers likely play a key role in the consumption of ELT textbook content because they participate in the choice of the textbook (however insignificant that may be), help implement the textbooks into a curriculum and inspire their students to engage with the content.

From these arguments, we can infer that students and textbooks come and go, but the teacher remains (Masuhara, 2011). However, in many cases, teachers are forced to *repurpose* textbook content to suit the needs or cultural contexts of their students. For this reason, Harwood (2014) asks: '1) How do most teachers see the value of their ELT textbooks? 2) How closely do they adhere to the content? and 3) How do they manipulate the materials to meet the needs of their students?' (p. 154). Harwood (2014) admits that answering such questions draws varied responses and represents an area of EFL textbook consumption research seldom explored. This suggests that ELT textbook content is part of a larger system of reflexive consumption negotiated between the students and their teachers, who try to read the atmosphere of the classroom ecology (Blyth & Thoms, 2021; Kramsch, 2008; Steffensen & Kramsch, 2017; Van Lier, 1997) in the process of delivering English lessons to fulfil the goals of a particular curriculum.

In addition to a lack of research in the way ELT textbooks are used in situ (Littlejohn, 1992, 2012; Smith, 2021; Wohlwend, 2011) or how teachers are forced to manipulate the contents, Tomlinson (2011) and Harwood (2014) speculate there are few studies exploring their use inside and outside of the classroom, involving the consumption habits and perspectives of students, or differentiating classroom from external use. There appears to be a pressing need for student perspectives regarding ELT textbooks as contributing devices to their failure or lack of enthusiasm to learn English (Chen, 2010; Harwood, 2014; Lee, 2014; Littlejohn, 1992, 2012; Rahimi & Hassani, 2012; Song, 2013; Tomlinson, 2011; Xiong & Qian, 2012). Harwood (2014) further asks if ELT textbooks are necessary anymore or in what conditions can learners achieve their language learning goals otherwise? Asking these questions suggests that consumers, especially students, may be a *muted group* (Harwood, 2014; Smith, 2021). Hence, research attention should be drawn to EFL textbooks, the opinions of numerous stakeholders in a community's EFL education system and their effectiveness in that system, so that those perceived *muted* groups are given a voice.

By discussing the varied elements of ELT textbook production, sources influencing and delineating the habits of consumption are revealed. Thus far, the literature appears to suggest a *conditioning* of consumption in textbook users via the standardization of English content in production (Curdt-Christiansen & Weninger, 2015; Gray, 2010; Harwood, 2014; Littlejohn, 1992, 2012; Mesthrie, 2006; Tomlinson, 2011). If so, between the consumption and production of ELT textbooks, there may exist a reciprocal link born in economic incentivization driven by the promise of perceived, global and upward socio-economic mobility associated with acquiring English language skills (Cameron, 2012; Canagarajah, 2016; Curdt-Christiansen & Weninger, 2015; Rubdy & Tan, 2008; Smith, 2021; Smith, 2021).

It may be important to note here that the connections we are constructing mean to underscore how teachers, as consumers, carry out textbooks in class and how students may interpret them. Not only does that serve as an important investigation towards understanding consumers and ELT textbooks but also parries a line of criticism often levelled against CDS or similar engagements that concentrate on discourse analysis. Critics (i.e. Breeze, 2011; Hadley, 2013; Waters, 2009) of critical discourse studies (to which the field of study is now more commonly referred) (Wodak & Meyer, 2016) have said that the problem is the analyst's assumption that all audiences interpret a text the same way that they do, which may not be the case. For this reason (and something that will be explored in more depth in Chapter 2), the literature noted in the following sections underpins critical analyses of textbooks and points to their insufficiencies as a need for critical frameworks specializing in the multimodal discourses in textbooks. The highlights and discussions that follow continue to give purpose to the triangulated analysis proposed in this book and shore support for the need to include students and practitioners in those methods.

The Problem of Authentic English

Although there may be a reciprocal relationship between production and consumption of ELT textbooks, the larger gear in the dynamic may well be found in production. Although ELT textbooks are designed for use inside classrooms, their design and production will always be sourced in conditions outside the classroom (Harwood, 2014; Littlejohn, 2012). For this reason, *authentic* English in EFL textbooks may be problematic because it begs the question: *To whom is the linguistic content deemed authentic?* (Gilmore, 2011). Mestrovic and Ahmed (1997) argued that contemporary society forces people to learn how to feel or act so it is not surprising that measures of *McDonaldized* culture (i.e. Franklin, 2003; Littlejohn, 2012; Ritzer, 1993) infiltrate the content of language learning textbooks. That enforcement results in a kind of artificially contrived authenticity (Earl et al., 2002) in content that feels more generic and less real, especially when students leave EFL classrooms feeling that they are learning the way Americans speak. While Mestrovic and Ahmed (1997) paint the concept of authenticity as something that consumers feel is worth achieving, despite rising socio-economic and political inequities, Earl et al. (2002) warn, in their research about assessment reform in language learning, that *authentic* may be unachievable, and to present English content as such might equate to presenting a kind of rhetorical distortion that students might find demoralizing if their real-world communications ever contradict their language learning investments.

Several studies demonstrate the misalignment between commonly spoken variations of English and the linguistic challenges featured in ELT textbook lessons. The absence of common lexical items, such as 'well' in textbook content (Lam, 2010), a general mismatch between live speech and textbook dialogues (Cullen and Kuo, 2007; Timmis, 2010) or misguided instruction for common, semantic choices, such as the difference between interrogative and imperative when requesting help (Tomlinson, 2011), are only a few examples that point to the problem of authenticity in ELT textbooks. Perhaps this is the reason why students and practitioners, if given a choice, prefer materials with authentic language use in entertainment or social media (e.g. films, music, literature or internet sources) (Bell & Gower, 2011; Earl et al., 2002; Gilmore, 2011). Gilmore (2011) speculated the reason why students preferred *real-world* material was the robust variance in discourse exposure that stimulated a wider range of communicative competencies.

Kramsch (2008) agrees the quest for *authentic* target language is a problematic endeavour. While Bell and Gower (2011) and Gilmore (2011) sympathize with the desire for authentic language and cultural relativity in ELT textbook content by consumers, Kramsch (1993) reminds us that the term 'authentic' refers to natural speech used in a non-pedagogical discourse in reaction to prefabricated or *artificial language* found in ELT textbooks. Cultural relativity, Kramsch (1993) argues, is left at the door of the classroom, 'not because the educational culture of the language class reflects by necessity the dominant culture of the institution, but because teachers could not teach if they did not make pedagogical choices' (p. 183). Furthermore, communicative exchanges found in ELT textbooks usually involve two or three speakers, who interact uniformly, each having equal measures of agency (Kramsch, 2008). Real speech, of course, is nothing of the sort. This suggests that *authentic* language may not be achievable in classroom discourse using ELT textbook material.

McDonaldized English

Littlejohn (1992) argues that ELT textbooks have become a centralized commodity of production in standardized English consumption used by deskilled educators for a contemporary capitalist society (Cameron, 2012; Gray, 2010; Harwood, 2014; Kubota, 2011; Rubdy & Tan, 2008). The production of ELT textbooks has a direct educational impact on *classroom consumers* and led to the *McDonaldization* of EFL materials (Littlejohn, 2012). In a general context, the concept of *McDonaldization* (Ritzer, 1993) is nothing new and informed Franklin's (2003; 2005) research on the appearance of *McJournalism*. That research was informed by Mestrovic and Ahmed's (1997) observations, that many aspects of American society have devolved into a kind of artificial niceness, and Ritzer's (1993) *McDonaldization* of social acceptability and etiquette, where people are constantly taught how and what to feel. For Ritzer (1993), McDonaldization characterized that entrapment within a 'highly controlled, bureaucratic and dehumanized nature of contemporary . . . social life' (Franklin, 2005, p. 138) and gives evidence that the processes of that fast-food brand, to which the neologism refers, have transcended their industrial boundaries to influence other aspects of American life (Franklin, 2005). Franklin (2005) believes those aspects include packaged products such as holidays or university programmes, each reflecting the McDonald's business strategy by prioritizing 'efficiency, calculability, predictability and control, where quantity and standardization replace quality and variety as the indicators of value' (p. 138). Those standards, Franklin (2005) argues, create uniformed cityscapes of business chains, where cities like Toronto, London or New York, for example, appear somewhat indistinguishable. Hence, one might infer that the institutions that monopolize ELT textbook publications, with an equal preference for centralization (Franklin, 2005; Littlejohn, 2012), are also indistinguishable and impose a kind of homogenized, global field of EFL culture with all the hallmarks of McDonaldization (Franklin, 2005; Ritzer, 1993). Within these industries, the emergence of 'Mcjobs' (Franklin, 2005, p. 139) ensures that producers and consumers of any product become 'deskilled' (Littlejohn, 2012) or 'disempowered' (Franklin, 2005). Littlejohn (2012) argues that contemporary, global ELT textbook publications and their consumers are no exception to that devolution in language education.

McDonaldization associated with ELT learning may have led to the emergence of deskilled teachers heeding only an institutional curriculum or teaching to the test – completely lost without textbook guidance and thus deskilled as educators (Littlejohn, 2012). According to Littlejohn (2012), McDonald's business stratagem requires a strict adherence to 'deskilled work routines for its employees and fixed language scripts for interactions with their customers to generate a totally predictable, globally standardized McDonald's experience' (p. 291). Littlejohn (2012) points out that *McDonaldization* is evident in standardized teacher training and textbook materials used in classrooms. Some ELT textbooks provide instructions for the students and teachers how to use the content, in addition to instructing them how to talk to each other, as evidence supporting this connection (Littlejohn, 2012, p. 293). The educational impact suggests that ELT textbooks play a role in *dehumanizing* both teachers and their students in a very efficient and predictable method. By making language lessons and outcomes predictable and efficient, some ELT students may obtain the ability to score highly in assessment exams such as the IELTS (International English Language Testing System) but remain remarkably ill-equipped to participate in spontaneous conversation or even enjoy casual English exposure. However, rather than *deskilled* or *dehumanized*, it may be more accurate to note that if one subscribes to Littlejohn's (2012) assertions, McDonaldization in ELT textbook content and dependency on those publications in EFL curriculums in expanding-circle cultures may serve to devalue teacher and student investments in language learning because of its capacity for presenting the rhetorical distortions against which Earl et al. (2002) warned.

Perhaps Littlejohn's (2012) assertion of the *McDonaldization* of ELT textbooks hints at *indigestible* content, corroborated in several studies. Marginalization of student audiences, Matsuda (2002) criticizes, is blatantly apparent in ELT textbooks where the content reflects only inner-circle situations. This affects student perceptions and attitudes that they will never be part of that community (Matsuda, 2002). In a study centred around the opinions of rural Thai students of their ELT textbooks, Boriboon (2004) found that learners saw content to be too authoritative or controlled. Boriboon's (2004) observations showed the incongruity between ELT textbook content and the context of student's daily lives negatively affected their progress in learning. Sakai and Kikuchi (2009) point to rising issues of demotivation in EFL high school classes in Japan. Their investigations identified numerous, highly demotivating factors, not least of which were the contents of ELT textbooks. Nguyen's (2011) study draws attention to the lack of intercultural pragmatic practice in ELT textbook content for Vietnamese high school programmes. Instead of illustrating real language patterns that native English speakers follow, many textbook dialogues are designed with the predication of native speaker intuition (Nguyen, 2011). Sherman (2010) implies a significant source of demotivation found in cultural representations in Korean ELT textbooks. In an investigation revealing biased depiction of non-native English-speaking characters, Sherman (2010) identifies this as a demotivating factor contributing to the lack of interest in EFL classes. The studies noted earlier describe critical issues with ELT textbooks used in expanding- or outer-circle nations such as Japan, Thailand, Vietnam and Korea. These critical studies point to EFL textbooks as predictably efficient language learning artefacts, published under controlled and calculable measures to ensure maximum global sales (Harwood, 2014; Gray, 2010; Littlejohn, 2012; Smith, 2021). The unfortunate side effect of these McDonaldized publications is that not all tastes are meant for every culture, so it remains the duty of teachers to *un-deskill* themselves and repurpose the material so that the investments student make in the learning materials and the time to study are given fair value (Smith, 2021).

Standardization and Class in World Englishes

The needs of EFL students have changed rapidly over the last few decades to accommodate their membership in an ever-expanding circle of global English-speaking communities (Syrbe & Rose, 2018). However, EFL speakers have needs that extend beyond the parameters of 'foreign' into domestic contextualization (Syrbe & Rose, 2018). Those needs contend with the plurality of standardizations in *World Englishes* and are a source of relevant concern for consumers of globally published ELT textbooks in expanding-circle nations. Therefore, a question arises if a variety of English is being negotiated with the EFL in their textbooks?

Scholars of World Englishes have argued that certain English standards such as 'Received Pronunciation' (RP) or 'General American' – the latter being a preferred variation in many expanding-circle nations (Smith, 2021) – are not necessarily the most common variations of English in use (Syrbe & Rose, 2018). Mauranen (2012) argued that exposing students to more variety may be a more viable pedagogical choice because 'imposed standards are different from the natural forms that arise in groups and communities' (p. 6). The common sentiment suggests that greater exposure will enable a greater capacity to understand Englishes used in various communities of practice. Syrbe and Rose (2018) further maintain that familiarity with communities of practice, such as the capability of students to laterally move between different English speech communities, is a much more valuable language learning investment than isolating one's language skills to one standard.

When using the General American standards of English that most globally published ELT textbooks follow, it falls on instructors to help their students prepare for global uses of that variation (McKay, 2012). To achieve more globally adaptive language learning in classrooms, Matsuda and Friedrich (2012) have three suggestions: (i) teach the most salient variety of English for students based on their geopolitical positions, (ii) teach the instructor's own variety and (iii) use an established variety and feature lesson components that compare it to another variety (Syrbe & Rose, 2018). Unfortunately, there is a dearth of materials that feature alternative varieties of English beyond RP or General American, so instructors must be willing to seek out or create their own (Syrbe & Rose, 2018).

In addition to an absence of variation of English in globally published ELT textbooks, the unrealistic neutrality of *social class* in ELT textbooks fails to render an accurate representation of the world (Luke, 2015). The lack of a working-class representation, for example, abandons the recognition of an entire class of language learners (Block, 2015; Canagarajah, 1999; Harwood, 2014; Hu, 2005; Lee, 2006; Song, 2013) and may serve to adversely affect the learning experience.

Collectively, the lack of English variation and neutralized social classes resonate in the content of the 'teacher's guides' that accompany many ELT publications, arguably serving to *deskill* teachers by presenting a standardized discourse, complete with all the *right* answers and all the right forms of behavioural rules befitting an English teacher (Curdt-Christiansen & Weninger, 2015; Gray, 2010). Additionally, an overall feeling of decontextualization or generalizability, perhaps inspired by the standardization of English and social classes (Dendrinos, 2015; Tomlinson & Masuhara, 2017), presents all EFL learners in the same light, as if they were all the same age and in the same *foreign* location. Some studies, such as Linse's (2007) study of the appropriacy of American or British bedtime stories in early childhood EFL programmes, do step into this area of research. However, little attention is given to children's ELT materials or what an educational impact they may have on EFL learning in early education.

Critical Studies of ELT Textbooks

Foucault (2003) warned that information from media, such as news organizations, or from institutionally endorsed sources, such as teachers, can become fixtures of truth in the minds of audiences because of 'the way it is delivered, in this tone, by this person, at this time' (p. 525). It is reasonable to include textbooks and their contents into Foucault's (2003) warning about information received (Thoma, 2017). Remembering, as noted earlier, that a textbook can be perceived as a tactile promise of knowledge, it is not surprising that the fixtures of truth to which Foucault (2003) refers become measures of trust in the textbook that curriculum stakeholders choose for their students (Cho, 2013; Connelly & Clandinin, 1988; Giroux, 1983, 1988, 2017; Savignon, 2002; Smith, 2021; Shor, 1992). That measure of trust in textbooks relates to the value of their education and learning because it is a kind of social investment risked by language learners, motivated by social and material interests (Canagarajah, 1993, 2006, 2016;

Ortactepe, 2013; Savignon, 2002). The implied institutional endorsement that textbooks carry (Curdt-Christiansen & Weninger, 2015) validates their contents as valued realities a student must learn.

In textbooks, what passes for knowledge is often ideologically founded (van Dijk & Atienza, 2011). Critical studies of textbooks are the keys to unlocking power relationships and ideologies in textbook content that might otherwise remain unnoticed and consumed by students and practitioners without challenge. In this way, perceived social unfairness in textbook content (i.e. Ahn, 2014; Choi, 2008; Lee, 2009; Lee, 2011; Lee, 2014; Matsuda, 2002; Sherman, 2010; Shin et al., 2011; Song, 2013; Taylor-Mendes, 2009; Yim, 2014), interpellated under the umbrella of education (Apple, 1985; Canagarajah, 1993, 2006, 2016; Curdt-Christiansen & Weninger, 2015; Dendrinos, 2015; Fitzgibbon, 2013; Gray, 2010; Harwood, 2014; Littlejohn, 1992, 2012; Song, 2013; van Dijk, 2011), is given just exposure.

Despite a variety of research foci on textbooks in general, many studies appear to look at ELT textbooks (Smith & Sheyholislami, 2022), such as studies that underscore superior human agency in Christian-based textbooks for K-12 courses (Agiro, 2012; Sharma & Buxton, 2015), marginalized discourse communities and identity (Eriksen, 2018), cultural marginalization of indigenous people (Maposa, 2015), the 'othering' of immigrant voices (Gulliver, 2010), racism and *whiteness* evident in multimodal discourse (Harper, 2012), nationalism (Vinall & Shin, 2018), imbalanced gender representation where male social actors (Van Leeuwen, 2008) possess most or all forms of agency (Giaschi, 2000; Mustedanagic, 2010; Setyono, 2018) and membership criteria for *citizenship* or belonging to a particular national entity (Ververi, 2017). Rising from these perceived narratives of social iniquities, language learning textbooks, particularly ELT textbooks, receive the largest share of investigative attention.

In a general sense, most of the studies focused on gender representation, where the findings exposed males as the dominant social actors in all forms of discourse (Ahour & Zaferani, 2016; Amerian & Esmaili, 2015; Baghdadi, 2012; Giaschi, 2000; Gungor & Prins, 2010; Healy, 2009; Lee, 2014; Marefat & Marzban, 2014; Mustedanagic, 2010; Setyono, 2018; Sherman, 2010; Stockdale, 2006; Thomson & Otsuji, 2003). Some investigations drew attention to marginalized identities or communities, where the discourse appears to present or omit information that positions certain demographics as *them* and/or *not us* (Machin & Mayr, 2012). Studies featuring social conditioning (e.g. Chiu, 2011; Borhaug, 2014), where some communities are contrasted against inner-circle social standardizations (Chu, 2015; Eriksen, 2018; Maposa, 2015; Song, 2013; Thompson, 2013; Xiong,

2012), result in *othering* certain groups as less important to the construction of national identities (Camase, 2009; Popson, 2001), academic research (Lee, 2011) or national immigration policy (Gulliver, 2010). Additionally, while many studies examined how genders or particular discourse communities were *presented* or *not presented* (graphically and textually), few address *multimodality* in their theoretical frameworks or methodologies, choosing instead to employ unique constructions of critical discourse studies (e.g. Camase, 2009). This suggests a significant gap in approaches to analysing the multimodal discourse in textbooks.

Some studies appear to stand out from the rest, in terms of the impact or reach of their social inequity, such as *whiteness*, unfavourable African-American portrayal in history, Asian racism and issues related to immigration (e.g. Gulliver & Thurrell, 2017; Fitzgibbon, 2013; Pellegrino et al., 2013; Harper, 2012), but these studies do not appear to sufficiently inform, in terms of the quantity of articles, the seriousness of the social injustices they've exposed. Additionally, studies surrounding the design and interpretation of a school curriculum (Svendsen & Svendsen, 2017), falsification of Palestinian and Jewish communications (Osborn, 2017), the dismissiveness of anthropocentric climate change in Christian-based textbooks (Agiro, 2012), the ideological squaring (van Dijk, 2011) of nationalism versus international, where the former term is presented, by contrast, to be preferable to the latter term (Vinall and Shin, 2018), call for more investigation and imply a more considered approach to engaging multimodal discourses in future research.

Critical Studies in Expanding-circle Contexts

As was noted earlier in this chapter, some critical analyses of EFL textbooks have revealed consistent biases, often favouring inner-circle cultures as the preferred model (Ahn, 2014; Choi, 2005; Giaschi, 2000; Kachru, 1992; Lee, 2009; Liggett, 2009; Matsuda, 2002; Sherman, 2010; Shin, Eslami, and Chen, 2011; Smith, 2020; Song, 2013; Taylor-Mendes, 2009; Yim, 2014). In other words, under their attractively designed covers, some ELT textbooks contain insidious models of monocultural politics (Hong & He, 2015) and social realities that tighten ideological tensions in EFL classrooms that negatively affect learners from expanding- or outer-circle cultures (Curdt-Christiansen & Weninger, 2015; Canagarajah, 1993, 2016; Choi, 2005; Weninger & Kiss, 2013; Dendrinos, 2015; Song, 2013). The vignettes featured in Chapter 2, 3 and 4 that showcase frameworks for understanding multimodal discourses in ELT textbooks take place in Korean contexts, so we inform those analyses with a brief review of literature that underscores critical discourse studies in Korean EFL education. However, it is important to remember that although this book showcases Korean EFL learning, the implementation of the featured frameworks can achieve commensurate insights in any language learning context that prioritizes the textbook as a necessary investment in a course curriculum.

Bemoaning the lack of foresight on the impact that ELT textbooks might have on Korean learners, Baik (1994) appears to warn against the insidious potential of their contents, which may not be seen for years to come. Years later, we see some research in Haggerty and Fox (2016) with results that resonate Baik's (1994) warning and point to other issues in Korean EFL culture as consequential to learner motivation. In a study that examines motivations to learn English in relation to high-stakes English language testing in Korea, Haggerty and Fox (2016) found that the motivation to learn is greatly seeded in Korea's *Su-neung*, (Korea's equivalent to the Scholastic Aptitude Test used in the United States), among other measures in Korea's high-stakes testing culture. Considering the *Su-neung* is Korea's final stage for K-12 education, it is curious that despite all the investment in learning functional English (Biggs & Tang, 2007; Canagarajah, 2016), it appears declarative knowledge inspired by the EFL *testing culture* to which Haggerty and Fox (2016) give their research attention is the preferred model or system of English learning. In other words, the silence of ELT textbooks, in the context of scholarly research into EFL learner motivation, may be explained in their implied demotivating potential.

In a critical reflection of power relations and ideologies found in secondary school reading comprehension materials from global (specifically, American) ELT textbook publishers, Choi (2005) found that underlying hegemonic interests in the content of the reading materials place America first among all cultures, which appear socio-economically dependent on the former, with no consequence of their own on the world stage. Choi's (2005) findings are reflected in Lee (2006), whose content analyses of several ELT textbook publications used in primary school classes revealed counter-intuitive tendencies in cultural depictions which young learners found contrastive to their own (Korean) identity. Ihm (1996), in an earlier and apparently multimodal study, although it is not explicitly mentioned, looked at the cultural content of illustrations in EFL learning materials for primary school learners (i.e. *Let's Go!* series by Cambridge University Press) and found they presented *inner-circle* social realities and standards. Ihm (1996) implies that the sociocultural narratives throughout ELT textbook publications can be a positive inclusion in EFL classrooms for the purpose of understanding foreign cultures. However, as already noted, those positive assumptions appear to be overshadowed by Lee's (2006) findings of a hidden curriculum in EFL materials (Weninger & Kiss, 2013), where certain cultures promoting certain ideologies and social realities are given priority over all others (Curdt-Christiansen & Weninger, 2015; Canagarajah, 2016; Pennycook, 2004). In another, unspecified, critical multimodal analysis of *New American: Inside and Out* (Kay & Jones, 2008), a popular ELT textbook used in elementary schools in Korea, Chao (2011) found consistent biases in favour of the target culture, assumed to be inner circle, and a general universality of all other cultures. Chao's (2011) findings suggest that for audiences, all other cultures to whom most of the readership likely belongs are indeed *othered*. That kind of discrimination was noticed by Lee (2011), who investigated situational meanings in EFL textbook content used in Korean K-12 schools. Lee (2011) found that people of inner-circle countries were presented as 'law-abiding, capable of getting things done, and living in a society that respects equality . . . educated in a way that gives them a sense of personal responsibility' (p. 52). Despite failing to meet the criteria enforced by KICE (i.e. KICE, 2001) for providing appropriate content, Lee (2011) notes some outdated publications are still being used in some institutions and recommends recontextualization in class by teachers and for students to be critical of perceptibly bias content that marginalizes them. Lee's (2011) recommendation is echoed in Song (2013), whose critical study of EFL textbooks used for high schools revealed equal measures of cultural biases favouring inner-circle cultures. For all the reasons noted here, it is not surprising that there haven't been more studies, such as Smith (2021), that claim that globally published ELT textbooks play a key role in perpetuating EFL learning anxiety among Korean students.

The literature reviewed here is not meant to represent an exhaustive collection of critical studies of ELT textbooks. However, these studies sufficiently outline a gap in literature for examining the multimodal discourse in ELT textbook content and what power relations and ideologies emerge in the multimodal fabric of each opened page, how that multimodal fabric is negotiated in situ and how the consumers of that content account for the hegemonic interests they negotiate in each lesson. In other words, no studies appear to engage in a triangulated approach that foundational scholars have been calling for decades (i.e. van Dijk, 2011; Wodak & Meyer, 2016).

A textbook, much like an image, is a static thing on its own. However, we know they are artefacts of a pedagogical culture that serve as vehicles or instruments in the conveyance of certain social realities. In the context of globally published

ELT textbooks, those social realities are invariably inner circle in nature (Smith, 2020). By analysing an ELT textbook in a triangulated approach, we are seeing a static text 'in action' or 'in situ'. From that perspective, we begin to see a blossoming of consequences of potentially marginalizing textbook content as their multimodal discourses are negotiated between students and practitioners in the pedagogical culture of EFL. By completing the triangulation with accounts from individual participants of that bloomed negotiation, we can corroborate inferences made in the first two frameworks featured in this book.

Chapter Summary

This chapter discussed some of the social politics involved with ELT textbook production and how that can translate into problematic issues for students and practitioners. In those discussions, it appears that for global publishing markets the needs and concerns of students and practitioners are overshadowed by political interests to maximize sales. A review of critical studies of textbooks in general, that is, textbooks used in K-12 or university programmes, revealed that globally published ELT textbooks draw the most attention. From that review, the need for critical analyses and evaluation is underscored by the lack of research featuring power and ideologies in the multimodal discourses of ELT textbooks. To meet that lack of research, this chapter calls for a triangulated approach to crisply delineate issues and problems that students and teachers face in ELT textbook use. In the chapters that follow, this book constructs a step-by-step procedure that students and practitioners can follow regardless of their position in that pedagogical culture. In Chapter 2, the call for stronger attention towards multimodal discourse in textbooks is met. The first of three frameworks featured in this book emerges from scholarly foundations in multimodal and critical discourse studies.

Discussion Questions

i. Think about some of the language learning textbooks or materials that you have used over the years, as a student, a student-teacher or a practitioner. How consequential were they in your course of study? What were some of their qualities that stood out to you? What did you appreciate or not prefer about them? Did you ever question the contents? Why or why not?

ii. According to Gray (2010), PARSNIP (politics, alcohol, religion, sex, narcotics, -isms and pork) represents topics that globally published ELT textbooks avoid. Do you believe that neutralizing potentially controversial topics is a necessary form of censorship in ELT production? Why or why not?

iii. According to Smith and Sheyholislami's (2022) literature review of critical discourse studies of textbooks used in secondary schools and up, most appear to target ELT publications. Why do you think ELT textbooks draw the most attention from researchers?

In Text – Addressing Multimodal Discourses in ELT Textbooks

English language teaching and learning is a diachronic continuum in which students and practitioners synchronize their professional breathing. In other words, if change is the lifeblood of the language teaching profession (Harmer, 2003), then it is reasonable to assume that change in language learning materials, such as textbooks, is part of that professional respiration.

A multimodal approach to analysing ELT materials has been given even more relevance due to our increased participation in digital/online learning engagements. As we have already noted, as per the onset of online communications, the world once *read* is now, perhaps much more than ever, the world *seen* (Kress, 2010). Not only is it easier to have and produce multimodal texts, but they are also tempting to use in a pedagogical sense, given the content that students and practitioners in language learning have access to on Facebook, Twitter, Instagram, TikTok, etc. It is more colourful, visual, aural and, frankly, more exciting than the conventional forms of content from which language praxis is traditionally negotiated. Thus, there is the need for a multimodal discourse approach to analysing ELT material to appreciate the potentiality, complexity and multiplicity of meaning-making mechanisms in those texts. An increase in online language learning programmes means that they will have more multimodal discourses in learning materials and require a measure of multimodal literacy to deliver, design, analyse and negotiate a course curriculum. Perhaps online language learning engagements will be the preferred format, surpassing the preference for conventional classes, and if so, have much more multimodal discourse in their activities and linguistic materials.

The Multimodal Discourses of ELT Textbooks

In the context of ELT textbooks, most are decontextualized into formulaic lists of expressions that promise acceptable entry into passable live speech (Curdt-Christiansen & Weninger, 2015, p. 16). Contrastively, visual representations in textbooks are not decontextualized but rather highly contextualized (Bateman, 2014; Bezemer & Kress, 2008; Gray, 2010; Jewitt, 2009; Kress, 2010; Lemke, 1989). In other words, the visual discourse recontextualizes the lessons on a *Gestaltian* field of meaning (Lemke, 2002; Machin, 2007, 2016; Machin & Mayr, 2012) that presents certain cultural realities as preferred models (Curdt-Christiansen & Weninger, 2015). Equipped with the armaments (vocabulary, semantic choices, pragmatic linguistic models, etc.) to participate in the contrived or highly specialized social realities, encouraged in the practice of ELT textbook content, students are shown what to say, when and where to say it, and in what forms those expressions are deemed suitable, as per the visual constructs in textbooks (Curdt-Christiansen & Weninger, 2015; Canagarajah, 2016; Jewitt, 2009; Kress, Jewitt, Bourne, Franks, Hardcastle, Jones & Reid, 2004). For this reason, ELT textbooks condition students to develop a fluency with the cultural realities they contain because with that understanding comes the implied capability for fluent speech. Gray (2010) points out a gap in research may lie in the visual formatting and design aspects of ELT textbook publishing alongside the sociocultural conditioning that the content appears to prescribe. A specific move towards the inclusion of visual discourse in rigorous analyses brings with it a new level of understanding that few have ventured to examine (Curdt-Christiansen & Weninger, 2015; Gray, 2010; Wodak & Meyer, 2016). Therefore, multimodal critical discourse studies may shed greater light on social injustices in content that may otherwise go unnoticed by students and practitioners.

In this first framework for understanding multimodal discourses in ELT textbooks, we ask: What are the power relations and ideologies in the multimodal discourse of an ELT textbook? By revealing how the world of English (Cortez, 2008) is presented to non-native English-speaking students in a foreign publication, we may begin to see a picture of the power relations and ideologies in the content and anticipate what pedagogical eventualities manifest in classroom negotiations or how consumers value that lesson content in their language learning investments. In what follows, we ground our design in foundations of critical discourse studies and multimodality, give illustrative details about the construction of the critical multimodal analysis template, then show how it can be used to analyse the multimodal discourse in a popular, globally published ELT textbook.

Critical Discourse Studies

Before we discuss critical discourse analysis, it is important to note this book uses the pluralized term 'critical discourse studies' (CDS). van Dijk (2016) argues that CDS is a more appropriate term because the pluralization reflects the various critical research methods, approaches, models and agendas involved in that field of research. To situate CDS and multimodality in contexts relevant to this book and its proposed frameworks, we should briefly discuss some foundational research in discourse analysis and systemic functional linguistics (SFL).

First proposed by Zellig Harris (1952) to analyse language beyond the level of the sentence, discourse analysis (DA) 'examines patterns of language across texts and considers the relationship between language and the social and cultural contexts in which it is used' (Paltridge, 2012, p. 3). DA also helps us understand how language presents different perspectives of social reality and how it constructs or establishes relations and identities between participants (Paltridge, 2012). In other words, DA helps us analyse an utterance as a communique and not just a product of grammatical flow (Gee and Handford, 2013) because 'grammar can tell us what *I pronounce you man and wife* literally means, but not when and where it actually means you are married' (Gee and Handford, 2013, p. 2). By extension, perhaps CDS can tell us why the expression *man and wife* is not *wife and man* or even who is doing the pronouncing and why it must be pronounced in the first place. To do so is to examine power relations, hegemony and ideologies that may only manifest with some measure of clarity in macro-perspectives of discourse (van Dijk, 1993).

Halliday (1978) saw language as socially constructed, requiring a social semiotic approach to clarify its use beyond the limitations of structuralist traditions (Bhatia, Flowerdew & Jones, 2008). Emerging from Halliday's (1978) work, systemic functional linguistics has profoundly influenced many fields of research (Bhatia et al., 2008), including discourse analysis and (multimodal) discourse studies (Jewitt et al., 2016). Halliday's (1978) SFL argues that grammatical structure in English presents a system of options for meaning-making from which speakers or writers select to serve their specific social contexts (Machin & Mayr, 2012). Verb transitivity, simply who is doing what to whom and how, plays a key role in meaning-making (Machin & Mayr, 2012). Multimodal discourse analysts have used SFL (i.e. Halliday & Matthiessen, 2014) in their explorations, leading to the development of systemic functional multimodal discourse analysis (SF-MDA).

In more specific terms, the frameworks proposed in this book partially draw upon Halliday & Matthiessen's (2014) *metafunctions* in SFL, such as the ideational – where reality, as we experience it, is made up of processes that consist of the *goings-on* or what is happening, doing, sensing, meaning and being and becoming, not only in clauses but in the visual transitivity of multimodal discourses (Machin & Mayr, 2012) – and the interpersonal – where *mood* and *modality* give meaning to how people express their attitudes and positions/stances in textual and multimodal discourse. The metafunctional concepts of meaning-making partially inform the construction of our critical multimodal analysis template, featured in this chapter, and the semi-structured interview coding procedure, featured in Chapter 4.

CDS, emerging from DA traditions, is a critical form of inquiry into social problems that manifest in discourse (Fairclough, 1992; Fairclough & Wodak, 1997; Gee, 2004; Kress, 1993; van Dijk, 1993; Wodak & Meyer, 2001). The emergence of CDS finds close association with Norman Fairclough's *Language and Power* (1989) and its roots connect, for example, with Bakhtin (1981) and the essays of W. E. B. DuBois (b. 1868–d. 1963) (Zamir, 1995) but perhaps most directly with two seminal publications – *Language and Control* (Fowler et al., 1979) and *Language as Ideology* (Hodge & Kress, 1989) (Flowerdew & Richardson, 2017; Rogers et al., 2005). Those publications played a key role in encouraging linguistic scholars from a variety of different backgrounds to pursue rigorous investigations of language and society (Flowerdew & Richardson, 2017). In the years that have followed, CDS emerged from interdisciplinary beginnings, seeded in scholarly research at separate institutions where social theory began weaving into linguistic investigation (Flowerdew & Richardson, 2017; Rogers et al., 2005).

From early 1990s research in methods of DA by Teun van Dijk, Norman Fairclough, Gunther Kress, Theo Van Leeuwen and Ruth Wodak, CDS was partially inspired by critical social inquiry and critical linguistics, aimed at underpinning ideological characteristics in linguistic processes of discourse (Fairclough, 2013; Flowerdew & Richardson, 2017; Wodak & Meyer, 2016). By bringing criticality to language analysis, CDS includes social manifestations of power relations and ideology (Fairclough, 2013). As already noted, CDS is not a neatly contained method but a 'problem-oriented interdisciplinary research movement, subsuming a variety of approaches, each with different theoretical models, research methods and agenda' (van Dijk, 2011, p. 357). However, despite the differences, each finds a common goal in exploring evidence of social injustices and inequities in discourse, whether they be micro-structures of power relations, such as a doctor–patient interaction, or macro-structures of cultural ideologies sometimes found in textbook contents or systematic distortions of human representations and constructed identities (Flowerdew & Richardson, 2017; van Dijk, 2011).

For Huckin (2002), CDS is unique for several reasons: (a) it is not experienced in a vacuum but in a real-world context, (b) it is open to integration between text, discursive practice and social practice, (c) it is concerned with societal issues, (d) it requires the researcher to take an ethical stance in the process of analysis, (e) it supports a view that discourse is socially constructed, (f) it endeavours to be accessible to a broad, non-specialist audience. Bearing these tenets in mind, it is not surprising that DA and CDS attracted researchers of education and textbooks (in particular) because no textbook, in any curriculum, is neutral in expressing, either implicitly or explicitly, a particular social reality (Auerbach & Burgess, 1985; Curdt-Christiansen & Weninger, 2015; Macgilchrist, 2017). Additionally, the classrooms in which they are frequently used are social ecologies (Hu, 2005; Kramsch, 2008; Van Lier, 2015) constantly in flux with the live negotiation of textbook content between students and their teachers (Littlejohn, 1992; Smith, 2021).

In education research, CDS is an attractive choice to find meaning in textbooks (Rogers et al., 2005). For example, Sinclair and Coulthard (1992) developed a detailed framework for investigating the negotiations between teachers and students in their classroom interactions, then later developed an equally elaborate framework in their content analysis of textbooks. As for ELT textbooks, investigations featuring CDS (i.e. Ahn, 2014; Canagarajah, 1993; Lee, 2009; Matsuda, 2002; Sherman, 2010; Shin et al., 2011; Song, 2013; Smith, 2021; Taylor-Mendes, 2009; Yim, 2014) highlighted power relations and ideologies that could be consequential to language learning in expanding-circle communities. Since ELT textbooks have received increased attention from researchers trying to identify oppressive characteristics in their contents, it is not surprising that a variety of CDS have served to identify social injustices in textbook discourses, challenged them (as per the studies noted here) and effected some drive towards change (Fairclough, 2013; Flowerdew & Richardson, 2017; van Dijk, 2016; Wodak & Meyer, 2016). This book continues that drive towards change and in the coming chapters, it manifests from one's understanding of social injustices in multimodal discourses and how they exercise curriculum reflexivity in situ with that content.

Multimodality

In the term 'multimodality', a mode is a means for making meaning, such as speech, writing, image, sound or colour, so multimodality refers to people using multiple means of meaning-making (Jewitt et al., 2016; Kress & Van Leeuwen, 2006; Norris, 2019). Modes are semiotic systems of representation that can take the form of gesture, gaze, spoken discourse, layout, print, music, just to name a few (Norris, 2004). More and more, these semiotic systems, driven by parallel directions of research, are formed by accretion into a single category to unify all manner of meaning-making (Kress, 2010). However, multimodality is diachronic, reflecting the changing world of communication that was drastically elevated with the birth of digital formats, tuned to the vibrations of technological innovation (Kress, 2010). Additionally, different modes of meaning-making inspire varied potentials for choices in specific instances of communication (Kress, 2010). Those differences are seen with more clarity through the lens of cultural variance, where modes of meaning-making find varied resources of representation (Kress, 2010).

As with CDS, Kress (2010) argues there is no theory accounting for the present state of communication or how that might encapsulate multimodality, but consistency lies in the connection between semiotic resource and social construction. In other words, despite there being no current universal theory accounting for multimodal communication (Kress, 2010), the fluctuations of multimodality can at least be read and predicted in the social eventualities that affect communication. Some common premises of multimodality are: (1) that meaning is achieved in a variety of semiotic resources, (2) that meaning-making is achieved by multimodal wholes and (3) that the study of meaning requires an accounting of all semiotic elements in a multimodal whole (Jewitt et al., 2016). For these reasons, multimodality is a necessary approach for examining ELT textbooks and the representations they illustrate because such compositions of image and text are constituents of a larger field of meaning (Jewitt et al., 2016; Machin, 2007; Machin & Mayr, 2012). Smith (2021) found that while many studies give attention to how a community or group is represented, few studies give sufficient attention to (or were theoretically informed by) any multimodal frameworks outside of Kress and Van Leeuwen (1996; 2006). That apparent gap in research suggests that a lack of attention to the visual discourse in textbooks allows for certain social realities to go unquestioned as they are negotiated between students and practitioners.

Wodak and Meyer (2016) suggest that meeting Jewitt et al.'s (2016) premises may be achieved in reconstructing the ways that multimodal texts can present social realities or standards that maintain power or domination of certain discourse communities. In that reconstruction, multimodality meets the common drive of CDS and gives partial reason why the term 'lens' was chosen to categorize domains of analysis in the forthcoming framework. Wodak and Meyer (2016) maintain that the union of CDS and multimodality requires the consideration of three key points: (1) that CDS is not a specific form of analysis but a programme of many theoretical models and methods, (2) that criticality seeks to question 'how things are, why they are like that, and how they could be different' (Wodak & Meyer, 2016, p. 183) and (3) that criticality and multimodality should focus on currents of power and ideology within social constructions and how dominant truths move through them (Wodak & Meyer, 2016). Visual elements in multimodal texts often enable power and ideology to masquerade as objective representation (Wodak & Meyer, 2016). Therefore, visual constructs have a powerful capacity for insinuation (Curdt-Christiansen & Weninger, 2015; Dendrinos, 2015; Gray, 2010; Littlejohn, 2012; Smith, 2021) by eliciting emotional responses that are processed with more instinctive alacrity than verbal discourses (Wodak & Meyer, 2016). One might infer, by reminding us of these key points and special attention to visual modalities, Wodak and Meyer (2016) are hinting at the insidiousness of visual content, asking researchers to be mindful not to underestimate the potency of those meaning-making mechanisms.

Necessitating Multimodal CDS for EFL Textbook Content

Looking to the most prominent representations of methodologies and contextual attention in the literature, such as studies of gender representation and marginalized/dominated communities in ELT textbooks, it is surprising none (or few) have explored or used the diverse, scholarly works that multimodal discourse studies presently offer (i.e. Bateman, 2014; Jewitt, 2009; Jewitt et al., 2016; Kress, 2010; Ledin & Machin, 2020; Machin & Mayr, 2012) for the analysis of textbooks.

Bearing in mind that discourse analysis questions *what* is said and *how* it is said (Gee, 2004), by extension, multimodality asks the same questions but acknowledges discourse as something beyond linguistic means. Gray (2010) claims that imagery in some ELT texts appear to employ strategies associated with advertising, and very little of this area of research is mentioned in the literature associated with production and consumption of ELT textbooks (Curdt-Christiansen & Weninger, 2015; Weninger & Kiss, 2013). The impact of imagery allows for much more visual modality in the delivery of English content (Gray, 2010). The tendency for many native English speakers to refer to photographs as *taken* rather than *made* implies a resonance between the image presented in the textbook and its unquestionable reality as something available to be taken from the real world (Gray, 2010). Gray's (2010) observation suggests that a photo taken rather than made also mitigates agency, whereby seemingly objectionable content is not produced by the publisher but rather taken from the real world to be digested as one pleases without ideological responsibility. This observation reveals an opening for the analysis of multimodal discourse and imagery in ELT textbooks that recent research is drawn to (i.e. Ahour & Zaferani, 2016; Amerian & Esmaili, 2015; Baghdadi, 2012; Giaschi, 2000; Gungor & Prins, 2010; Healy, 2009; Lee, 2014; Marefat & Marzban, 2014; Mustedanagic, 2010; Nofal & Qawar, 2015; Sadeghi & Maleki, 2016; Sahragard & Davatgarzadeh, 2012; Setyono, 2018; Sherman, 2010; Smith, 2020; Soylemez, 2010; Stockdale, 2006; Tajeddin & Janebi, 2010; Thomson & Otsuji, 2003), but few have undertaken or outlined specific, procedural analyses to validate their findings and subsequent discussions and conclusions.

For Bateman (2014), images and text are multiplied by each other, resulting in a greater summation of meaning than either occurring alone. While language was considered the main artery for communication, subordinating other modes of meaning-making, Norris (2004) warned that position limits one's understanding of the complexities involved with multimodal discourse. Images are a transmission for reality, rather than simply representative of it, and are linked together to form an ideologically *Gestaltian* fabric woven by social institutions where visual elements are created and consumed in a field of meaning (Kress & Van Leeuwen, 2006; Ledin & Machin, 2020; Machin & Mayr, 2012). Kress and Van Leeuwen's (2006) observations also draw attention to the connection between CDS and multimodality, noting the former predictably evolved to become part of a larger enterprise of meaning-making in the form of social semiotics (Kress, 1993; Van Leeuwen, 2005). Therefore, as an approach to critical studies of ELT textbooks, multimodal CDS (MCDS) may prove to yield far richer harvests of ideology and power relations because multimodality is a broad throughway for the conveyance of meaning in many forms (Kress and Van Leeuwen, 2006; Machin & Ledin, 2020). In other words, in an ELT textbook, CDS may only address *half the picture*.

Text and image are multiplied by each other (Bateman, 2014), so it is reasonable to assume that multimodal studies of ELT textbooks can increase our understanding of their impact on language learning (Hruska, 2004). We have also shown that ELT textbooks draw research attention because they represent a key component in ELT programmes for material reference, linguistic inquiry, learner practice and communicative interaction (Cunningsworth, 1995; Richards, 2014; Song, 2013; Tomlinson, 2011; Tomlinson & Masuhara, 2017), but also contain instances of social unfairness in their multimodal discourses (i.e. Ahn, 2014; Lee, 2009; Matsuda, 2002; Sherman, 2010; Shin et al., 2011; Smith, 2021; Song, 2013; Taylor-Mendes, 2009; Xiong & Qian, 2012; Yim, 2014). MCDS can provide the necessary lenses for seeing the highly specific social standards acquired by EFL students, under the banner of education (Apple, 1985; Gray, 2010; Harwood, 2014; Littlejohn, 1992; Song, 2013).

Schools of any type, especially with EFL learning programmes in expanding-circle nations, often force students to use certain textbooks (Lee, 2011; Xiong & Qian, 2012; Smith, 2021). In this way, they are also pressuring students to become passive consumers of whatever ideology is presented in their classrooms instead of encouraging them to become active producers of meaning (Gee, 2004). However, few studies engage in explicitly noted methods of analysis, such as the forthcoming framework in this book, to unveil how the visual transitivity in ELT textbook content frames, omits, foregrounds, backgrounds, insinuates certain social realities and what degrees of certitude power relations and ideologies are conveyed. MCDS may also assist in revealing those social injustices that have become normalized or standardized by the ELT textbook industry under the umbrella of language education (Littlejohn, 2012; Smith, 2020). In other words, MCDS can help us understand the integration of text, discursive practice and social practice (Huckin, 1997), as it manifests in ELT textbooks and their use in classrooms. Considering the social gravitas ELT textbooks represent and the apparent lack of research on their multimodal discourses, operationalizing MCDS may result in richer yields, illuminating otherwise unnoticed discourses with sharper clarity, while striving to fulfil one of the core aims of CDS – to instigate change (Fairclough, 1992).

As we have already noted, van Dijk (2016) insists on using the pluralization of CDA as 'CDS', referring to the diversity of analytical approaches. This is important to mention because it reflects the pluralistic nature of CDS, making it a suitable tool for coupling with other methods for more potent analyses in multiple modes of meaning-making (Jewitt et al., 2016). Canagarajah (1993), Kubota and Lin (2006), Littlejohn (2012), Sherman (2010), Song, (2013), and Xiong and Qian (2012) are just a few demonstrative examples of critical studies identifying oppressive characteristics of multimodal content in some ELT textbooks without using multimodal analysis as a theoretical framework, informing the analyses. Where CDS identify social injustice manifested in textbook content and challenge it to initiate some drive towards change

(Fairclough, 2013), the theoretical principles of multimodality examined here point to a more robust accounting of that content, improving the mindfulness of researchers and consumers in realizing the insidious delivery of inner-circle social realities. Additionally, MCDS can assist school administrators or EFL programme developers to make informed decisions on textbook selection (Fitzgibbon, 2013) that might go unchecked in lieu of brand recognition (Gray, 2010; Harwood, 2014; Littlejohn, 1992; 2012) enjoyed by many global EFL textbook publications.

However, textbooks are not the same as they once were, even thirty years ago. The term 'textbook' is now used to describe a multitude of items (Bell & Gower, 2011) and not a singular artefact of EFL culture. It is important to remember that global ELT textbooks are presently marketed to an audience overwhelmed with digital multimedia and all the visual stimuli those formats can deliver. Bell and Gower (2011) describe global ELT textbooks as one-size-fits-all, expensive, multimedia package, with (1) a dedicated website of auxiliary components such as (2) workbooks and (3) student books to which (4) teacher's manuals and (5) study strategy guides support the curriculum with (6) fully downloadable audio components supplementing a variety of (7) online games, activities and (8) homework assignments leading to (9) prefabricated exams and assessment packages. In other words, Bell and Gower (2011) appear to imply that the term 'ELT textbook' is a misnomer, so this book regards those publications as digitally interactive English language teaching (DIELT) programmes because the new nomination reminds us that ELT textbooks are, in every sense, a multimodal engagement by the consumer and should therefore necessitate a multimodal approach for any analysis.

Kress (2010) argues that images are no longer the providence of visual support but serve to deliver, with equal or greater potency, the ideology of a particular multimodal text. On a platform such as ELT textbooks, where text and image are often richly balanced, images and text further meaning and narrative (Bateman, 2014). In other words, visual discourse fuels the drive of a textbook's ideological vision (Kress, 2010). If one subscribes to Fox's (2004) arguments that a curriculum is a rhetorical accomplishment, then it is reasonable to assume multimodal textbook content is connected to classroom negotiations, where that rhetoric is given further legitimation via teacher's instruction.

Considering that ELT textbooks are likely designed towards earning generic acceptance in global markets (Harwood, 2014), it is not surprising that some measure of development and design focuses on visual semiotics as much as textual content. Therefore, equal measures of critical attention should be given to all the visual elements in EFL textbooks, as is given the textual content, in order to meet Jewitt et al.'s (2016) third premise of multimodality: to account for *all* forms of meaning-making in a particular multimodal whole.

Building a Framework for Critical, Multimodal Literacy

This chapter has explored foundational literature in CDS and multimodality and found an unfortunate dearth in analytical procedures that draw focused attention to multimodal wholes in textbooks (Wodak & Meyer, 2016). As there is no single, accepted form of MCDS, an integrated synthesis of scholarly frameworks was used to create a critical multimodal analysis template (CMAT) towards operationalizing a critical analysis of the multimodal discourses in ELT textbooks. CMAT, outlined in following sections, draws from Machin and Mayr (2012), Serafini (2014) and Wodak and Meyer (2016).

For Serafini (2014), those who are not able to read multimodal wholes are illiterate in the twenty-first century. Therefore, Serafini's (2014) framework for analysing visual and multimodal ensembles, while a composite of different approaches primarily inspired by Fairclough (2013) and Kress and Van Leeuwen (2006), gives the lion's share of analytical attention to visual modality. Serafini (2014) addresses perceptual, structural and ideological dimensions in multimodal text by connecting the dimensions to each other for a clear process of analysis that can easily coalesce with other frameworks. Although Serafini's (2014) framework appears simplified, the full extent of the framework's inquiry involves nearly fifty questions.

According to Wodak and Meyer (2016), visual modalities can reflect, deflect, mask, highlight, pervert or constitute social realities. In their framework for critically analysing visual and multimodal texts, Wodak and Meyer (2016) designed a procedure suitable for large sets of data, such as the multimodal discourse in a textbook. The five key steps in their design include assessing the discourse genre, capturing manifest content, reconstructing latent elements, assessing composition, followed by critical evaluation (Wodak & Meyer, 2016). Wodak and Meyer (2016) admit they are not proposing a standard scheme for MCDS but underpin how one might operationalize their approach towards large data. CMAT attempts to operationalize their approach by integrating specific questions of visual elements explored in Serafini's (2014) framework.

From Machin and Mayr's (2012) multimodal CDA framework, we borrow from their treatment of analysing semiotic choices, which highlights attributes of visual and textual devices, including (but not limited to) iconography, denotation, connotation, gaze, identity, colour, how the discourse is situated in the settings and what degrees of salience cause certain elements to either stand out or recede (Machin & Mayr, 2012). Additionally, we incorporate verb processes and transitivity, nominalization and presupposition to complement the visual transitivity that their multimodal CDA achieves.

The Critical Multimodal Analysis Template

The critical multimodal analysis template builds on the research of Wodak and Meyer (2016), Serafini (2014) and Machin and Mayr (2012) for the specific purpose of analysing large data, such as textbooks. The template in Table 2.1 poses a series of questions, each within a particular lens designed to reveal ideology and power relations in the multimodal content of ELT textbooks. The term 'lens' was chosen because it is hoped the term will inspire research that measures visual content on par with textual content, rather than as a supporting mode of meaning-making (Norris, 2019; Kress & Van Leeuwen, 2006). Put simply, lens reminds the analyst to *look* as well as read (see Figure 2.1). The procedure for critical inquiry, outlined in Table 2.1, requires one to observe all the multimodal content on each page or opened section of an ELT textbook as part of a system of meaning-making.

Rationale behind Framework Selection

It is important to remember that MCDS are problem-oriented movements (van Dijk, 2011), so framework choices and design depend on the problem. However, selecting multiple frameworks can be tricky, so Jewitt et al. (2016) suggest assessing their compatibility by gauging the synergy appearing between them, in addition to their capacity to answer the research question. At first, Wodak and Meyer (2016) presented a near-perfect framework in 'Critical Analysis of Visual and Multimodal Texts' (p. 189) because it was designed to (a) be used for large, multimodal data such as may be found in textbooks (p. 190) and (b) focus on critical multimodal analysis. However, the visual inquiry posed by Wodak and Meyer (2016), specifically the inventories of visual elements in ELT textbooks, appeared too ambiguous to achieve the specific focus warranted for all the potential mechanisms of meaning-making in a textbook. Wodak and Meyer

Table 2.1 Critical Multimodal Analysis Template (CMAT)

Lens	Inquiry
Holistic Lens	1. What is presented in the multimodal ensemble (ME)? What is the topic? What are the goings-on?
	2. What are the spatiotemporal and sociocultural contexts?
	3. Who are the apparent producers and audience of utterances and/or meaning?
	4. What is the purpose of the lesson? How does that align with the visual discourse?
	5. To what extent is the culture or topic institutionalized?
Inventory Lens	6. What is the register of the textual and visual elements?
	7. What dots, lines and shapes are presented in the ME? What characteristics do they have? Do they make a pattern? What social meaning/theme do they appear to convey/teach?
	8. What colours are used in the ME? How do they differentiate, frame or emphasize other elements in the ME? How are the students meant to translate or understand the colours, culturally or emotionally?
	9. What are the sizes and shapes of all elements in the ME? What relations of power do they convey about emphasis or recession?
	10. What is denoted in the ME? How do the textual denotations compare to the visual inventory? What does the denotation appear to teach?
Latent Lens	11. What structures of social reality are presented? What themes or meanings do they convey? What symbols, signs or recurring patterns support them?
	12. What are the textual or visual connotations in lessons? What cultural meanings or messages are conveyed in the ME?
	13. What is the ideological mood and modality in text? How does it relate to the visual discourses?
	14. Does the ME make sense or appear complete? What is the cohesion and coherence in the multimodal discourse? Is the lesson persuasive?
	15. What are the textual or visual silences in the lessons? What is missing? What ideological meaning do their expected or unexpected silences convey?
Compositional Lens	16. How do the visual and textual inventories relate to each other?
	17. How is gaze operated? Do participants connect with other participants? What does gaze 'offer to' or 'demand of' the students?
	18. What vectors manifest in the lessons? Do they connect participants and objects in the ME? What do those connections imply?
	19. Does any multimodal design separate students from elements in the ME?
	20. What are the angles of perception for the audience?

(Continued)

Table 2.1 (Continued)

Lens	Inquiry
	21. What is the visual transitivity? What are the participants and objects doing? What is foregrounded or backgrounded? Emphasized or de-emphasized?
	22. What interpersonal connections manifest between the students and the ME?
Critical Lens	23. What does the analysis of the ME in the textbook reveal about the broader social, cultural and institutional issues surrounding this educational programme?
	24. How can ideologies and power interests be described in the emphasized or silenced elements within the ME?
	25. How is power supported, challenged or concealed by all the modes in the ME?

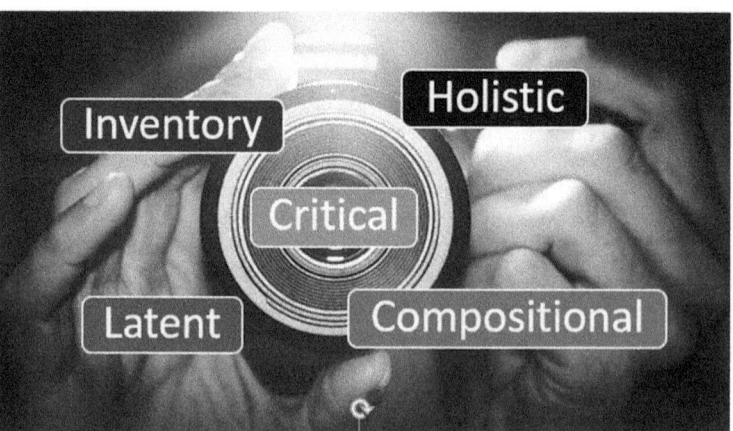

Figure 2.1 The lenses of CMAT.

(2016) even admit as much, encouraging analysts to embellish their framework because it was designed to be receptive to integration for various forms of critical inquiry. Therefore, using Wodak and Meyer (2016) as the foundation of inquiry, Serafini's (2014) 'framework for analysing visual and multimodal ensembles' (p. 34) and Machin and Mayr's (2012) multimodal approach to CDS were added to embellish inquiry of visual modalities in each multimodal ensemble (ME), such as an EFL textbook. Each draw close attention to perceptual, structural and ideological inquiry of visual modalities, strongly influenced by SFL and Kress and Van Leeuwen (2006) to delineate a visual grammar of multimodal discourse. The integrated synthesis of these frameworks results in a more robust, balanced and detailed method of critical inquiry for visual and multimodal ensembles (Kress and Van Leeuwen, 2006; Serafini, 2014). Considering the lack of any commonly accepted framework for MCDS, the need to include multiple frameworks for developing CMAT heeded Charmaz and McMullen's (2011) warning that sufficiently critical, qualitative inquiry requires multiple angles of observation. Furthermore, CMAT is an engagement of many forms of data, requiring a commensurately diverse 'conceptual and methodological toolbox' (Wodak & Meyer, 2016, p. 202) for analysis. For these reasons, the frameworks that inspired the construction of CMAT achieve more concise reconstructions of all the mechanisms for meaning-making and a thorough accounting of power relations and ideologies in the multimodal discourses of ELT textbooks.

For Littlejohn (1992, 2012), ELT textbooks are Trojan horses led willingly into global EFL classrooms with little consideration for what may be within. To see all instances of potentially objectionable content, practitioner-researchers and consumers of ELT textbooks may need to learn how multimodal, especially visual, elements talk (Serafini, 2014). If text is only half the picture of one-size-fits-all, multimedia packages masquerading as ELT textbooks (Bateman, 2014; Bell & Gower, 2011; Kress & Van Leeuwen, 2006), the resonance between Machin and Mayr (2012), Serafini (2014) and Wodak and Meyer (2016) may offer a compelling lens for broad, sharp perspectives of the whole picture. Additionally, operationalizing CMAT may provide strategies and procedures for encouraging multimodal and visual literacy (Serafini, 2014) in EFL education by empowering educators and students with a critical understanding of the materials they use in classrooms.

Vignette: A CMAT-Driven Analysis of *Top Notch 2*

In this vignette, CMAT is used on a popular textbook publication for university EFL programmes in China, Japan and Korea (Fitzgibbon, 2013; Smith, 2020). Prior to reporting on the results of the analysis towards understanding the power relations and ideologies in the multimodal discourse of that publication, we briefly remind the reader of the importance of ELT textbooks in Korean post-secondary perspectives because that contextuality will corroborate with the other frameworks in Chapter 3 (classroom observations) and Chapter 4 (interviews).

Language learning textbooks are easily accessible for evaluation and analysis because they are static time capsules that feature samplings of language and culture for student audiences (Weninger & Kiss, 2013). However, those samplings are richly illustrated with visual discourses that serve a hidden curriculum of social values and ideologies difficult to label or source, other than projecting them as preferred models of social reality (Weninger & Kiss, 2013). That ambiguity insidiously legitimizes the social values and ideologies in ELT textbooks because, for many students, language learning textbooks are a kind of *curricular tender* wherein a promise of education is negotiated (Giroux, 2007; Harwood, 2014; Gray, 2010; Littlejohn, 2012). In the specific contexts of Korean post-secondary EFL courses, a textbook is not only a vehicle for a teacher's pedagogical vision (Apple, 2001; Littlejohn, 2012; Curdt-Christiansen & Weninger, 2015) but a nesting-ground for ideological systems that few dare to question (Pennycook & Candlin, 2017) because so much of the content is used in an EFL course curriculum (Smith, 2020).

It is important to remember that ideology, as it may arise in the findings revealed in this vignette, refers to a structure of social values aligned with certain political views that become legitimized and preserved in a particular hierarchy of power relationships (Curdt-Christiansen & Weninger, 2015; Fairclough, 2013; van Dijk, 2011). Curdt-Christiansen and Weninger (2015) maintain that *ideology* in language learning

> is not simply any system of beliefs; it is the dominant political, educational, or cultural value system that secures its legitimacy through institutionally circulated discourses, and through the impact of these discourses on readers/ viewers/listeners . . . textbooks, sanctioned in most cases by government bodies, are thus an important vehicle in this process of legitimation. (p. 3)

This study presumes that no textbook is devoid of presenting a particular social order (Auerbach & Burgess, 1985). Language learning textbooks, often connected with powerful publishing institutions (Gray, 2010; Harwood, 2014, Littlejohn, 2012), need to be examined for their capacity to present unquestioned agendas or cultural values under the guise of authorized, official texts (Curdt-Christiansen & Weninger, 2015). It is important to bear in mind some of the critical research supporting these assertions were highlighted earlier in this chapter (i.e. Ahn, 2014; Sherman, 2010; Song, 2013; Yim, 2014). In this way, as textual and visual discourse constructs subjectivities in the content, so do language learners begin to see delineations of *us* and *them*, for example, as preferable interpellations of truth (Curdt-Christiansen & Weninger, 2015; Fairclough, 2013).

In the context of Korean post-secondary EFL courses, the insufficiencies of curricular design give textbooks more weight in a course of study (Lee, 2006; Littlejohn, 2012), but some literature suggests that ELT textbooks are not deserving of the dependency (Canagarajah, 1993; Cortez, 2008; Lee, 2015; Song,

2013; Sung, 2008). *Top Notch 2: Student Book* (Saslow & Ascher, 2006) is one of the most popular textbooks used in Korean university EFL courses and was the second highest seller for post-secondary EFL programmes from 2008 to 2013 (Fitzgibbon, 2013). The contents of *Top Notch 2* (*TN2*) appear to be much like many other ELT textbook publication marketed to expanding-circle cultures and involve a myriad of supplemental digital media and website material in addition to the textbook (Bell & Gower, 2011; Brown, 2011; Gray, 2010; Grossman and Thompson, 2008; Harwood, 2014; Littlejohn, 1992; 2012; Tomlinson, 2011). However, only the *Student Book* will be examined because it is largely the source of classroom activity and from which the curriculum of a typical Korean university EFL course is drawn.

Findings

In this section, we will look at findings gathered from CMAT (see Table 2.1) for analysing Unit 5 (Saslow & Ascher, 2006, pp. 50–1) and Unit 6 (pp. 62–3). Students participating in subsequent frameworks will have studied various listening, speaking, reading and writing activities involving vocabulary, dialogue practice and grammar exercises on pp. 62–3 (Saslow & Ascher, 2006). The topics in that unit addressed personal care, appearance and eating well.

The open-faced page units were analysed and referenced in the findings as a *multimodal ensemble* (ME) (Kress & Van Leeuwen, 2006). These MEs were analysed as if they were singular fields of meaning presented to the reader, and it is important to remember that this study assumes the multimodal inventories analysed in CMAT are interwoven fabrics in a field of meaning (Kress, 2010; Machin, 2016). Elements of those inventories (colour, shape, gaze, vectors, etc.) may yield meaning on their own but have significantly different meaning due to size, composition or placement in their fields of meaning, which may emphasize or de-emphasize them. Food is a good metaphor in support of this assertion – while flour, water, tomatoes, milk, lemon juice and seasonings may not be particularly significant culinary choices on their own, put together and/or prepared in certain ways, they can become an appreciated dish in many cultures around the world: pizza. Let us assume, then, that the MEs (Saslow & Ascher, 2006, pp. 50–1 and pp. 62–3) are *Gestaltian* dishes wherein a buffet of meaning tantalizes the viewership.

Unit 5: 'Personal Care and Appearance'. For copyright reasons, we are unable to share the exact visual reference of *Top Notch 2*, Unit 5 and Unit 6 (Saslow & Ascher, 2006, pp. 50–1 and pp. 62–3). Instead, we can offer maps of those units (see Figures 2.2 and 2.3), so that the forthcoming analysis inspires one's visualization of the lessons.

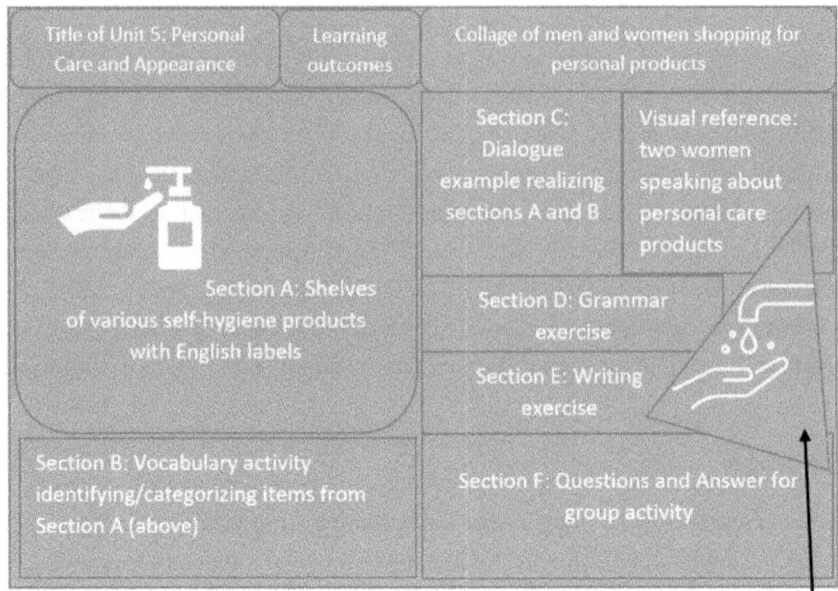

Figure 2.2 Unit 5 ME map of Saslow and Ascher (2006, pp. 50–1).

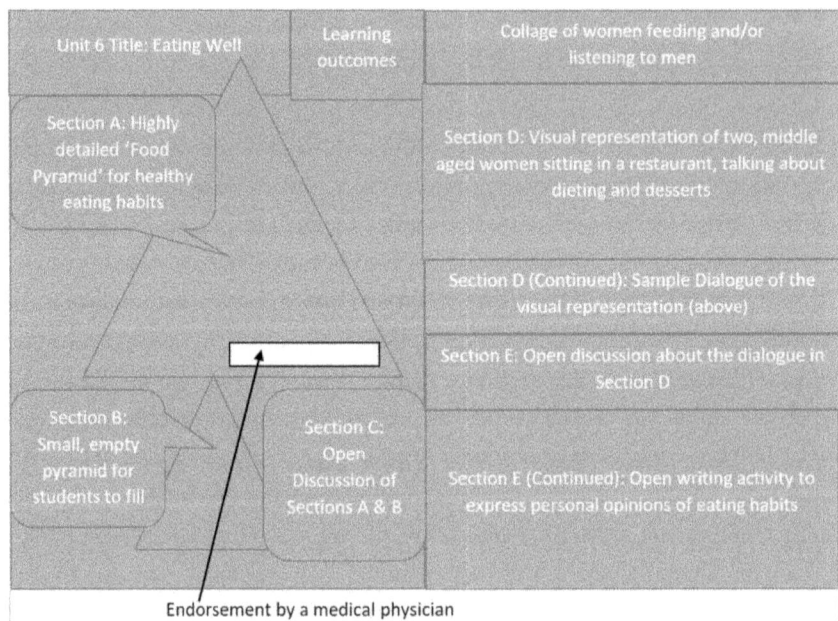

Figure 2.3 Unit 6 ME map of Saslow and Ascher (2006, pp. 62–3).

Unit 5, entitled 'Personal Care and Appearance', features five activities involving vocabulary, listening, comprehension and speaking practice. The left page features a large, colourful image of three shelves, lined with multiple personal hygiene products, indicated implicitly 'for men' or 'for women' on the labels (e.g. a thumbnail illustration of a man shaving his beard or a woman shaving her legs). A pair-work assignment beneath the shelves asks the students to write the featured products in a categorized table. The right page features three sections: a conversation dialogue example, followed by a comprehension check and a contextual writing completion activity. The bottom right features a *What about you?* section where students are asked to fill out a small chart. Spatiotemporally, the left page is ambiguous because the products could be contemporary or decades old, but on the right, the women speaking with each other in the photo appear to be in a contemporary office setting. The banner at the top of the right page features several images of customer and staff interactions in a pharmacy or health care section of a store. Four women and two men are featured in the ME but only two women, Mieko and Noor (Saslow & Ascher, 2006, p. 51), are speaking. The audience is assumed to be English language learners. The purpose of the lesson appears to teach about some vocabulary pertaining to 'personal care and appearance' products as well as conversations people might have in an office or in a store about those things. While the text denotes Brazilian cosmetics and a Japanese visitor's communicative challenges in Brazil, the visual discourse appears focused on personal grooming products, as evidenced by the shampoo and conditioner floating awkwardly and on an angle in the lower-right space below the dialogue as if directed at the two women. The composition of the shampoo and conditioner in the field of meaning is contrasted against all other objects on the page that are structured in a grid, suggesting emphasis and connecting it with Mieko and Noor's conversation. There appears to be an institutionalized assumption that with EFL instruction comes the bonus of learning how to take care of one's personal hygiene and appearance and feel comfortable to speak of such matters publicly. Items such as aspirin, cough medicine and shaving cream, and razors, for example, are presented as essential and generic personal care products in any culture, even though in a Korean context, some of these items would not appear in the average Korean household. Additionally, of those generic products featured on the left, at least half of them appear to be marketed for women.

The register of text appears to be instructional with a dialogue featuring a casual exchange between businesswomen in an office environment. However, the register of the visual discourse diverges from the textual because the entire left panel of the ME displays health care products. Bullet points mark the five, large activity sections and each appear isolated from each other. The lines on the shelves and the subtle spaces between the products imply categorical association between them and add to the overall narrative that the lesson is teaching one about personal hygiene rather than EFL. The myriad of colours featured on the left draws the eye and emphasizes those items. The grassy green and golden yellow hues framing the shelves add to that emphasis, which is lacking on the right. The red, white and blue bullet points resonate with inner-circle cultures, adding to the overall inner-circle perspectives of personal care, despite the dialogue between two people from different, expanding-circle cultures.

Sections B and E (see Figure 2.2) each invite the students to fill in personal information and the green banners highlighting those tables appear to encourage the students to 'go' or be willing to reveal personal information or opinion. This appears to be one example of how colours associated with international traffic signals appear to be utilized in various activities. In addition to colour choice, the left section highlighting personal care and appearance products projects the lion's share of emphasis on the ME. The shampoo and conditioner floating on the right panel could easily have come from the shelves featured on the left. The textual denotation, already noted earlier, does not match the visual representation because there is very little visual representation, other than the two pictures on the right, that gives emphasis to the exchange between Mieko and Noor. In other words, the unit title 'Personal Care and Appearance' could easily be modified to include *Products* because they are visually emphasized.

The structures of social reality presented in the lessons suggest that EFL learning must include lessons about personal grooming from inner-circle perspectives. Presenting all the 'personal care and appearance' products in a line, side by side on levelled shelves of equal distance and height, suggests that all of those products are the same for everyone. The connotations of the dialogue suggest English is a lingua franca in Brazil for speakers of Japanese who need to buy cosmetics. The connotations of the visual discourse support a narrative that English capability is a requirement for personal care and appearance because the emphasized products are labelled in English. Considering that the labelling on the products is English, it is assumed that these products are being sold in Brazil because that is where Mieko and Noor are having a conversation. For this reason, the ideological force of the visual and textual discourses presents English as a lingua franca in Brazil and an implied requirement for personal grooming. Those discursive devices effectively *other* the speakers because neither belong to nor are presently situated in an inner-circle culture. For these reasons, the ME does not feel complete because it does little to give visual or textual representation for Brazilian culture, Japanese culture or any expanding-circle nation to which both speakers in the lesson belong. Instead, the lesson appears to teach vocabulary and eventualities around personal care and appearance that does little to justify why there should be two businesswomen in Brazil having a conversation about cosmetics.

The silencing of the Japanese and the other woman suggests the necessity of English skills not only for communication in Brazil but for understanding personal care and appearance. The presence of the two women in the lesson doesn't appear to make sense and effectively silences their respective cultures. While vectors do not appear significant on the page, there is an ambiguous connection between the photographs of Mieko and Noor and the personal care products in proximity to their conversation (shampoo and conditioner). Each are visually *angled* on the ME and connected in that way. The association between these two floating visual devices appears to give each a resonating connection that implies a silencing of the cultures of the two women because de-labelling the shampoo and conditioner suggests the cultures to which the speakers in the dialogue belong are not worth mentioning. However, by contrast, giving very distinct English labels to the products on the left implies more resonant agency for the language and the products on which it is used.

Compositionally, the visual and textual discourses do not completely relate to one another because the conversation on the right does not correspond to the emphasis on personal care products on the left. Gaze does not appear to offer to or demand anything from the students and that silence may diminish the potential for students to connect with the lesson. However, gaze does emphasize connections between the participants on the page. The connected participants are not gender-mixed; men are speaking with men and women are speaking with women. The perceived differences separating the students from certain elements in the ME are the silencing of the cultures of Japan and Brazil, the misalignment of the visual and textual discourses and the persistent narrative that learning English helps one overcome language challenges *and* achieve personal hygiene. Korean university students connect with the Japanese and Brazilian women because they each belong to expanding-circle nations. Therefore, they also share in the cultural silencing of those women in this lesson.

Critically, the visual and textual discourses present inner-circle sociocultural perspectives as preferable to any other, despite the conversation taking place in a non-inner-circle culture. That narrative is supported by silencing those expanding-circle cultures effectively presents them as *others*, unworthy of even a label written in Brazilian or Japanese. In this way, the power of inner-circle personal care products is emphasized because they are given labels in English. Any measure of agency afforded to Mieko and Noor, as independent businesswomen, is diminished by the content of their dialogue which centres on the acquisition of cosmetics, as if their professions come second place to their physical appearances. This assertion is underpinned by Mieko's comment that she'd love to get some cosmetics 'that these lovely Brazilians wear' (Saslow & Ascher, 2006, p. 51). The topic of conversation delegitimizes their professional status in the lesson and adds to the concealment of their sociocultural representation in the visual discourse. The overall emphasis on inner-circle products overshadows the women as *others* by presenting English as the assumed lingua franca of Brazil and the preferred cultural model of personal care and appearance.

Unit 6: 'Eating Well'. This unit will be given additional attention in later chapters because the content will be showcased in Chapters 3 and 4. There are five activity sections in the lesson. On the left, a food pyramid with descriptions written on either side of it towers above a smaller, empty pyramid where students are invited to fill in some spaces with writing. The right panel includes two sections with multiple activities, including a listening exercise of a conversation featuring two women in a restaurant, followed by comprehension questions and a yellow section entitled *What about you?* where students are invited to fill in personal information about food choices. Spatiotemporally, the context appears contemporary and centres around a conversation in a restaurant. Socioculturally, the visual discourse points to an emphasis on *inner-circle* perspectives of food, exemplified by the typical or generic food choices given attention in the food pyramid on the left. The primary producers of text in the ME are the two women, named Iris and Terri on the right, and include two more men and women above in imaginary exchanges, totalling four women and two men. The audience of this lesson are assumed to be EFL students for the purpose of learning about food choices and what English dialogue might occur in a restaurant, but that purpose appears to be only loosely associated with the unit goals, listed top left, in a small green box. What appears to be institutionalized in this EFL lesson is the assumption that learning about food and English invariably includes dieting and food choices that are limited to inner-circle palettes. Considering the unit name, 'Eating Well', implies an instructional narrative for healthy eating choices, those assumptions appear to normalize the necessity for understanding inner-circle foods in English.

The inventoried register of text in the lesson is casual dialogue about dieting and eating and vocabulary of common inner-circle foods. The visual registry appears to be more instructional than casual and features a large food pyramid as the model of healthy eating habits because those shapes are traditionally associated with power and agency. The pattern that emerges in those repeated shapes on the left suggests the completed food pyramid is superior to the empty pyramid the students must fill, as if to imply their commitment to English must also include a subscription to healthy eating habits. This lesson features a myriad of colour combinations in reflection of the visual representations of food items, but it is hard to overlook the red, white and blue bullet points marking every section. Those persistent bullet points appear on every page in the textbook and resonate with those colours normally associated with inner-circle cultures. The textual denotations are conversations about nutrition, diet and vocabulary of apparently inner-circle foods in each of the learning activities. The visual preference for inner-circle cultures appears to legitimize the instructional nature of the denotations to learn the specified eating habits.

The structures of social reality that emerge, then, appear to point to inner-circle perspectives of healthy consumption habits as the model against which all others are measured. For Serafini (2014), the triangular shapes would represent dynamic action or conflict, suggesting that image of the large food pyramid is a visual challenge to the audience. The connotation, then, may be that inner-circle perspectives are superior because the pyramid is being presented as superior to all others for 'daily eating habits to avoid heart disease' (Saslow & Ascher, 2006, p. 62). The lesson feels incomplete because it presents a one-sided view of food and consumption habits as the only options for continued health. This assertion is supported by the silencing of all other cultural perspectives to which EFL students, to whom this lesson is aimed, likely belong.

Compositionally, the visual and textual inventories relate to each other in so far as they promote inner-circle perspectives of food. However, the two Asian people speaking in a kitchen on the top right appears to place them in a lesser social status, as if to suggest Asian people are likely to be found preparing food rather than eating it, as featured in the conversation between Terri and Iris. Gaze operated between the participants and does not demand or offer anything with the audience. The only vectors that manifest are the lines that appear on either side of the smaller, empty pyramid, pointing directly up at its larger partner – the implied model of healthy eating habits. The differences that separate the students from the elements in the lesson appear to be the lack of reference to any other culture, either textually or visually. That lack of inclusivity diminishes the potential for any interpersonal structures to develop between the students and the English lesson and may be partially the reason why one professor, featured later in this book, decided to change the food pyramid to a food *pagoda* during class.

Critically, then, the broader sociocultural and institutional contexts surrounding this lesson appear to promote continued *inner-circlism* as the preferred model of social habits against which all others are silenced. The ideological force of the lesson appears to rest in the interpellation that the ability to speak English affords one the capacity to develop healthy eating habits. This is extraordinarily ironic because according to the World Health Organization (WHO, 2020), inner-circle nations such as the United States, Canada, Australia, the United Kingdom and New Zealand have among the highest rates of adult obesity compared to all the nations, in addition to the highest percentages of heart disease worldwide. In this way, power is supported by the visual discourse to legitimize the quality of healthy eating habits from an inner-circle perspective while concealing those dietary and lifestyle habits of other cultures.

Chapter Summary

This chapter began by discussing the multimodal discourses of ELT textbooks, followed by theoretical frameworks of critical discourse studies and multimodality. After arguing the need for MCDS of textbooks, we showed the formation of CMAT, a framework for analysing multimodal discourses in ELT textbooks, followed by a rationale behind its design and construction. Finally, a vignette, featuring the use of CMAT analysing two MEs, has shown how CMAT helps us see the holistic, inventoried, latent and compositional mechanisms in all the modes of meaning-making, towards a critical revelation of power relations and ideologies. A discussion of these findings will be forthcoming in Chapter 5. However, in following chapters, we will see how the content that we've examined, using CMAT, is negotiated by students and practitioners in a Korean university EFL classroom.

Discussion Questions

i. In a Foreword for Serafini (2014), James Paul Gee asserts that those who are not able to read multimodal wholes are illiterate in the twenty-first century. Do you agree? Why or why not?

ii. Jewitt et al. (2016) remind us that meaning is achieved in a variety of semiotic resources. Find an example of a 'multimodal ensemble' online – it can be a website page, an advertisement or an internet meme. Using the 'Inventory Lens' on CMAT (Table 2.1), try and list all the semiotic resources that you can find. Did you discover anything that you did not notice the first time? If so, has meaning in the ensemble changed?

According to the analytical findings of 'Unit 6' in the vignette, English-speaking capability is connected to healthy eating habits. How does the researcher reveal that this connection is projected in the multimodal ensemble? Do you agree with the findings? Why or why not?

3

In Class – Negotiating Multimodal Discourses 'In Situ'

In traditional classrooms, there are so many things that occur that can have an impact on learning and acquisition for students and practitioners. The classroom, the occupants, the instruments of learning and the typical *goings-on* one might expect to see in classrooms form a unique ecology in which textbooks play a significant role, especially in the contexts of foreign language learning (Kramsch, 2020; Kramsch & Zhang, 2018; Macgilchrist, 2017; Van Lier, 2004). As teachers, we also learn and acquire an understanding of ourselves as we develop a professional craft in a reflexive praxis that shapes our pedagogical vision in the rhetorical accomplishment of a curriculum (Fox, 2004; Smith, 2021). In the context of this book, the professional craft that we continuously develop in classrooms necessarily includes knowing how to negotiate, deliver, resist, transform, appropriate or neutralize the multimodal discourses in one's textbook. In what follows, we take a closer look at curriculum and ELT textbooks and critical pedagogy (CP), and use those to inform the design and construction of our second framework: a multimodal analysis of visually recorded English classrooms.

In this second framework for understanding multimodal discourses in ELT textbooks, we ask: *How do students and practitioners negotiate the multimodal discourses in their ELT textbook during class?* This second question draws attention to the findings in CMAT, where we begin to see some evidence of social unfairness in the data (discussed in Chapter 5), by asking how those discourses may be negotiated *in action* (i.e. Littlejohn, 1992; 2012; Smith, 2021). In specific terms of the featured vignettes, where we look at an ELT textbook in a Korean university classroom, this question inspires several peripheral questions, such as: *How do Korean students relate to the multimodal content? Does it inspire them to achieve greater English proficiency or demotivate their learning experience? Do the students appear to resist or subscribe to the content?* As for the instructors:

How are they presenting the power relations and ideologies in the multimodal content? Are they resisting, transforming, appropriating or neutralizing (Cortez, 2008) *any of the multimodal discourses in classroom negotiation?* By revealing how the world of English (Cortez, 2008) is presented to L2 English-speaking students in a foreign publication, especially during class time, we may begin to see a picture of the power relations and ideologies in the content and anticipate what pedagogical eventualities manifest in classroom negotiations or how students and practitioners value the lesson contents in their language learning investments. In what follows, we anchor this second framework in studies of curriculum and critical pedagogy, and then show how it can be used to build an analytical framework for looking at multimodal interactions in an EFL classroom.

Curriculum and ELT Textbooks

When light is shone through a prism, the resulting delineation of hues in that spectral beam helps us understand those fractured constituents of light. Bearing this in mind, to ask what curriculum *is* entertains a loaded question (Fox, 2019) because the illumination that a curriculum endeavours to achieve requires a similar fracturing to see its constituents. For Fox (2019), how we define it and where we happen to be (i.e. geopolitically) says a lot about our beliefs, assumptions and knowledge (BAK) (Woods, 1996) about education and teaching.

It is also important to explicitly delineate the difference between 'syllabus' and 'curriculum' at this point because the author has witnessed students and practitioners use the terms interchangeably. A syllabus is a specific and flexible description of activities and instruction in a particular subject, while a curriculum is much wider in scope and serves to align courses with the pedagogical visions and methodologies of an institutional programme of study. The umbrella term of curriculum, in the classical *Greek* sense, was channelled by Cicero: 'Hae sunt exercitationes ingenii, haec curricula mentis' [These are the spurs of my intellect; the courses my mind runs on] (Egan, 2003, p. 10). In lighter terms, Egan (2003) reminds us that for Cicero, *curriculum* is the *content* that he is studying at that time – and it may, indeed, be true that is what curriculum is to him *in that place* and *in that time*. However, in the context of language learning, which serves as a polestar for this branch of theoretical reasoning, *content* is not a sufficient platform on which to build explanation for its envisioned learning outcomes or how it is written, received, enacted, learned, assessed and finally accomplished in the larger sense of a completed course of study (Biggs & Tang, 2007; Connelly & Clandinin, 1988; Fox, 2004, 2019; Earl, Hargreaves & Schmidt, 2002; Stoller, 2015; Wiggins & McTighe, 2005). Some language instructors envision their *curriculum* as unending frameworks for a student's life, long after the components of a syllabus are achieved in a course of study, so that their students can face linguistic challenges on their own. Bearing that perspective in mind, Fox (2004) presents an elegant summation of curriculum that 'itself may be viewed as a kind of rhetorical accomplishment' (p. 1) and further argues that its renewal is linked to its dynamic discursivity with education policies in certain communities (Fox, 2004). Therefore, Fox (2004) encourages a discursive approach to curricular analysis because it draws on and accounts for educational stakeholder voices and intentions.

Again, it is important to remember that ELT textbooks are not only tactile vehicles for a portion of the course curriculum but an implied spring of trust, continuously replenished as the teacher and the learner negotiate meaning in the content (Savignon, 2002; Smith, 2021; Wiggins & McTighe, 2005). For some teachers, whether in language learning or elsewhere, the beginning and end of a curriculum is bound to the syllabus in the textbook or their favourite lessons, where *learning* becomes a lesser preference to *teaching* (Wiggins and McTighe, 2005). Considering that ELT textbooks often serve as the curriculum for many language programmes (Richards, 2014; Tomlinson & Masuhara, 2017), the underlying risk of that over-investment could limit lessons to declarative, text-centred activities following fixed linguistic challenges, rather than nurturing functional knowledge (Biggs & Tang, 2007; Curdt-Christiansen & Weninger, 2015).

In the following sections, we explore critical pedagogy as a bedrock on which to build a second framework for analysing multimodal interaction in a classroom. The analysis includes a consideration of the multimodal discourses in an ELT textbook and how they can be accounted for, negotiated, delivered, resisted, transformed, appropriated or neutralized in situ.

Classroom Negotiations and Critical Pedagogy

We chose to inform the creation of a multimodal interactional analysis, for the purpose of seeing ELT textbook content used in live classrooms, with principles of critical pedagogy because the framework includes students as active negotiators of the content they are instructed to digest. Built on foundations set by Paolo Freire's *Pedagogy of the Oppressed* (1970), critical pedagogy deals with the critical nature of education, where *the classroom* is seen as a socially constructed and politically motivated fulcrum of diachronic ideologies (Giroux, 1988; 2004; 2007; Giroux et al., 1988; McLaren, 1988; Kumaravadivelu, 2006; Norton & Toohey, 2004; Shor, 1992; 2014). For Freire (1970), students are powerless in their education and subjected to the *checks and balances* reflective of a modern banking system, where teachers and the curriculum serve as the authority. In Freire's (1970) *banking system*, students are exorcized of any creativity and intellectually bound to a cyclical mechanism of dominance transmitted under the guise of increased knowledge and skill. Seeking to level the playing field, Freire (1970) proposed an educational framework that allowed for students to engage in critical co-investigation of educational challenges. That co-discovery of knowledge by Freire (1970) does not diminish or inhibit creativity through controlled or prescribed revelations of truth that 'maintain the submersion of consciousness' (p. 81) but 'strives for the emergence of consciousness and critical intervention in reality' (p. 81). Freire's (1970) inception to free the minds of oppressed people (students, in this case) served to inspire other researchers like Giroux (1988; 2004; 2007; 2017) and Shor (1992) to give form to CP, where students are active participants in the implementation of a particular curriculum, rather than mere receivers of it. In an EFL context, CP is a heuristic that helps diminish social unfairness while helping EFL students and practitioners recognize and challenge issues of domination in the classroom (Kumaravadivelu, 2006). Therefore, students are enabled to draw informed attention to the multimodal discourses in their ELT textbooks, where certain ideologies often go unchallenged (Smith, 2021).

For Giroux (1988; 2004; 2007), one of CP's central tenets draws focus on those situations or places where social agency is denied. Of course, inspired by Freire's (1970) directed focus, Giroux (2004) sees language education as a prime example of denied agency, where students (and teachers) are sometimes compelled to follow a curriculum prescribed by greater powers in a particular community or by the state. Education, Giroux (2017) insists, should produce critical thinkers who contribute to the culture of democracy, ensuring its continued prosperity. Considering that ELT textbooks may be the vehicles of a particular social, political and cultural agenda, normally used in classrooms where social agency is often denied by disenfranchised students, a framework inspired by the tenets of critical pedagogy research can inspire students (and practitioner-researchers) to think critically of the textbook content they consume (Giroux,

2007). Empowered with increased confidence in the engagement of linguistics challenges, students are enabled to build an identity in the language they seek to learn (Giroux, 2017). In this way, Giroux (2007; 2017) maintains that CP enables students and teachers to transform learning in the classroom into a live negotiation rather than a matter of mere consumption. In an EFL context, Giroux's (1988; 2004; 2007) argument appears to suggest that CP enables users of ELT textbooks to actively transform content in situ, rather than simply consume it to meet the requirements of a prescribed curriculum.

Shor (2014) echoes Giroux's (1988; 2017) claims of denied social agency, the reciprocal nature of learning and diachronic power relations in classroom environments. For Shor (1992; 2014), knowledge is in a constant state of change and only empowers those who can wield it to change their condition. By conceptual extension, in an EFL context, where English learning is often a socio-economic investment (Canagarajah, 2006) to improve one's condition or status, EFL education thus becomes a hegemonic commodity. If education suppresses intellectual curiosity and the development of skills, as is sometimes found in test-driven cultures such as Korea, Iran, Japan and China (i.e. Song, 2013; Lee, 2014; Matsuda, 2002; Rahimi and Hassani, 2012), something has gone terribly wrong in the education process because it no longer serves to enlighten but rather suppresses those who cannot afford the socio-economic investment that high-stakes testing, such as in expanding-circle nations (e.g. Haggerty & Fox, 2016), often requires.

Critical pedagogy encourages students to question *what they know* and *how they came to know it* (Shor, 1992, p. 260), empowering them to be critical thinkers while building resistance to domination. Drawing inspiration from Freire's (1970) research, Shor (2014) also recognized the work of clinical psychologist Jean Piaget (b. 1896–d. 1980), who encouraged a reciprocal relationship between a student and their teacher within a centred pedagogy. In such a curriculum, where the student(s) and their teacher enjoy a revolving transmission and consumption of knowledge, one-way knowledge is avoided (Shor, 2014). In this environment, Shor (2014) maintains, students are enabled to develop critical thoughts of their learning experience and 'make meaning and act from reflection, instead of memorizing facts and values handed to them' (p. 12). In an EFL context, Shor's (2014) CP encourages the combined effort between students and their teachers to think critically of the content in the ELT textbooks because political ideology resides in classroom discourse as much as through textbook content. By recognizing the importance of classroom discourse as perhaps part of a greater culture of learning (i.e. Cortazzi & Jin, 1996), Shor's (2014) CP draws focus on EFL materials-in-action (Littlejohn, 1992; 2012) and contributes to a theoretical framework informing critical studies on the use of EFL textbooks.

Approaches in critical studies of EFL textbook use, from the perspective of CP, issue challenges to problematic, sociopolitical, value-laden content such as issues of cultural marginalization, stereotyping and inner-circle secularization (Lee, 2009, Rashidi & Safari, 2011; Xiong, 2012) because they have become interpellated (Fitzgibbon, 2013; Gray, 2010) and *McDonaldized* in predictably efficient and highly controlled EFL learning systems (Janks, 2010; Kumaravadivelu, 1999; Littlejohn, 2012; Pennycook, 1994; 2008; Sayer & Meadows, 2012; Smith, 2021). It is not surprising, therefore, beginning with Freire (1970), that Giroux (2017), Shor (2014), and Pennycook and Candlin (2017) encourage the questioning of naturalized assumptions (Gray, 2010; Janks, 2010), especially in classrooms. By keeping this policy in mind, teachers are given the opportunity to become agents of critical pedagogy (Pennycook & Candlin, 2017), participating with students to deconstruct social unfairness in the classroom negotiations of multimodal discourses in ELT textbooks.

Canagarajah's (1993) ethnographic study of EFL classes in Sri Lanka revealed issues of cultural alienation from textbook content. Resonating with Littlejohn's (1992) assertion that sees ELT textbooks as *materials-in-action*, supported by Shor's (1992) speculation that classroom discourse can also be a medium of concern for CP, Canagarajah's (1993) study puts a spotlight on the values and beliefs that textbook content forces on students. Describing the study as a critical ethnography, Canagarajah's (1993) ideologically sensitive observations of a particular curriculum to which the textbooks adhere informs EFL culture. The textbook under scrutiny in Canagarajah's (1993) critical ethnography, *American Kernel Lessons* (O'Neill et al., 1978), drew considerable ire and resistance from Sri Lankan students. Canagarajah (1993) describes the textbook content as a shallow representation or version of *American* culture, promoting white, male, inner-circle values, which many of the Sri Lankan students resisted because it was so counter-intuitive to their own culture.

For Shin and Crookes (2005), CP informs an investigative study of two Korean EFL classrooms. The study implemented measures of CP to stimulate debate in EFL settings traditionally stereotyped as offering only test-driven curriculums while restricting student participation beyond one-way consumption of *state selected* EFL materials (Shin & Crookes, 2005). Channelling CP to inspire earnest student participation in classroom discourse, Shin and Crookes's (2005) study attempted to stimulate critical debate about social issues using pre-designed learning materials. The change in classroom activity was well received by both classes because many students, while recognizing Shin and Crookes's (2005) classes were not focused on their test-driven education system, nevertheless engaged in spirited debate and expressed positive reactions at the opportunity. Again, we see resonance with Cortazzi and Jin's (1996) culture of learning (Cortazzi & Jin, 1996) because Shin and Crookes's (2005) study challenged naturalized assumptions (Janks, 2010) that East-Asian students are passive participants in a test-driven education system. By dispelling such a stereotype, Shin and Crookes (2005) have shown CP to be a valued framework for addressing critical issues on East-Asian classrooms while informing a critical study on the use of ELT textbooks.

In a study discussing the ideological implications of EFL learning in Tajikistan, Fredricks (2007) addresses Islamic perspectives of English or inner-circle Christian secular pedagogies often found in ELT textbooks. For Fredricks (2007), one successful approach in EFL classrooms in Dushanbe, Tajikistan, delivered English reading instruction using some approaches inspired by CP. In support of the apprehension towards ELT textbook content, felt by the predominately Islamic student base in Dushanbe, Fredricks (2007) points out that a study at the International Islamic University of Malaysia found at least half of the students to consider ELT textbooks as delivery systems for non-Islamic, *inner-circle* cultures. To mitigate student reluctance to engage the EFL materials, Fredricks (2007) altered some of the contexts of the lessons and offered the students choices for English texts, some of which included stories of cultural or historical significance to Islamic communities around the world. By giving the students relevant and non-secular choices in reading instruction, Fredricks (2007) achieved a more positive response, improving motivation to learn in EFL classes. Additionally, the CP that Fredricks (2007) applied created a dynamic, reciprocal learning environment where the lessons served to inform the teacher how to use EFL material. Informed in this way, Fredricks (2007) was able to stimulate a more meaningful connection between English and the students by mitigating their immersion into secular, inner-circle social standards that appear all too frequently in ELT textbooks.

Critical pedagogy also has critics of its own. Resistance to principles of CP may have manifested in existing institutions, where an accepted curriculum of fixed measures of declarative knowledge (Stoller, 2015; Biggs & Tang, 2007) had also served as delivery systems for social standards and power relationships in hegemonic cultures (Pennycook & Candlin, 2017; Shor, 2014). Pennycook (2004) notes that some critics see *inner-circle* or North American CP aligned with democratic individualism and may be a hegemonic force of its own accord.

According to Gore (1992), Giroux (1988) may have overlooked his social position as an academic theorist as one purveying a *regime of truth*, giving one pause to consider that CP may represent an undemocratic application in the agency that it affords teachers in the process of empowering their students (Ellsworth, 1989). In an EFL context, while admitting that CP aids in the understanding and negotiation of certain power relations and political interests, Johnston (1999) reserves critical concern for the nature of power in classrooms that the teacher *gives* students, rather than something which manifests democratically in classroom discourse. Also, Johnston (1999) disagrees with Pennycook's (1994) assertion that education is primarily political in nature and regards it to be only one facet of a much larger social phenomenon within a classroom environment. Finally, Johnston (1999) condemns the use of language by many critical pedagogists as one reminiscent of a military jargon, reflective of the era of *liberation* and *revolution* in South America, where it was conceived, and warns, 'there will be no revolution . . . I believe [CP] would find a broader hearing if it did not require its adherents to dress themselves up linguistically as Che Guevara' (p. 56). Despite these criticisms, students in the twenty-first century have become increasingly aware of the value of their language learning investments and textbooks that are at the heart of that negotiated exchange (Smith, 2021). While CP research informs a viable framework for examining the negotiated, multimodal discourses of ELT textbooks, there are some gaps in research that require attention.

Lin (2004), in developing a reflexive, feminist approach to a critical pedagogical curriculum, addresses noteworthy issues by discussing methods of practice that do not strictly adhere to the universal positions set by earlier founders of CP. Lin's (2004) concerns with CP appear to reflect one of Johnston's (1999) assertions that critical pedagogy is not a method but one that requires a micro-management of individual classrooms on the part of the teacher. Such responsibility on the shoulders of teachers, as already noted by Gore (1992) and Ellsworth (1989), suggests a requirement for some measure of guidance in CP theory, but according to Lin (2004), it is difficult to find such instructional literature accessible to schoolteachers and, specifically, EFL educators. Lin (2004) also points out that more research is needed to inform global EFL educators trying to contextualize CP for their respective locales. Ramanathan and Morgan (2009) appear to agree with Lin (2004) because they insist an essential approach for EFL teachers to apply CP is by linking theoretical frameworks with their respective classroom practices. However, Lin (2004) notes the lack of literature in CP that delineates the 'gendered pattern of the division of education labor' (p.

285) in expanding-circle countries, where women are often socially pressured to fulfil maternal roles.

Ramanathan and Morgan (2009) insist that CP is essential for novice EFL teachers because many continue to see their job as one focused on the pure elements of English language rather than the socially constructed issues through which language flows (Sharifan, 2009). Social issues, such as power relations, identity development and ideology, are directly relevant to teachers and students in EFL learning (Sharifan, 2009). However, Pennycook (2008) contends that CP should not be a static heuristic but one continuously reflexive and open to question because issues of social dominance and lack of social agency can arise in situ where, for example, a Hindi teacher with Muslim students can become a culturally incendiary situation (Ramanathan & Morgan, 2009). Hence, Ramanathan and Morgan (2009) caution EFL educators to think carefully about *what is critical* and *what is not critical* in the context of their students because some social realities presented in EFL textbooks that may appear objectionable to them, especially if they come from an inner-circle culture, may be acceptable practice to their students. In other words, Ramanathan and Morgan (2009) advise EFL educators to be mindful of CP lest it becomes a form of social injustice of its own accord.

For Freire (1970), CP represented an existential conceptualization, continuously reaffirmed in the politicization of learning, where social standards of dominant classes are legitimized through classroom discourse, perpetuating social injustices (Cox and Assis-Peterson, 1999). In an EFL context, CP is especially required to mitigate the insidious application of social dominance which sometimes masquerades in the multimodal discourses of ELT textbooks as necessary, technical and linguistic forms (Curdt-Christiansen & Weninger, 2015; Kumaravadivelu, 2006; Smith, 2021). Research informed by CP (i.e. Canagarajah, 2005) normally results in positive student response to the innovations and interventions that research inspires. Therefore, it is reasonable to assume that CP can improve EFL education by informing instructional use of ELT textbooks in situ.

In the context of more contemporary education, Shapiro (2015) and McLaren (2016) disparage the unchecked consumption of class time that test-driven education is given in expanding-circle nations. Shapiro (2015) points out that the most creative and inspiring educators are likely undiscovered as such regimes empty 'education of anything that cannot be measured and tested in a standardized form' (p. 8). For this reason, Shapiro (2015) developed a CP of peace, outlining principles centred around community, a life of meaning, critical citizenship, compassion and empathy, and hope and possibility. In Shapiro's (2015) CP, educators and students are encouraged to realize our perceptions of the world are one of many possibilities and to ask: *Whose reality am I learning?* and *What interests compel me to apprehend it this way?* (p. 18). In the context of this book, Shapiro's (2015) CP challenges test-driven education systems and sufficiently informs critical research into ELT textbooks because it inspires instructors to engage in reflexive praxis (Pennycook & Candlin, 2017), such as in Korea's highly prescribed, post-secondary programmes.

For McLaren (2016), CP asks how we arrive at common understandings and the relationship between power and knowledge. By extension, McLaren (2016) suggests that hegemony resides in all forms of education and certainly in textbooks. Concerned with how the content of learning material benefits dominant groups and subverts others, McLaren (2016) argues that for CP, the challenge lies in the moral choices of educators and student negotiations of their textbook contents. In the context of critical ELT textbook research, McLaren (2016) suggests that teachers should be wary of how content can misrepresent or marginalize non-inner-circle perspectives and how such awareness can reveal a deeper understanding of how a student processes knowledge.

Increasingly, a trend emerges in the literature that points to curriculum studies and critical pedagogy as co-anchors in a triangulated study that highlights the multimodal discourses of an ELT textbook. In the following sections, we discuss the construction of our second framework in this triangulation, towards understanding how the multimodal discourses in an ELT textbook are negotiated, delivered, resisted, transformed, appropriated or neutralized in situ.

Building a Framework for Analysing Multimodal Interaction In Situ

The findings presented in the forthcoming vignette feature a recording of EFL instruction in two Korean universities classroom and focus on how the textbook content is used in each class and how that reflexive transformation is rooted in an instructor's beliefs (Banes et al., 2016; Meschede, Fiebranz, Möller & Steffensky, 2017), assumptions and knowledge (BAK) (Woods, 1996) about language learning. Reflexivity is an instructor's recognition and challenge of conventional teaching practices in dialogical and relational situations such as a classroom environment (Cunliffe & Easterby-Smith, 2004; Pennycook & Candlin, 2017). Using a novel multimodal analysis of visually recorded English classrooms (MAVREC), designed specifically for analysing interactions in EFL classrooms, attention is drawn to how EFL instructors negotiate and reconstruct the contents of their textbooks with students during class and what pedagogical affordances, if any, that gives to EFL learning. While there is no shortage of literature concerning reflexive teaching practices (i.e. Banes et al., 2016; Clark & Dervin, 2014; Fox, 2004; Smith, 2021; Turner, 2010; Widdowson, 2004), MAVREC fills a niche that is not as thoroughly considered in language learning – one that observes how a teacher reconstructs textbook content *impromptu* or *in situ* and how their students negotiate that reconstruction. As we have already shown, ELT textbooks are often published for reasons less pedagogical than financial (i.e. Gray, 2010, Harwood, 2014, Littlejohn, 2012; Smith, 2021) and drawn from a singular publishing mould for global audiences to which students seldom find cultural affinity (i.e. Canagarajah, 1993; 2005; Song, 2013; Sherman, 2010; Weninger & Kiss, 2013). For these reasons, MAVREC may help students and practitioners continuously shape a syllabus and classroom delivery of the multimodal discourses in their ELT textbooks by giving due attention and consideration to relevant, curricular commonplaces (Connelly and Clandinin, 1988; Null, 2016) that affect EFL learning in that expanding-circle culture.

What Are Curricular Commonplaces?

Drawn from Schwab's (1969) work on curriculum, where he contends that *rhetoric* is as relevant to curricular design and its implementation as are the traditional connections with natural sciences and behavioural psychology, the term 'commonplaces', translated from a term in Latin implying *community*, was meant to invoke a word or phrase that is accepted as a *communal truth* (Null, 2016). In other words, common-sense or conventional wisdom finds resonance with the term, such as 'schools should meet the needs and interests of students' (Null, 2016, p. 28). Writers and speakers (e.g. teachers) can rely on their understanding of the commonplaces to persuade participants in that culture to subscribe to their views (Null, 2016). By considering curriculum as a form of rhetoric, Schwab (1969) presented a novel perspective to educators that their efforts in classrooms include interaction with the classroom ecology and the students in a kind of rhetorical accomplishment of a pedagogical vision (Connelly and Clandinin, 1988; Fox, 2004; Null, 2016; Smith, 2021). While Schwab's (1969) commonplaces differ than those of Null (2016) and Connelly and Clandinin (1988), this book collectively uses them to inform part of MAVREC's design. Each commonplace is a facet of the larger structure of the curriculum and without the collective, it can become misaligned with the pedagogical vision (Null, 2016). However, there is a challenge in balancing each commonplace because on their own, each commonplace cannot inform the design and maintenance of a curriculum (Null, 2016).

The MAVREC – A Multimodal Analysis of Visually Recorded English Classrooms

MAVREC is a framework for seeing how the multimodal discourses in ELT textbooks are negotiated, delivered, resisted, transformed, appropriated or neutralized in class (see Table 3.2). However, MAVREC is a two-part framework that first investigates the curricular commonplaces of a curriculum in the analytical procedure (see Table 3.1). Practitioners must either know or seek answers to questions surrounding curricular commonplaces before the questions of MAVREC can be addressed because they contextualize unique variations in that pedagogical culture.

Bearing in mind the work of Schwab (1969), Null (2016), and Connelly and Clandinin (1988), the curricular commonplaces that have the strongest effect on EFL learning in expanding-circle nations are *students, teachers, milieu, subject* and *textbook*. These commonplaces stand out because this book is focused

Table 3.1 The Curricular Commonplaces in an EFL Programme

Subject	What is the subject? What are the common and expected learning outcomes for the subject? Is the subject consequential in the society? To the student? To the teacher? To the milieu? Why or why not?
Milieu	Who or what constitutes the milieu surrounding EFL? What concerns do they have? What are the social, political and/or economic consequences? What is the level of the institution? How prestigious or populous is the institution?
Students	Who are the students? Is EFL important to them? Why or why not? What is the relationship between the students and the other commonplaces in this table? What have they studied thus far? What motivations or demotivators do they have in EFL learning?
Teachers	Who are the teachers? Is EFL teaching important to them? Why or why not? How are the teachers trained to teach EFL? What are their BAK about EFL teaching? How do they relate to the other commonplaces?
Textbook	What textbook was chosen for the EFL course and by whom? Do the students and teachers know the material and/or the classroom ecology? How much of it must be used to fulfil a prescribed syllabus? How does the textbook relate to the other commonplaces?

Table 3.2 Multimodal Analysis of Visually Recorded English Classrooms (MAVREC)

Delivered	Does the instructor present the lesson to students as it is presented in the textbook? How are the students responding? How does the instructor present any of the visual aids or speak of any of the images in the lesson? How did the students respond?
Transformed	Does the instructor provide alternative visual or metaphoric reference in lieu of the content? How did the students respond? Does the instructor make the linguistic and cultural references relevant in a Korean context during classroom discourse? Do the students appear confused or accepting of the content?
Neutralized	Does the instructor change or skip any part of the lesson? Why? Was the change explained? How did the students respond?
Resisted	Are there any uncomfortable silences in the classroom discourse? Does this appear related to the content of the textbook or the negotiation of the content?
Appropriated	What were the physical or behavioural responses while negotiating the content? What auditory (i.e. speech), visual (i.e. gaze), action (i.e. gesture, posture, movement, facial expression or touch) or environmental (i.e. proxemics) (i.e. Smith, 2021) signifiers or peculiarities occur among the students or the instructor during the lesson?
Negotiated	Overall, how did the students and instructors relate to the multimodal discourses in the textbook? Does the multimodal content appear familiar, strange or dismissed as unimportant to the lesson? How and why was this noticed?

on globally published ELT textbooks in expanding-circle countries where the institutional milieu commonly applies extrinsic pressure on students and practitioners in a test-driven pedagogical culture (Haggerty & Fox, 2016; Paik, 2018; Smith, 2020). As per the forthcoming vignette, considering the scholarly attention given to ELT textbooks in Korean university contexts (Ahn, 2014; Chun et al., 2017; Song, 2013; Smith, 2021; Thompson & Lee, 2018) and teacher self-efficacy in relation to their understanding of certain curricular commonplaces (Wyatt, 2016; 2018), textbook was added by the author as a commonplace in Table 3.1 because of its consequential connection to EFL learning in expanding-circle cultures (i.e. Macgilchrist, 2017; Smith, 2021; Smith & Sheyholislami, 2022). By including that commonplace, this study presumes that the teacher may achieve more fluency with the rhetorical accomplishment to which Fox (2004) refers in the delivery of textbook material. Table 3.1 gives a detailed description of the questions that practitioners might ask about the curricular commonplaces.

Once answers to the questions in Table 3.1 are acquired, the researcher may find more fluency with the rhetorical accomplishment to which Fox (2004) refers in analysing the negotiation of textbook material. The questions listed in MAVREC (see Table 3.2) were partially inspired by Norris's (2004) video transcription analysis, *mediated* discourse analysis (Scollon et al., 2011) and studies of action-oriented approaches to multimodal interactional analysis for classroom observations and examinations of video-recorded transcriptions (Cortez, 2008; Jewitt, 2006; Nelson et al., 2008; Scollon, 1998; Wohlwend, 2011). By endeavouring to answer these questions in situ (Wohlwend, 2011), the researcher will be noting 'how actions are made meaningful and social *in situ* rather than in representation, looking at interaction … semiotic practices, and discourses in contexts' (Wohlwend, 2011, p. 3). Each question considers the multimodal interactions of the students and instructors during the negotiation of the multimodal discourses in the ELT textbook.

Sample Vignette of MAVREC

In this second vignette, featuring MAVREC, we see how student and instructor interactions are extremely informative, especially when an instructor's perspectives and their respective roles are integrated with qualitative analyses (Duff, 2007; Duff & Van Lier, 1997). The forthcoming classroom observations will focus on how the content that was examined in Chapter 2 (i.e. CMAT), specifically Unit 6 (Saslow & Ascher, 2006, pp. 62–3), is negotiated as the instructor takes the class through a lesson.

Data Collection and Participants

Two instructors from different universities, who met the minimum prerequisites (e.g., native-English-speaking EFL instructors; at least fifteen years of post-secondary teaching experience in Korea; minimum education of an MA in Applied Linguistics or TESOL-related education), allowed the researcher entry into their respective classrooms for observation. In those classrooms were forty-seven Korean university students (25/22) who all shared a common goal of requiring the completion of an English communication course as compulsory towards their respective undergraduate degree programmes. All participants in this vignette (instructors and students) signed detailed consent forms prior to participation. The data examined in this vignette are two recordings of live university EFL classrooms at a university in Cheong Ju City, Korea. The videos were recorded on separate days in May 2019, using a test-proctoring camera built into the front wall of the classroom, next to the instructor's podium.

Findings

The findings of both classroom analyses (hereafter referred as classes X and Y) include a transcription of the audio (see Appendices A and B) from the video recording and feature the live negotiation of *Top Notch 2: Student Book – Unit 6: Eating Well* (Saslow & Ascher, 2006, pp. 62–73). It is important to note that each of the instructors participating in this study used the same textbook (Saslow & Ascher, 2006) in their respective courses. The findings of MAVREC presented in the next few sections follow the MAVREC framework, detailed in Table 3.1 and Table 3.2.

Curricular Commonplaces: EFL Learning in Korean University Programmes

In Chapter 1, we briefly explored textbooks and EFL learning in Korean or expanding-circle contexts. Here, more details are given for the specific context of Korean university EFL courses.

Subject. The subject is a fourteen-week, first-year, university English communication class that is compulsory for every student towards the completion of their undergraduate degree programme. The common or expected learning outcomes for these types of university courses in Korea are to achieve a minimum of 70 per cent (B-) score and a moderate level of English communication in speaking, reading and writing capabilities. This subject is consequential in Korean society because English language skills relate to upward socio-economic mobility (Paik, 2018; Smith, 2021). However, studying English is a subject of considerable stress and frustration for many students because while it is connected to one's status in Korean society, it is rarely utilized by students in their post-academic careers, unless they go abroad or need to use it in a very specific way, such as in teaching or another profession. While the English language education industry can be a fruitful career venture, educators become sources of extrinsic motivation because they are always trying to find ways to inspire their students to learn. As for the institutional or personal milieu in Korea, such as school administrators or parents or students, English language learning is big business and connected with the prestige and capability of that institutions' public image.

Milieu. In this category, we can see that parents or family of students, institutional stakeholders and government policymakers overshadow EFL education in Korean society. For parents, their concerns are usually associated with the fiscal investments in language that are associated with language learning. For institutional stakeholders, the investments that students make in attending classes at their institutions are a revenue stream that they feel is connected to the quality of their classes. Considering that Korea is a test-driven society in terms of language learning (i.e. Haggerty & Fox, 2016), continued student investment in institutions is a priority for most administrators. As for policymakers, social concerns surrounding EFL learning have led to numerous attempts to reconcile several problems related to the differences between K-12 and university education.

Students. The students in this vignette are forty-seven (25/22) in two university classes, all around nineteen to twenty-three years of age. While EFL is important to them, in terms of upward socio-economic mobility (Paik, 2018), many see English language learning as a source of frustration because whether they enjoy learning English or not, some measure of proficiency is required to complete their degree programmes. Considering that Korea is a Confucianist-based social structure, it is reasonable to assume that many students study English because of extrinsic motivators rather than intrinsic ones. While they are connected to EFL through the milieu in Korean society, their strongest and most immediate connection to English language is through their teacher, with whom they build an appreciation for learning the language in post-secondary classrooms.

Teachers. The teachers in the context of this vignette are very experienced EFL instructors who have lived in Korea for more than fifteen years each and who have taught courses at the university level for nearly all that time. EFL is important to them because it is their career, and they have invested a lot of time in practice and training to be in the positions that they hold at the university. While their beliefs, assumptions and knowledge about EFL may be different, they each have expressed to the researcher that if students make an investment in language learning, then they should receive a commensurate return on that investment.

Textbook. The textbook used for this vignette is *Top Notch 2: Student Book* (Saslow & Ascher, 2006). First, it is curious that the textbook used in these two university courses is so old. Korean universities occasionally use up surplus publications that they have in their respective libraries or stores rather than ask the students to purchase new copies because they are a cheaper option. In any case, this textbook was the most popular choice for EFL programmes in Korea from 2008 to 2013 (Fitzgibbon, 2013). It is a generic, globally published ELT textbook used in expanding-circle EFL programmes around the world and presents intermediate reading, writing, speaking and listening tasks in a variety of topics.

Now that we have a better idea about the curricular commonplaces of EFL learning in Korean contexts, we have set the contextual stage for understanding how the multimodal discourses in the ELT textbook were negotiated, delivered, resisted, transformed, appropriated or neutralized in situ.

MAVREC – Class X

Does the instructor present the lesson to students as it is presented in the textbook? How are the students responding? Instructor X appears to follow the sections of Unit 6 (Saslow & Ascher, 2006, pp. 62–73), but at the beginning of the lesson his discussion about eating healthy uses only parts of the textbook even though he follows the topical agenda. For example, he skips the practice dialogues in the Q&A sections of D and E (see Figure 2.3) and uses them as a backup activity only for those students who have finished other activities ahead of their classmates. The students respond favourably to these digressions from textbook material; this is discussed in more detail in physical and behavioural responses (discussed further).

Does the instructor provide alternative visual or metaphoric reference in lieu of the content? Does the instructor make the linguistic and cultural references relevant in a Korean context during classroom discourse? Do the students appear confused or accepting of the content? How does the instructor present any of the visual aids or speak of any of the images in the lesson? How did the students respond? Instructor X provides only one alternative visual device to replace the food pyramids featured in Unit 6 (Saslow & Ascher, 2006, p. 62) but frequently challenges students to imagine how the textbook content might manifest in a real-world context. For example, he jokingly states that wine may be a healthy choice in one's dietary habits but urges the students not to drink 20 glasses of wine because it may not be as healthy (see Appendix A). Student response to these personal asides and jokes is collective laughter.

In some cases, the alternative visual aid, a Korean version of a food pyramid called a 'food pagoda', appears to capture much more student interest than any of the textbook content, and students appeared to eagerly engage that supplemental material and discuss it with their groups.

Instructor X also uses the textbook as a peripheral guide to the lesson. He notes: 'and here we have the food pyramid . . . what about here in Korea? Do you have a food pyramid?' (see Appendix A, 8:33). Students respond with silent contemplation of the textbook. Instructor X continues: 'it's called *the* food pyramid?' He emphasizes the definite article 'the', as if to encourage some of them to challenge the ownership of 'food'. Instructor X continues: 'I remember at the high school' (referring to a previous position) 'they used to have the food pagoda . . .' (see Appendix A). Instructor X emphasizes 'pagoda', and many students disregard the textbook and look at the handout. The students respond in happy discussion with the instructor and with their peers.

Instructor X transforms the visual representations in the textbook so that they appear relevant from a Korean perspective. He gives reference to a common alcoholic beverage in Korea – soju – and makes a joke about alcohol consumption. Students respond to this with laughter and the segment quickly changes to a discussion about healthy consumption habits in Korea. Instructor X also shares personal information with his students, noting that he hates *gachi* (eggplant in Korean), choosing to use the Korean word, then adds that he loves *sam-gyeop-sal* (BBQ pork lettuce wrap in Korean) to demonstrate how someone might use the expression 'I'm a big <insert favourite food> eater'. While the textbook activity (Saslow & Ascher, 2006, p. 66) uses many dietary examples, each appears to be only identifiable with inner-circle cultures, so the students do not respond eagerly and mumble among themselves quietly without much discussion. However, as soon as Instructor X claims, 'I'm a big sam-gyeop-sal eater' (see Appendix A), the students immediately laugh and engage in happy discussion with each other, not giving the textbook much attention, even though they are fulfilling the linguistic challenge. These enhancements by Instructor X include a Korean perspective, to which the students, in all cases, appear to thoroughly enjoy.

Does the instructor change or skip any part of the lesson? Why? Was the change explained? How did the students respond? We have already noted that Instructor X decides to skip several sections in the textbook and replace one of the visual representations in the textbook with his own, supplemental handout. However, Instructor X also draws attention to habits and engages in a lengthy discussion that draws it towards 'eating habits'. The digression from the textbook lasted almost ten minutes, and all students appear to be fully engaged in the discussion, taking notes, participating with the instructor and discussing matters within their groups at the various tables around the classroom. Instructor X does not appear to give an explanation as to why he is digressing from the textbook content. Rather, he seamlessly segues from the textbook to open discussion in Korean contexts in a way that suggests that the textbook content should be neutralized or transformed in that way. During the discussion, the volume of discussion around the class rose, but also appeared to lessen whenever the students were asked to look at their textbooks. Instructor X asked all students to discuss food items, things that they prefer or not prefer to eat or drink in their regular dietary habits and specify whether those choices are driven by health concerns or matters of taste. Instructor X added common expressions of polite refusal of food, reflective of the textbook content but from a Korean perspective. Student response and engagement were considerably attentive during this discussion.

Are there any uncomfortable silences in the classroom discourse? Does this appear related to the content of the textbook or the negotiation of the content? Silences occurred whenever the students were compelled by Instructor X to read and contemplate the contents of the textbook. For example, the food pyramid in Unit 6 (Saslow & Ascher, p. 62) silenced much of the class, but when Instructor X replaced that content with his own 'food pagoda' handout, student resistance lessened, and activity increased. The same reaction occurred when the students were asked to create excuses for refusing food or to express preference; textbook choices seemed to confuse the students but when they were replaced with Korean options by Instructor X, they eagerly participated in the linguistic challenge.

What were the physical or behavioural responses while negotiating the content? Did any auditory (i.e. speech), visual (i.e. gaze), action (i.e. gesture, posture, movement, facial expression or touch) or environmental (i.e. proxemics) signifiers or peculiarities appear among the students or the instructor during the lesson? Often, when Instructor X is pointing to the textbook, students disregarded their own books and only watched the instructor. It is important to note that for many students, the proximity of their textbook was more distant from them, at their respective tables, than their notebooks, in which the students kept a record of Instructor X's notes on the board.

Additionally, at other points of transition where Instructor X is walking around the classroom and not enforcing their attention to the textbook content (see Appendix A) when students are discussing the content), students appear less interested in the textbook content and more engaged with the prescribed English-speaking practice in live discussion. In some cases, students are not even looking at their book and some have even closed them. Overall, most of the students appeared to enjoy the frequent digressions from the textbook by increasing the volume of their discussion, sitting perceptively upright in their chairs, drawing closer proximity to their notes and fixating their gaze on the instructor during the live discussions. These reactions also occurred when the instructor provided alternative visual or metaphorical explanations of the textbook content – for example, provided a Korean context by discussing Korean foods or by seamlessly using textbook content in a real-world context for Korean society. Contrastively, whenever the instructor asked the students to engage in the textbook content without transforming it, students were noticeably distant in their proximity from the book and engaged in lacklustre and almost quiet discussion.

Overall, how did the students and instructors relate to the multimodal discourses in the textbook? Does the multimodal content appear familiar, strange or dismissed as unimportant to the lesson? How and why was this noticed? Building on the findings in the previous question, there appeared to be many student expressions of bemused curiosity, especially when looking at the food pyramid in Unit 6 (Saslow & Ascher, 2006, p. 62). While the textual contents and the linguistic challenges appeared interesting to many students, such as learning how to politely refuse food or knowing how to explain their own food items in a food pagoda, much of the visual discourse in Unit 6 (Saslow & Ascher, 2006, pp. 62–73) appeared to distract student engagement. On a positive note, lexical curiosities, such as explaining the different types of vegetarianism or providing a clear definition of 'poultry', seemed to gain student interest and compel Instructor X to give detailed attention to those items outside of the textbook's lesson sequence.

MAVREC – Class Y

Does the instructor present the lesson to students as it is presented in the textbook? How does the instructor present any of the visual aids or speak of any of the images in the lesson? How did the students respond? Overall, Instructor Y follows the sections in the textbook quite closely and deviates only to recontextualize content or skip sections deemed unimportant to the lesson in the interests of time management. At the beginning of the lesson, Instructor Y introduces the topic for five minutes without drawing attention to the textbook. Then he introduces unit goals and tries to describe the textbook's agenda. Throughout the lesson, the students appear to enjoy the deviations from the textbook but return to solemn contemplation when asked to engage in some of the activities.

As in the classroom of Instructor X, Instructor Y held up the textbook and pointed to the visual discourse of the unit's lessons as he spoke about them. There was no PowerPoint presentation, but the students appeared to enjoy sharing the experience with Instructor Y, rather than look down to their respective pages. Whenever Instructor Y wanted the students to look at the textbook for any length of time during the class, it was solely to draw attention to the linguistic challenges. He purposely ignored almost all the visual contents of the textbook. Student response to this silencing of the visual discourse in the textbook was inconsequential and did not appear to affect the flow or the rhythm of the negotiated exchanges in the classroom during any of the lessons. For the most part, students were attentive and active during much of the discussion, especially when Instructor Y was drawing attention away from the textbook and writing on the whiteboard.

Does the instructor provide alternative visual or metaphoric reference in lieu of the content? If so, how did the students respond? Does the instructor make the linguistic and cultural references relevant in a Korean context during classroom discourse? Do the students appear confused or accepting of the content? In almost every situation, Instructor Y is providing alternative references to some parts of the lessons by adding a Korean context or perspective. However, that alternative perspective manifests in discussion rather than using alternative visual aids. For example, at the beginning of the lesson, Instructor Y explains the meaning of a food pyramid in great detail, noting that the top of the pyramid indicates lesser frequency and the bottom of the pyramid indicates higher frequency of daily food consumption. The fact that he felt it was important to describe this suggests that he is aware of student confusion and guesses many of the Korean students had not seen it before or know what it is meant to illustrate. From the student point of view, these supplemental asides appeared to inspire more classroom discussion because the atmospheric volume notably increased. Students began to take notes whenever these asides occurred.

Already in these findings, it was revealed that Instructor Y used several Korean language lexical items to capture student attention. Items such as *banmal*! (slang speech), *jon-daet-mal* (polite speech) appeared to earn student attention in the negotiation of the multimodal contents that might have seemed counter-intuitive to Korean culture. By using elements of Korean culture in his exchanges with the students, Instructor Y provides a contextually cultured relief-platform on which the students might stand to face the linguistic challenges in the lesson. This is evidenced, perhaps most noticeably, by Instructor Y noting that he was a big *Gamjatang* eater (a traditional Korean pork bone stew) to which the students reacted with laughter and agreement. He says: 'I had Stew last night . . . I had stew last week . . . I think I'm going to have stew tomorrow!' (see Appendix B).

To this statement, students erupted in laughter and appeared to appreciate that a foreign national would enjoy a popular dish that is quite common in Korea. In several cases, Instructor Y tried to bridge linguistic challenges by transforming the content of the textbook to reach students on a sociocultural level but still use the language activities as a platform on which to build.

To elaborate on what was highlighted earlier in this section, Instructor Y may have been trying to appeal to Korean sensibilities in the delivery of the activity involving refusal of food (Saslow & Ascher, 2006, p. 64). He explained why it is important to refuse food by invoking the Korean word *jon-daet-mal* (polite speech). These explanations were given at several points in almost every activity to contextualize the content from the perspective of a Korean.

Does the instructor change or skip any part of the lesson? Why? How did the students respond? Whenever Instructor Y skipped a section, the students seemed to agree. When attention is drawn to a particular lexical item, such as asking if students ever heard of the word 'serving' (see Appendix B), the students appear to enjoy those frequent diversions from the textbook, even though from the instructor's point of view, those lexical diversions serve to prepare students for upcoming activities. From the beginning to the end of the class, Instructor Y follows the activities in the book but permits frequent digression if the classroom discourse is robust.

Unit 6 (Saslow & Ascher, 2006, pp. 62–73) presents an inner-circle perspective of food. In that capacity, the genre of the multimodal content in this lesson appears to be relevant to the linguistic challenges in the activities. However, Instructor Y underpins a cultural contradiction, somewhat coyly, by noting that rice, a daily staple of many nations around the world, not to mention Korea, is listed in the same category of portion control as pasta or potatoes (see Figure 2.3). While this book does not intend to embark on an explanation of the nature of rice and carbohydrates, it is important to note that in those nations, where rice is consumed at nearly every meal and used synonymously in regular dialogue with dinner (i.e. in Korean language the question 'Did you have rice' equates to 'Did you have dinner?'), the food pyramid represented in Unit 6 (Saslow & Ascher, 2006, p. 62) would be a matter of cultural insult to those students from expanding-circle countries who would likely use the textbook because it clearly illustrates that frequent consumption of that item is wrong. Student response was somewhat subdued, and the atmosphere of the classroom felt awkward as many of the students quietly tried to understand the food pyramid (Saslow & Ascher, 2006, p. 62). For several minutes, the atmosphere of the class was momentarily cheerless, and many students exchanged looks of quiet bemusement with each other while looking at the food pyramid.

Considering the abundance of visual discourse offered in Unit 6 (Saslow & Ascher, 2006, pp. 62–73), Instructor Y avoids as much of it as possible and draws attention to the concepts and topics for communication that the unit inspires: lifestyle and dietary choices. In this way, Instructor Y silences the lesson's visual discourse and the one-way inner-circle logic that they appear to support (Curdt-Christiansen & Weninger, 2015).

Instructor Y changes some of the lessons to recontextualize and, in one case, chose to skip over several grammar-focused sections that were apparently deemed unimportant in the context of the English communication class. For example, at (see Appendix B), he asks the students their opinion whether a particular section in the unit's lesson is important – he is speaking about a grammar section. The students agree that section is not as important as the other communication practices and activities. Students responded to this happily and quickly moved on to the next page. Student response to Instructor Y's question, in this case, is a notable example of his style that maximizes every opportunity to empower students in the classroom choices. At 32:00 (see Appendix B), he says: 'before the mid-term exam, you remember we talked about the difference between acquisition and learning? . . . If you were the teacher of this English communication course, would you spend a lot of time on this?' Student response to the instructor's question is quite positive. Many students shake their heads, silently indicating that they do not mind, a common error in communication among Korean students. Some students were already looking ahead to the next page and reading the fresh material. By empowering his students to participate in the decision, Instructor Y appears to be negotiating the material with his students and the response was always positive. Student participation during textbook activities was earnest and attentive, the discussion was robust and energetic, and the general atmosphere of the classroom was active and perceptibly rose in volume whenever Instructor Y asked the students to do something.

Instructor Y explains the unit's learning outcomes (see Figure 2.3) at the beginning of the lesson as something that people from inner-circle nations might consider healthy. He is careful not to use language that expresses complete certitude of those perspectives. While it is reasonable to assume that topics surrounding healthy diet and lifestyles are meaningful to Korean students, the genre of the multimodal content does little to connect it to them or their culture. In other words, the interpretations and the BAK (Woods, 1996) of their instructor give the topic some relevance for Korean society. Student response to lexical items such as the food pyramid category 'legumes' (Saslow & Ascher,

2006, p. 62) is confusing but they become visibly relaxed when Instructor Y explains that *kong-na-meul* (Korean language) (see Appendix B) is a type of legume that in English is termed 'bean sprouts'. Instructor Y prioritized the Korean perspective in this case by noting a lexical item on the pyramid using the Korean word to connect students to the pyramid. Student response was first an audible and collective 'Ahhh!', and the cultural relevance of *kong-na-meul*, as something that is extremely common in Korean dishes and consumed almost daily, must have sufficiently connected the students to the food pyramid because the discussion that followed was much more robust and louder than before.

Are there any uncomfortable silences in the classroom discourse? Does this appear related to the content of the textbook or the negotiation of the content? Students were often initially confused about some of the content, as evidenced by their silence or their facial expressions at several points in the video. However, those awkward silences diminished when Instructor Y transformed the content to appeal to the students' sociocultural norms. Those brief moments of uncomfortable silence precipitated Instructor Y's interjections using Korean references (already noted in this section) and were quickly replaced by robust discussion. Perhaps most noticeable of these silences were the points when Instructor Y was speaking about 'rice' and the food pyramid (Saslow & Ascher, 2006, p. 62). Instructor Y may have noticed the awkward silence that followed his instruction to examine the food pyramid, particularly the prioritized categories equating to good health. The construction is emphasized on the first ME of Unit 6 and bears the hallmarks of an inner-circle standard against all other cultures could be measured. By spending a few moments focusing on rice, Instructor Y notes: 'Okay up here (he points to the top of the pyramid) you have white rice . . . but here . . . (indicating a lower section) whole grain also includes rice . . . what's the difference here' (see Appendix B). After spending a few minutes focusing on a Korean staple, such as rice, not only has Instructor Y drawn attention to a familiar item to break the uncomfortable silence, but he has also drawn attention to the idea that the pyramid was not projecting a Korean perspective. He notes that those food items are *tan-su-hwa-mul* (Korean, meaning carbohydrates) but gives no attention to carbohydrates to which we might find more common in inner-circle cultures. It was noticeably clear that as soon as the instructor offered a Korean reference to the topic, relevant to the activity, the students were able to situate themselves and participate more enthusiastically with their peers. Hence, while uncomfortable silences among the students occurred in moments when identifiable elements of their culture appeared to be marginally represented, such as rice on the food pyramid given lesser visual agency than pasta or potatoes (Saslow & Ascher, 2006, p. 62), or when social manners, such as making excuses to refuse food, appeared counter-intuitive to Korean culture, they also dissipated whenever Instructor Y included a Korean perspective.

What were the physical or behavioural responses while negotiating the content? Did any auditory (i.e. speech), visual (i.e. gaze), action (i.e. gesture, posture, movement, facial expression or touch) or environmental (i.e. proxemics) signifiers or peculiarities appear among the students or the instructor during the lesson? Whenever Instructor Y transitioned to new content, he would hold up the textbook and point to the new page. The students appeared to be more keenly engaged, indicated by many of them sitting forward, to pay close attention to Instructor Y's gestural and personally engaging speeches that often see him walking towards the seated students. For example, when Instructor Y was deconstructing the conversation between Terry and Iris (Saslow & Ascher, 2006, p. 65), he gestured dramatically to make his point speaking about past, present and future.

The intensity of student engagement with the textbook content appeared to diminish whenever they were instructed to look at the visual discourse, especially when Terry and Iris (Saslow & Ascher, 2006, p. 63) were speaking about having cake. In other words, as with Instructor X's class, the students appeared less interested in the visual discourse of the textbook content but more engaged with the prescribed English language practice. In most cases, students appear to focus on the material only at the instruction of their professor and not of their accord or interest. During those periods of enthusiastic engagement with the language activities, the volume of discussion in the classroom rose significantly.

Overall, how did the students and instructors relate to the visual components of the lesson in the textbook? Does the multimodal content appear familiar, strange or dismissed as unimportant to the lesson? How and why was this noticed? Instructor Y's students exhibited expressions of bemused curiosity, especially looking at the food pyramid (Saslow & Ascher, 2006, p. 62). While the content did not appear confusing to any students, other than the lexical item 'legumes' (see Appendix B) to which Instructor Y initiated some discussion, most of the culturally informed dialogue surrounding food in most of the lessons required careful explanation by Instructor Y to situate it in a Korean context. Those situated contexts were usually predicated on awkwardly silent student response to the content.

Moving Forward

If we accept Littlejohn's (1992) assertion that ELT textbooks are, indeed, ideologically laden *Trojan horses*, then seeing how the multimodal content *speaks* (Serafini, 2014, p. 36) *in situ* can confirm the insidiousness of the social realities that CMAT revealed in Chapter 2. Building from those revelations, MAVREC underpins physical and behavioural student responses to the presentation of the lessons, their visual contents, constructed realities, believability, enjoyment and general pitch by the instructor who practises live negotiations of that content. Operationalizing MAVREC can demonstrate a strategic and procedural framework that serves two purposes: (1) it highlights *textbooks in action* in EFL classrooms and reveals their negotiated content through the instructor's pedagogical vision and (2) enables EFL learning stakeholders (including students) to be more informed in using, choosing and/or teaching ELT textbook content by seeing the results of that material during classroom consumption. For these reasons, MAVREC empowers participants in expanding-circle EFL learning programmes with demonstrable data that can be cross-referenced with the findings in CMAT.

Chapter Summary

This chapter began with an illustration of a typical classroom ecology that one might expect to find in EFL contexts and features textbooks as a common focal point in that pedagogical culture. The illustration underscores the importance of understanding the complex relationships that form between students, practitioners and their textbooks, and how the contents from the latter are negotiated in classrooms. Building from that pedagogical context, a question is premised about how to operationalize an analytical framework for seeing textbooks negotiated in live classrooms. Starting with theoretical principles of critical pedagogy, underscoring how students and practitioners share a cooperative engagement in EFL learning, a brief discussion of multimodal interactional analysis helps introduce a basic framework for analysing ELT textbook use during class time, where the multimodal discourses in lesson contents are actively negotiated between teachers and students. Our second framework, MAVREC, emerged from the discussion and was used in a sample vignette in a Korean university EFL classroom with the same course professor featured in Chapter 2. While the findings presented in this chapter feature how instructors negotiate, deliver, resist, transform, appropriate or neutralize the multimodal discourses of an ELT textbook in situ, they will be discussed in more detail in Chapter 5. In what immediately follows, we will see how students and practitioners, whose voices have been disregarded by many stakeholders in the production of ELT textbooks, are given a chance to account for and give value to the contents of their textbooks.

Discussion Questions

i. Why do you think that globally published ELT textbooks often serve as the syllabus and/or curriculum for language learning programmes?

ii. Schwab (1969) and Van Lier (1997, 2004, 2015) talk about 'classroom ecologies' in this chapter. In the context of ELT textbooks, what does this term mean and how does it contribute to the understanding of content that is negotiated between students and teachers?

iii. Think about some of the language learning textbooks or materials that you have used over the years, as a student, a student-teacher or a practitioner. Discuss some of your recollections using MAVREC as a guide to understand how they were negotiated, delivered, resisted, transformed, appropriated or neutralized in class.

4

In Mind – Accounting for Multimodal Discourses in ELT Textbooks

The third part of our triangulated framework, towards a better understanding of the multimodal discourses in ELT textbooks for students and practitioners, is one that serves as the methodological equivalent of asking, 'now . . . tell us how you really feel!' We all have a public face and for some students in expanding-circle cultures, such as some in Asia, 'face' systems have very real social consequences that can reverberate across one's personal and professional life (Scollon et al., 2011). In other words, our publicly expressed values and judgements can be significantly different in private, especially when there are balances of power connected with the pedagogical culture in which that accountability is exposed. In simpler terms, students may hesitate to be critical of their textbooks because they may be considered a choice or extension of their instructor's pedagogical vision. Likewise, practitioners may be commensurately apprehensive because their director or someone else in senior management at an institution may have chosen the textbook for a campus-wide programme. Whatever the case may be, this framework is meant to bypass those potential conflicts of interest and retrieve a more reliable accountability for the multimodal discourses in an ELT textbook. In what follows, we explore ELT textbooks in expanding-circle contexts and then draw focused attention to Korean contexts of EFL learning because that is where our third step in the framework is situated. Informed by critical applied linguistics (CALx), a semi-structured interview coding framework is introduced and used in a vignette featuring students who have already participated in Chapter 3.

ELT Textbooks in Global Contexts

In the Introduction, we noted that although this book will feature the use of three frameworks in Korean university contexts, their implementation can achieve commensurate insights in any language learning context that prioritizes the textbook as a necessary investment to complete the course curriculum. Bearing this in mind, we explore student and practitioner perspectives of EFL learning, ELT textbooks and curricular commonplaces for EFL learning programmes in Korean society so that we have a platform on which to contextualize the vignettes presented in Chapters 2, 3 and 4.

Textbooks, in general, are sociopolitical commodities at the epicentre of a cultural tug of war to determine the circumstances involved with their production, distribution and consumption (Gray, 2010; Harwood, 2014; Littlejohn, 1992; Sherman, 2010; Wang et al., 2011; Sleeter & Grant, 2017) 'because they are not only textual artifacts but social and historical practices' (Curdt-Christiansen & Weninger, 2015, p. 11). Considering the investment made by ELT students and teachers requires a commensurate level of research by each into the materials which are expected to ensure that investiture (Canagarajah, 1993; Smith, 2021). Factors such as (a) fiscal costs of production receiving the lion's share of attention before content is even considered, (b) the widespread distribution of standardized ELT textbook content by publishers concerned far more with profits than pedagogy and (c) the struggle of writers inside the PARSIP prison are just a few issues painting a bleak picture of ELT textbook production (Gray, 2010; Harwood, 2014).

From a consumer's perspective, 'many students in the world hold an ambivalent, want-hate relationship with English' (Lin, 1999, p. 393) and classrooms are on the front lines of that struggle, where students negotiate and consume content that arguably leads to a certain measure of social domination. The consumption of ELT textbooks reflects production, where a lack of research in understanding EFL materials *in action* can only leave us to guess why the students would accept standardized, culturally alienating content divorcing them from the possibility of developing an identity *with* and ownership *of* the language they intend to speak (Bell & Gower, 2011; Brown, 2011, Canagarajah, 1993; Gilmore, 2011, Littlejohn, 1992; Harwood, 2014; Masuhara, 2011; Tomlinson; 2011). The educational impact of production and consumption of EFL textbooks has resulted in a growing desire for *authentic language* in classroom materials that may never be achievable (Gilmore, 2011; Earl et al., 2002; Kramsch, 1993, 2008). The *McDonaldization* of ELT textbook content has deskilled students and teachers (Littlejohn, 2012), and demotivated EFL students, who feel disenfranchised from the language they want to speak by culturally irrelevant content (Boriboon, 2004; Matsuda, 2002; Nguyen, 2011; Sakai & Kikuchi, 2009; Sherman, 2010). Additionally, native-speakerism marginalizes non-native English-speaking educators while positioning native-English-speaking teachers as unchallengeable experts in EFL education (Holliday, 2006), who blindly follow the classless linguistic paradigms in the multimodal discourses of ELT textbooks that do not exist (Block, 2015; Canagarajah, 1999; Curdt-Christiansen & Weninger, 2015; Harwood, 2014; Hu, 2005; Lee, 2006; Song, 2011, 2013).

In contexts of language learning textbooks, the educational *culture* in which they are conceived may be a commodity or a process that is mechanized in production and consumption to provide a sense of distinction, perhaps between brands or social statuses (Apple, 1985; Bourdieu, 1991; Cho, 2013; Gray, 2010). Hence, if one accepts textbooks as cultural commodities, they may be subject to the *ways and means* of production and consumption that impart an intrinsic social value (Curdt-Christiansen & Weninger, 2015; Giroux, 1983; Littlejohn, 1992, 2012; Harwood, 2014; Gray, 2010; Tomlinson, 2011). For Kubota (1999), EFL textbook authors tend to illustrate a cultural contrast between inner-circle ideologies and the target EFL student base, where 'fixed, apolitical, and essentialized cultural representations such as groupism, harmony, and de-emphasis on critical thinking and self-expression' (p. 12) envelope expanding- or outer-circle cultures. Therefore, it is important to remember textbooks are powerful cultural artefacts and valued commodities imbued with the promise of pedagogical value, shaped by the zeitgeist of global EFL learning momentum. These cultural artefacts, Gray (2010) maintains, are targeted by scholars from multiple angles of research because they are multifaceted products, designed around compromise and conciliation to appease multiple stakeholders with competing interests in a global marketplace (Brumfit & Mitchell, 1990; Sheldon, 1988; Harwood, 2014; Weninger & Kiss, 2013).

The intention here is not to condemn or advocate on behalf of ELT textbook designers or their publishers or the books themselves but to highlight those eventualities in production and consumption that impact education and, perhaps more importantly, students. In what follows, we look closer at Korean EFL learning and textbooks because that is where the vignette for this chapter is situated. From the CMAT used on a few ELT textbook pages, featured in Chapter 2, to a multimodal interactional analysis of students using those unit pages in class, featured in Chapter 3, we now give those same students and practitioners a chance to express how they account for the multimodal discourses in their textbooks. After discussing Korean contexts, we venture into principles of CALx, which inform our third framework: semi-structured interview coding.

EFL Learning in Korea

It is important to be mindful that this book problematizes the unquestioned use of EFL textbooks, the lack of critical attention to their multimodal contents and how poorly considered classroom negotiations of those contents might present challenges for EFL learning in expanding-circle cultures. However, these problems find numerous points of connection in a deeply complex web of issues revolving around EFL learning in Korean society (i.e. Ahn, 2011; Choi, 2008; Chun et al., 2017; Huh, 2004; Lee, 2011; Song, 2013; Thompson & Lee, 2018). To give some measure of clarity to this point, the author of this book once met a former Korean student in Canada who, despite a lofty International English Language Testing System (IELTS) score, could not order a cup of coffee from a Starbucks *drive-thru*. That sad reality is a real problem for some expanding-circle EFL students (Nam, 2005; Smith, 2020; Song, 2013). In Korean K-12 education policy, there is an influence echoing *Taylorism* (i.e. Taylor, 2004) that appears to have informed the design of model learning outcomes (LO) for a highly regulated EFL curriculum (Chun et al., 2017; Stoller, 2015) that the Korean Institute of Curriculum and Evaluation (KICE) pressures most Korean universities to follow (Haggerty & Fox, 2016). Those policies trickle down to the level of institutional milieu in Korean education, which feel compelled to give orders to instructors in their respective institutions that students *must* learn vocabulary by doing *this*, or it's the *only* way, or even, they *must* do precisely *this* to improve their language skills – like a mind-numbing litany of misinformed language learning prescriptions. In other words, many Korean university EFL programme LOs adhere to a test-driven (or numbers-driven) culture of language learning (Choi, 2008; Haggerty & Fox, 2016; Ryu & Boggs, 2016), so it is not surprising that *Taylorism* is an attractive consideration.

For Korean students, much like EFL students elsewhere, learning English is a socio-economic investment and an attractive commitment for political stakeholders involved with post-secondary education policy at the national level (Ahn, 2011; Canagarajah, 2016; Choi, 2008; Song, 2013). Those political stakeholders (e.g. KICE) promote a language learning curriculum that appears to (1) inhibit creative expression, (2) deny student involvement as informative to the syllabus and (3) adhere to seemingly antiquated methodological or theoretically established principles that overlook any other language learning phenomenon (Stoller, 2015). For Korean students, Stoller's (2015) observations certainly resonate with the current state of test-driven learning outcomes that university programmes expect their instructors to achieve. Unfortunately, test-driven learning outcomes in language learning do little to nurture creative expression or foster deeper learning and functioning knowledge to inform spontaneous communication (Biggs & Tang, 2007; Paik, 2018; Smith, 2020; Stoller, 2015). For Biggs and Tang (2007), declarative knowledge has been the traditional hallmark of university education, where students come to (literally) be indoctrinated with knowledge.

While it may seem that this study implies a preference for functional over declarative knowledge, the intention here is to note the latter tends to outweigh the former in a Korean EFL education to meet state-sanctioned evaluations (Ahn, 2014; Haggerty & Fox, 2016). The result is a Korean graduate who cannot order a cup of coffee from a Starbucks drive-thru or a student who knows, for example, what a *subjunctive verb form* is but not be able to say: 'I wish I *were able* to speak better English.' Ascough (2011) addresses that challenge in a framework for course development that integrates student needs, programme requirements and teacher expertise to nurture functional knowledge (i.e. Biggs & Tang, 2007). However, many new approaches to EFL learning in Korea stall under the weight of stakeholders such as deskilled instructors set in their ways (Lee, 2015), KICE or other federal entities fiscally connected to post-secondary institutions (Ahn, 2011).

Textbooks in Korean EFL Learning

Korea is a collectivist, ethno-centric culture where 'individuals are acutely aware of their obligations and responsibilities to those who have come before' (Scollon et al., 2011). In such a culture, those who are granted power and status within the collective are often revered and their actions rarely questioned (Adams & Gottlieb, 2017; Kohls, 2001). Bearing this cultural tendency in mind, an instructor's influence on their students is one of infectious commitment to learning (Dornyei, 2001, p.50). In most Korean university EFL programmes, textbooks have an instructor's implied endorsement (Ahmadi Darani & Akbari, 2016; Canagarajah, 2016; Dendrinos, 2015; Song, 2013; Weninger & Kiss, 2013; Wu, 2010; Xiong & Qian, 2012) pressuring students to follow the instructions therein and have faith that the linguistic and cultural models align with proven pedagogical practices (Cortez, 2008). Even the name *global* ELT textbook foreshadows the insidious potential such artefacts might have for Korean students eager to improve their socio-economic status in a *globalized* world (Huh, 2004; Lee, 2011; Song, 2011). Considering the desire for achieving participation on the world stage carries with it an implication that English communication skills are a global requisite, the term 'global textbook' attracts participants in EFL education because it bears a commensurately deceptive implication that the contents will help students achieve such worldly positioning. For these reasons, this book problematizes the unquestioned use of ELT textbooks and the lack of critical attention to their multimodal contents in compulsory English courses, on which many instructors and students lean for linguistic and cultural relativity in Korean university education.

In the context of EFL education in Korea, globalization, as a pedagogical consideration, is connected to the choice and use of textbooks. In 1995, a Korean government implementation (labelled *Se-gye-hwa* in Korean) was meant to kick-start a *globalized* approach to language education policy (Lee, 2011). During that time, plentiful government funding supported a national English education programme, which included teacher training, recruitment, curriculum assessments and investments of emergent technologies (Jung & Norton, 2002). Some Koreans even supported the idea of making English an official second language because of the expectation that English as a second language in Korea (rather than as a foreign language) would garner stronger foreign investment (Kang, 2000; Lee, 2011). Likewise, 'globalization' is a term that gained popularity in Korean society during that time because it implied the notion that Korea was a significant actor on the world stage. The term 'global English' was noted earlier as insidiously attractive to potential consumers because that generic moniker carries with it the implication that consumers of its contents will belong to an international community and, by extension, are considered economically and politically significant (Lee, 2011; Shin, 2003). For these reasons, the term 'globalization', in the context of Korean EFL education, bears a close relationship to its associated textbooks. KICE, a powerful, institutional entity informing wide networks of government officials involved with language policy and planning in Korea (i.e. Fitzgibbon, 2013; Haggerty & Fox, 2016; Lee, 2011), determined that ELT textbooks should facilitate a conductive and broadening measure of worldly understanding, leading to membership in a global community (KICE, 2001).

KICE's commitments, as an institutional stakeholder championing *Se-gye-hwa*, also reached Korean society at the local level. Many Korean people go to great lengths to achieve some measure of English fluency because with that capability comes perceived social, political and economic benefits (Ahn, 2011; Smith; 2020). In extreme cases, some parents had their children's tongues surgically altered so that their children might achieve better English pronunciation (Park, 2009). At the heart of these social consequences surrounding EFL education in Korea are the associated textbooks, where contents project white, middle-class lifestyles and cultural values as the preferred representation of contemporary *Anglo-centric* culture (Yim, 2007; Smith, 2020; Song, 2013). For those reasons, some Korean social commentators incorrectly regard *globalization* as synonymous with *Americanization* (Lee, 2011). That syllogism, Lee (2011) argues, should have been a warning for the policymakers of *Se-gye-hwa* to consider because it confirms the notion that EFL education is not a neutral endeavour but one that is ideologically laden (Auerbach, 1995; Auerbach & Burgess, 1985, Canagarajah, 2016; Curdt-Christiansen & Weninger, 2015; Pennycook & Candlin, 2017; Phillipson, 1992).

Student Perspectives

Much of the discussion thus far, regarding EFL learning in Korean society, continues to point to textbooks as socially consequential artefacts (Ahn, 2014). The purpose of this section further problematizes ELT textbooks in a Korean context by underpinning relevant factors in education, culture and politics (Weninger & Kiss, 2013). Prior to university, Korean students learn in a heavily structured, teach-to-the-test-driven primary and secondary school system that does little to prepare them for practical English speaking in a real-world context (Ahn, 2014; Baik, 1994; Choi, 2008; Haggerty, 2011; Song, 2013). Perhaps the Jovian maelstrom around which the climate of Korean K-12 education revolves is the *Su-neung* (in English, the Korean Scholastic Aptitude Test (hereafter KSAT)), where English is one of the core components (Ahn, 2011, 2014; Fitzgibbon, 2013; Haggerty & Fox, 2016; Hwang, 2003; Lee & Lee, 2016; Smith, 2020). The KSAT determines the course of one's academic career with far more consequence than any other test and a source of considerable stress for senior high school students (Ahn, 2014).

In post-KSAT learning engagements, such as university courses, EFL learning can be an intimidating experience for Korean students, enticing them to become strongly attached to learning materials, such as ELT textbooks, that may be undeserving of such dependency. English communication skills are not given robust attention in the pursuit of high scores in KSAT (Ahn, 2014; Choi, 2008; Hwang, 2003; Song, 2013), so when these students eventually come to university, their textbooks likely represent academic life rafts on which they drift along the ebbs and flows of post-secondary *interlanguage*. Hence, having no other platform of reference on which to tether their oral English challenges, it is not surprising their textbooks become trusted anchors to which they cling. In this context, the textbook becomes a prescription for not only (oral) linguistic but cultural appropriateness (Cortez, 2008), forcing students to lend it tremendous dependency.

Teacher Perspectives

To underpin such concerns over EFL and its associated materials over the past few decades, several studies point to various challenges in Korean EFL education and textbook content, and how educators and EFL education practitioner-researchers addressed those challenges. In a study looking at the relationship between Korean EFL learners' preferred learning styles and their textbooks, Lee (2015) found the former to be a referential indicator for the selection of the latter. Lee's (2015) findings imply that teachers may have more engaging classes by using textbooks as foundations on which to build learner-centric adaptations of the lessons they contain, rather than strictly adhering to each activity. However, globally published textbooks can present considerable contextual challenges for a Korean English teacher, wishing to build more engaging lessons.

In a case study looking at EFL educational materials between 1997 and 2001, Kim (2001) found that domestically published textbooks (i.e. *Sisa-yongeo-sa* series) appeared to be well received by students and teachers in primary and secondary public schools because Korean English teachers struggled to negotiate globally published ELT textbook contents. Although Kim's (2001) study underpins the misalignment between materials, curriculum and language learning methods, the study revealed that domestic publications diminished the challenge of following communicative language teaching methods in K-12 classrooms because they presented familiar cultural content to which teachers felt more confident to transform, adapt and teach to their respective students.

While communicative language teaching sharpens communicative comp-etence by bringing lessons closer to real-world application, by contrast, it has fostered the habit of teaching cultural and linguistic stereotypes as necessary artefacts of consumption in language learning (Kramsch & Vinall, 2015). Instructional practice that includes certain social realities, without considering to whom they are being taught, further explains why some inexperienced teachers use and trust textbook content and peripheral materials without question, especially if that content serves as a syllabus or simply fills a quota. Unfortunately, close adherence to textbook content allows for cultural biases to go unchallenged in EFL classrooms. In a quantitative study looking at the differences of opinion between pre-service and in-service secondary school English teachers, Kim (2015) found that pre-service teachers preferred strict adherence to textbook activities and syllabus requirements while in-service teachers preferred to allow for flexibility as per the needs of the students. In this way, Kim (2015) has revealed the tendency in younger generations of Korean

English teachers to follow a globally published ELT textbook syllabus rather than use their own beliefs, assumptions and knowledge (Woods, 1996) about language learning. Such publications persist in Korean K-12 education because it is far easier to follow a pre-made curriculum than to craft one from experience.

In a mixed-methods study looking at cultural representations in eleven globally published, university ELT textbooks (i.e. *Top Notch* series or *Interchange* series) and surveying 179 university students of that content, Sung (2008) found a mismatch between the cultural exposure in the content and the English activities. For Sung (2008), many of the examined ELT textbooks presented uninteresting and persistent biases in favour of imaginary, generic version of inner-circle ideals. Sung (2008) argues little effort had been made by the publishers to present a diverse discourse in their cultural representations. The quantitative findings reflect the qualitative analysis, where students appear somewhat ambivalent to their textbook content, finding no real consequence in the cultural exposure (Sung, 2008). For this reason, Sung (2008) advises teachers to repurpose the material for more context-specific lessons to mitigate disinterest. Wang et al. (2011) present a content analysis or *checklist* that teachers may use to make tailored selections of global ELT textbooks for their respective courses. Wang et al.'s (2011) checklist of considerations for textbook selection gives assistance to inexperienced English teachers preparing for Korean EFL classes and partially informs this book's approach to understanding their multimodal discourses.

Curriculum Connections to Expanding-circle Contexts

In addressing the challenges of EFL learning in Korea, several studies point to how educators and practitioner-researchers perceive and/or theorize how to better serve the public interest in EFL education or to meet the needs of their students. A key practice for many EFL teachers, to meet those needs of their students and to address the insufficiencies of their ELT textbooks, is to manipulate the content to best serve each teacher's particular classroom *ecology* (Richards, 2014; Smith, 2021; Van Lier, 1997). In a mixed-methods study of contextual autonomy in Korean EFL teaching methods, Eun (2001) looked at surveys and interviews of 146 middle-school students and teachers. The findings indicate that each group preferred autonomy in the classroom rather than following a prescribed curriculum because it allows for more fruitful explorations of English challenges that are otherwise overlooked in a teach-to-the-test curriculum (Eun, 2001). For Kang (2000), in most cases, Korean students are extrinsically motivated especially in EFL contexts. In a study looking at learner motivation in 234 middle-school students, Kang (2000) found that extrinsic motivation, that is, the external reasons and forces pushing for a student's increased capability in English (Dornyei, 2001), outweighed internal motivations, such as personal desires to learn. Kang (2000) argued that intrinsic motivation is an equally crucial factor in English acquisition for Korean EFL students (Dornyei, 2001; Ushioda, 2011) and implies that the contextual autonomy to which Eun (2001) refers would inspire educators to pay more considered attention to the uncritical usage of textbook content in their courses. Brundage (2007) also underscores that preference for autonomy in Korean classrooms. In a quantitative study looking at fifty-three foreign English teachers in Korea, Brundage (2007) found that teacher stress was related to the increased presence of micro-management by administrative entities in their respective institutions to follow a mandated curriculum. Administrative micro-management, Brundage (2007) argues, prevents the development of teacher autonomy and deskills the EFL educator profession to one motivated only for achieving test scores. Looking at teacher awareness and willingness to engage various strategies, Lee (2006) used a mixed-method study to survey and interview sixty different private academy and public institution EFL teachers and discovered that many were not informed enough and thus not capable of implementing curricular strategies. Lee (2006) argues that delivering an effective EFL classroom strategy was only possible when a teacher had a general understanding of many theoretical options available to them and appears to show conclusively that most of the EFL teachers they interviewed and surveyed were a kind of deskilled labour force, largely dependent on their respective EFL textbooks and their accompanying teacher's guides for all matters concerning curriculum and classroom delivery. Smith (2021), in a study that used Norris's (2004) framework for video transcription (the one that informed the design of MAVREC in Chapter 3), looked at the multimodal interactions of students using ELT textbooks in situ and found that a reflexive praxis, based on student performances and reactions of textbook content during class, informed the instructor of suitable and successful content for future lessons.

Insufficiencies in EFL teacher training exist in every expanding-circle nation, so it is not surprising that some students feel their courses, whether in a private academy or at a university, are uninspiring educational engagements (Ahn, 2014). In a study looking at the perceptions of Korean university students and teachers about their EFL curriculum, Nam (2005) reveals student preference for outcomes aligned with improved test scores (such as TOEIC, TOEFL, IELTS) rather than sufficient communicative competence. On the other hand, the teachers felt that communicative language teaching was an effective approach to language instruction. The implication of Nam's (2005) study appears to reveal that the socio-economic investment made by Korean EFL students is expected to yield verifiable results (such as good test scores) rather than the communicative competence that their teachers aimed to nurture. In other words, Nam (2005) appears to argue that communicative language teaching is not useful for achievable test scores, not because of the insufficiencies of communicative language teaching as a method of instruction but because of teacher inability to use it as an effective method for helping students face *all* their linguistic challenges.

In a quantitative study looking at native-English-speaking teacher's understanding of Korean contexts, Chang (2004) revealed heavy reliance on ELT textbook content for guidance in communicative language teaching rather than using one's BAK (Woods, 1996). According to Kim et al. (2018), in a qualitative study of twenty-three K-12 students and nine teachers at private academies around Seoul, Korea, major demotivators in EFL learning were found in a teacher's lack of clear delivery in the classroom and excessive dependence on grammar in the textbook contents. Considering the complex process of developing an identity with English as a competent speaker is predicated on the socio-economic desire to earn membership with that global community wherein greater academic performance is a higher probability (Canagarajah, 1993, 2016; Song, 2013; Thompson & Lee, 2018; Vasilopoulos, 2015), the textbooks on which insufficiently trained teachers rely so heavily can play a leading role in demotivating student performance.

Comparing EFL learning in India and Korea, Cha (2002) gives convincing evidence for significant differences, suggesting the necessity for tailoring curricular designs and the delivery of textbook content in localized contexts. Unfortunately, textbook content can play a role in diminishing the development of Korean student identity, as noted in Grant and Lee (2009), who revealed ways in which ELT textbook content appears to sustain narratives of privilege inherent in socio-economic, racial and linguistic classes. Those narratives of privilege appear to be relevant in global communities, suggesting that linguistic imperialism (i.e. Phillipson & Skutnabb-Kangas, 2017) remains a relevant concern in EFL education in Korea (Grant & Lee, 2009). In a mixed-method study of the opinions of native-English-speaking and non-native English-speaking teachers and their learners, Ahn (2011) found that idealized American English norms were being emphasized as the preferred type of English to learn in Korea.

All the studies featured in this section point to a misalignment between textbook publishing/production interests, which tend to be primarily fiscal (Harwood, 2014; Gray, 2010; Littlejohn, 2012), and the interests of ELT textbook consumers, such as students and practitioners. In Korean contexts, and likely for other expanding contexts too, a lack of teacher training results in an overabundance of dependency on textbooks, where some multimodal discourses are seen to project social realities that marginalize non-English-speaking consumers.

This chapter builds upon the frameworks explored in Chapter 2 (CMAT) and Chapter 3 (MAVREC) to achieve a triangulation of qualitative analyses. The third framework is driven by the need to find out how students and practitioners value the multimodal content that they have negotiated and asks: *How do students and practitioners value or account for the multimodal discourses in their ELT textbook during class?* In what follows, we explore CALx and use it, along with the literature we have reviewed thus far, to inform the design of semi-structured interview questions and construct a framework for coding the data that emerges from the use of these questions.

Critical Applied Linguistics

Applied linguists concerned with EFL learning should value the voices of students and practitioners, who are the end users of ELT textbooks in classrooms around the world. Whatever branches might spring from the central pedagogical vision of a curriculum or whatever digital format manifests in tandem within the ever-changing sociopolitical and technological landscapes that host language learning engagements, the core or heart of learning material in any course of study may always be a singular unit: the textbook (Macgilchrist, 2017; Tomlinson & Masuhara, 2017).

Considering the navigational direction of this book, thus far, towards issues of power and ideologies that manifest in the multimodal discourses of ELT textbooks and how they might affect education, CALx may serve as a beacon to which CP and curriculum theory find guided alignment. Where the ultimate concerns of CP may be one of democratic social agency in education (Cho, 2013; Freire, 2018; Giroux, 1988; 2007; McLaren, 1988), CALx encourages language education to include the revelation of power and ideology embedded in discourses that serve as vehicles for sociopolitical and economic agendas (Canagarajah, 1993; 2006; Fairclough, 1992; Gray, 2010; Harwood, 2014;

Littlejohn, 1992; 2012; Pennycook & Candlin, 2017; van Dijk, 2011). For EFL students, acquiring English does not mean memorizing language rules but experiencing language in a dynamic social environment where meaning is created (Curdt-Christiansen & Weninger, 2015; Cho, 2013; Fitzgibbon, 2013; Kumaravadivelu, 1999; 2006; Weninger & Kiss, 2013). While the areas of concern for CALx are spread across a broad social lens, for the purposes of this discussion, focus is maintained on ELT textbook material in the context of Korean post-secondary education.

For Pennycook (2008), CALx is a diachronic praxis, conceptualizing and implementing an amalgam of thought, desire and action. The continuous reflexive integration of theory and practice is a CALx concern and achieved in the validation of oppressed social agencies (Giroux, 2004; 2007). In an EFL learning context, social justice can be realized through praxis (Pennycook, 2008). It is important to note the research of some critical pedagogists (i.e. Freire, 1970; 2018; Giroux) (1988; 2004; 2007; 2017; McLaren, 1988; Shor, 1992; 2014) makes foundational arguments in support of praxis, explored later in this chapter.

Given that English language education (EFL or ESL) plays a leading role in applied linguistics research (Pennycook, 2008), one might infer that CALx problematizes language education to address issues of power relations and social inequities in language learning. In a study of power relationships between students and teachers at Kobe Shoin Women's University, Japan, Sakui (2007) illustrated challenges faced by thirty Japanese EFL teachers, such as classroom management, variance in socio-economic backgrounds of students, attitudes towards teachers and institutions, and poor regard for ELT textbook material by their students. The study found successful classroom management relied on the teacher's sophisticated understanding of power relationships in the content (Sakui, 2007). This suggests the participants (teachers) realized that power lies not only in the teacher but as something that should be shared with the students (Sakui, 2007). This realization enabled them to achieve praxis (Pennycook, 2008) by adopting different strategies of empowerment as per classroom management challenges (Sakui, 2007), which could change from day to day, resulting in an overall improvement of student performance and observed motivation in EFL classes.

In a similar study of elementary school student power relationships in EFL classes in Bogota, Columbia, Mendez and Garcia (2012) found that power in discourse appeared to change hands, be resisted, be exchanged and be exercised among the students depending on the classroom activity. Power relationships changed in the contexts of 'discipline, responsibility, fellowship, resistance, reproach, and silence during class activities' (Mendez & Garcia, 2012, p. 183). The results of Mendez and Garcia's (2012) study describe the ebb and flow of power relationships during classroom activities, serving to inform EFL teachers how to be reflexive with their respective lessons to match or counter the tides of such relations in power towards a more considered EFL learning experience. Each of these studies, in addition to those critical studies drawing attention to EFL education in expanding-circle cultures, noted in Chapter 2 (i.e. Ahn, 2014; Choi, 2008; Lee, 2009; Lee, 2011; Lee, 2014; Matsuda, 2002; Sherman, 2010; Shin et al., 2011; Smith, 2020; Song, 2013; Taylor-Mendes, 2009; Yim, 2014), serves as examples of CALx in their reflections of power dynamics in EFL classrooms (Iyer et al., 2014, Pennycook, 2008). These studies inspire change in the way that ELT textbook content is negotiated and accounted for by frequent consumers of their contents.

CALx informs us that EFL teachers from inner-circle cultures may be more connected with the politicization of education than they suspect (Pennycook, 2008). By accepting these teachers into their schools, academic institutions of expanding- or outer-circle cultures contribute to the continual spread of globalized, sociopolitical and economic standards, for which the English language serves as a delivery system (Apple, 1985; Auerbach & Burgess, 1985; Cho, 2013; Dendrinos, 2015; Giroux, 1983, 1988; Pennycook, 2008, 2010; Savignon, 2002; Song, 2013; Weninger & Kiss, 2013). That system is part of a greater EFL culture that forces students to learn English via specific, monolingual exchanges in global publications, with speakers using (typically American) forms of English (Kramsch, 2008) that systematically indoctrinate them as participants in those social realities (Curdt-Christiansen & Weninger, 2015; Canagarajah, 1993; 1997; 2006; Pennycook, 2008). However, there may be no way to avoid the delivery of those social realities (Kramsch, 2008; Weninger & Kiss, 2013) because, as has been noted already, no textbook in any curriculum is devoid of certain ideological narratives (Auerbach & Burgess, 1985; Bourdieu, 1991; Curdt-Christiansen & Weninger, 2015; Cho, 2013; Pennycook & Candlin, 2017; Phillipson & Skutnabb-Kangas; Savignon, 2002; Song, 2013). Hence, praxis must be achieved through a teacher's mindful connection or disconnection with those devices during class (Pennycook, 2008; Fitzgibbon, 2013). Kramsch (2008) argues that EFL 'education should include the development of a more flexible capacity to read people, situations, and events based on a deep understanding of the historical and subjective dimensions of human experience' (p. 391). Kramsch's (2008) observations also resonate with some of the pedagogical concerns of CALx, where subjective manifestations of human experience in ELT textbooks, unchecked by conscientious teachers, have the potential to become naturalized vehicles for social injustices (Janks, 2010). We have shown in some studies that global ELT textbooks contain sociopolitical neutralities that seem reflective of imaginary or non-existent, middle-of-the-road realities (i.e. Curdt-Christiansen & Weninger, 2015), CALx research reveals how the reasonableness of such content can be culturally marginalizing to some students because not all social norms are universal (Pennycook & Candlin, 2017). In other words, CALx recognizes that global ELT textbooks are vehicles of inherent discrimination because publishers approve content as widely reasonable as possible to maximize international sales (Gray, 2010; Harwood, 2014; Littlejohn, 2012; Pennycook & Candlin, 2017).

Building a Framework for Consumer Voices

It bears repeating that this chapter sets the stage for a deeper look at student and practitioner perceptions about their ELT textbooks. The interviews featured in the forthcoming vignette were deemed necessary to complete this book's triangulated analysis and partially inspired by an unpublished pilot study by the author in 2017. In that mixed-method study, Korean students who publicly displayed certain opinions in a particular context did not necessarily share those exact positions in private. The *mixed-methods approach* (given more attention in Chapter 5) of that study involved an online survey and semi-structured interviews with volunteer participants of the survey. The results of the online survey of over 150 Korean university EFL students showed they felt EFL textbooks were inconsequential to their EFL courses but did not have a negative regard for them. However, in private interviews, participants expressed significant levels of frustration and concern for the multimodal content, contradicting the survey results. After consulting two experts, who have more than fifteen years of teaching experience in Korean EFL education, it was determined that cultural motives may have pressured the students in the pilot study to give 'socially acceptable' answers in the questionnaire. The fear of online content coming back to affect people is a very real and common sentiment in Korea and may have influenced student responses in the questionnaire. Collectivist cultures, such as Korea, usually pressure community members to meet the approval of the common sentiment by performing actions with the group in mind, rather than the individual (Neuliep, 2020). In the context of this study, common sentiments regarding textbook choices and EFL culture are often cemented in administrative policies formed in the upper levels of KICE

(Choi, 2008; Huh, 2004). In the context of Korean culture, those who stand out from the group disrupt the harmony and risk appearing socially objectionable (Neuliep, 2020). Therefore, it is reasonable to assume that for online engagements, where one is not completely sure who sees the results, participants may select answers representative of a common sentiment rather than of individual opinion. Therefore, cautioned by the misalignment between the qualitative and quantitative analyses discovered in the pilot study, this chapter pins down student and practitioner opinion to corroborate what we have learned thus far.

Semi-Structured Interview Coding (SSInC)

The 'interview' portion of the semi-structured interview coding is constructed within a phenomenological framework of interactive inquiry (Chen, 2008; Charmaz, 2014; Creswell & Creswell, 2017; Wertz, 2011; Yin, 1994) to measure how students and practitioners account for the multimodal discourses in their ELT textbook content. Using interviews to corroborate the other parts of the triangulated analysis proposed in this book (CMAT and MAVREC) was partially inspired by Cortez (2008) and Holliday (2015), who believe that interviews 'get to the bottom of what is going on in all aspects of social behaviour . . . within specific social settings such as schools' (p. 51). As a social practice (Talmy, 2010), interviews may reveal to what extent the discursivity of multimodal content in an ELT textbook supports or impedes an expanding-circle university EFL course and the rhetorical accomplishment of a curriculum to which Fox (2004) refers. Four experts in EFL education in Korea were consulted during the design of the interview questions for the students (see Appendix I) for facing challenges of validity. Two experts (Carleton University, Canada, alumni), with extensive experience teaching at the university level in Korea and Japan, were consulted while designing the instructor's questions (see Appendix J).

The interview questions designed for the students and the instructors guided both groups to share their opinions: (a) EFL in Korean universities, (b) EFL to each interviewee personally, (c) to contrast those perspectives with the multimodal content of their ELT textbooks and (d) if such content serves to validate their investments in EFL education (Cortez, 2008). The 'coding' part of SSInC, informed by grounded theory (Charmaz, 2014, 2017; Straus Strauss & Corbin, 1994; Wertz, 2011), borrows from a few scholarly approaches to coding and SFL. In addition to Cortez (2008), Holliday (2015), and Talmy (2010) informing the construction of the interview questions, we borrow from Saldana's

(2016) Affective/Values coding framework to highlight or *code* evidence of expressions aligned with *values* or the importance placed on ourselves, others or a thing (p. 131), *attitudes* or 'the way we think and feel about ourselves, another person, thing, or idea' (p. 131) and *beliefs*, or our personal interpretations and perceptions (p. 132). According to Saldana (2016), beliefs are 'part of a system that includes our values and attitudes' (p. 131). From that amalgam of attitudes and values, interpretive perceptions form into beliefs that serve as a vehicle for personal experience and one's moral compass (Saldana, 2016), predicating 'rules for action' (Saldana, 2016, p. 131). In the context of the forthcoming vignette, those rules for action to which Saldana (2016) refers help delineate how the students and practitioners privately regard the multimodal content in their ELT textbooks.

We also borrow and augment the coding analysis with Machin and Mayr's (2012) overlexicalization, when noticeably repetitious and synonymous items occur in utterances that imply a kind of *over-completeness* in its expression. Overlexicalization attempts to over-persuade and usually appears in ideologically contentious exchanges or utterances (Machin & Mayr, 2012). We looked for overlexicalization in the three branches of SSInC, which we illustrate later in this section.

In Halliday and Matthiessen's (2014) interpersonal metafunction in SFL, mood and modality can give meaning to how people express their attitudes,

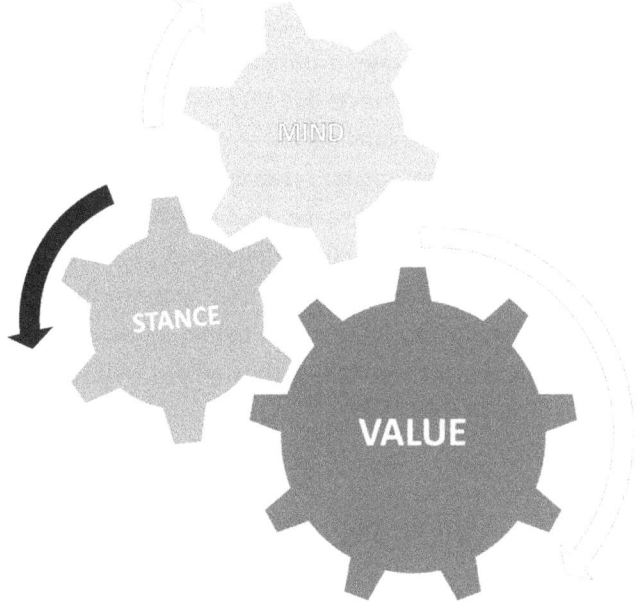

Figure 4.1 SSInC framework – Mind, stance and value.

positions and stances in discourse. For mood, the linguistic devices we look for are declarative (subject + verb), interrogative (auxiliary + subject + verb, except for wh-interrogatives) and imperative statements (verb – no subject (understood)). Declarative statements delineate who has the power to give information, while interrogatives, depending on the question, can reveal the relations between the person asking and the person listening (Young & Fitzgerald, 2017). Imperative statements reveal who has the power to command and what power tells us about the relationship between the commander and the person at whom it is being directed (Young & Fitzgerald, 2017).

When a speaker uses utterances that place themselves in between distinctive ideological or opinionated positions, Halliday and Matthiessen (2014) defines it as *modality*. The stances of modality are probability (the likelihood that the speaker feels something may occur), frequency (how many times the speaker feels something may happen), obligation (when the speaker/writer feels an urgency that something should be done) and inclination (how the speaker measures if they/someone/something will do something). Mood and modality are added to our analytical toolset in SSInC.

SSInC is a conceptual amalgam of Saldana's (2016) framework, overlexicalization (Machin & Mayr, 2012), and some components of Halliday and Matthiessen's (2014) interpersonal metafunction in SFL (see Figure 4.1). The framework features three categorical focal points to 'code' in a dialogue: mind, stance and value. In mind, we look for utterances that align with mood and evidence of expressions that indicate an *attitude* towards a person, place, thing or action. In stance, we look for utterances that align with modality and evidence of expressions that indicate our experiential *interpretation* of a person, place, thing or action. In value, we look for utterances that *positively or negatively express*, over-express, emphasize, overlexicalize (i.e. Machin & Mayr, 2012), background or silence a person, place, thing or action. Collectively, mind, stance and value inform each other, as visually implied in Figure 4.1. In the forthcoming vignette, we will see how this framework captures these points of interest in the interview transcriptions, so that we can corroborate the findings with those achieved in Chapters 2 (CMAT) and 3 (MAVREC).

Sample Vignette of SSInC

The third vignette in this book highlights a series of interviews that underpin the values of the multimodal content in Unit 6 (Saslow & Ascher, 2006), from the perspectives of the participating students and practitioners in Chapter 3. After transcribing the interviews, the transcriptions were analysed and coded with SSInC.

Data Collection and Participants

Following the classroom activity recorded in Chapter 3 (MAVREC), the researcher drew a random sampling of four volunteers from the pool of student participants from each class. Additionally, each of the instructors, who participated in phase two, completed semi-structured interviews. The total number of interviewee participants were four students and two instructors from two Korean universities. Recordings of the semi-structured interviews were transcribed verbatim.

The interviews gave students and their instructors the opportunity to account for the multimodal discourse in their ELT textbook in a setting chosen to inspire their uncensored, anonymously given opinions. The setting was important because Korea is a collectivist, ethno-centric society where individual expression is often measured by one's peers in public and a potential source of considerable anxiety (Neuliep, 2020). Operationalizing the coded, semi-structured interviews yielded insights from two angles: the students and their instructors. The two instructors (noted respectively as Instructor X and Y, as in Chapter 3) in this case were American, native English speakers, so it seemed imperative to include student interviews (noted respectively in the findings as Student X1, X2, Y1 and Y2) because their expanding-circle, cultural perspectives have a greater potential to account for the perceived social injustices yielded in CMAT and how they were negotiated in MAVREC. It should also be noted that while the interview questions for the students were composed in English, the students were encouraged to use their L1 (Korean language) if they felt uncomfortable or incapable of accurately conveying their answers. Although the researcher is competent in both English and Korean, the transcriptions (Appendixes E–H) are English and do not show the few Korean utterances that occurred during the interviews. While the English levels between the student volunteers varied from good to poor, all of the interviews were successfully recorded and transcribed verbatim in one of the instructor's offices at a national university in Korea (see Appendixes C–H).

Unlike structured interviews, 'semi' refers to a certain flexibility during the interview (Dornyei, 2007). While the interviewer provides structured guidance with a series of questions designed to evoke responses in alignment to certain research questions (Paltridge & Phakiti, 2015), the interviewee is encouraged to elaborate their responses (Dornyei, 2007) and share insights or opinions that inspire a live exchange of inquiry. The interview questions in those exchanges serve as probes and the elaboration they encourage provide an insider's perspective (Roulston, 2010), resulting in deeply enriched data collection of the social phenomena in question.

It is important to note that for each of the participants in this phase, they had just completed classroom recordings only one day earlier, so the negotiated multimodal content in the textbook was still fresh in their minds. As in Chapter 3, all participants (two instructors and four student volunteers), followed the classroom recording and observation, signed detailed consent forms prior to participating in the interviews.

Findings

The findings illustrated in this section use SSInC, which serves as an analytical toolkit for disseminating personal experience with a measure of value (Saldana, 2016; Smith, 2020). In the context of this book, SSInC helps us see how the Korean university EFL instructors and their students feel about the multimodal discourses in Unit 6 (Saslow & Ascher, 2006, pp. 62–73) *in private*, so that we can corroborate those insights with what we already know about how they were negotiated *in situ*. Furthermore, these insights reveal what pedagogical implications the insights afford Korean university EFL education.

Instructor X

Mind. For Instructor X, 'conversation' classes – a term used in Korea for EFL courses that focus on listening and speaking practice – are the most stimulating among the different types of EFL courses that his institution offers (see Figure 4.2). Although he hesitates to claim that he is qualified for his position, that hesitation is quickly reasoned. He claims, 'I don't have the know-how of a lot of theory, but I've been learning as I work' (see Appendix C), suggesting that his self-efficacy as a teacher is strengthened by lengthy, practical experience, despite the lack of former EFL teacher training.

Regarding his students, Instructor X's mind is one of compassion for their struggles as Korean L2 English speakers. He feels that Korean culture and language present significant cross-linguistic interference for EFL learning, so he encourages students to 'get the heck out of the country' (see Appendix C)

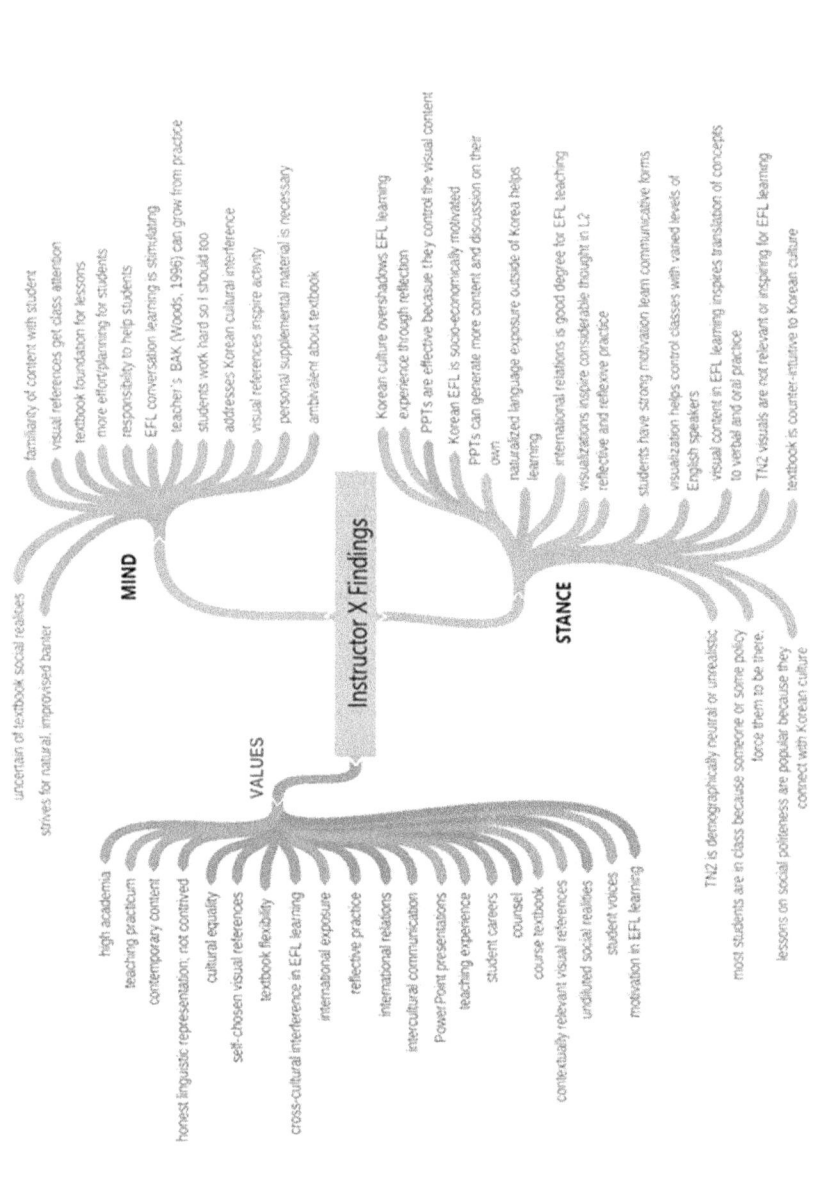

Figure 4.2 Instructor X findings.

because they need more international exposure. This attitude is demonstrated by the label he gives his students as '*Korean* English speakers' (see Appendix C), emphasizing the national moniker.

Generally, he feels the textbook offers a base on which to build his own class, but overall, the usefulness of the book, both visually and linguistically, is 'touch and go' (see Appendix C). He feels that visualizations are important for any language learning class, but his own referential choices are preferable to those presented in the textbook. For Instructor X, the textbook is 'eye-catching' (see Appendix C) but lacks visual relevance to his lessons and the context of Korean university EFL teaching. He feels the students do not find any social familiarity with the visual discourse in the textbook and prefers to repurpose some of the content with his own PowerPoint (PPT) presentations. He tries to see the content through the eyes of his students, demonstrated in his assertion that despite not paying attention to the cultural demographics represented in the content, he feels 'that would be important to the students' (see Appendix C). While Instructor X feels the content in the textbook can sometimes generate impromptu banter or discussion in class, some of the content is anachronistic. If he notices something, such as an old device or an old linguistic style in the content, he'll bring it to the attention of the students and make sure they understand it is not necessarily contemporary form.

Values. The coded transcriptions of Instructor X's interview revealed a mix of values that favour undiluted social realities, strong work ethic and cross-cultural understanding. He appears to value international relations as an educational necessity for EFL teaching and sees intercultural communication, travel and linguistic exposure as necessary components for language learning. He also appears to value reflective practice in teaching and thinks about his lessons and how he can help them 'make something of themselves' (see Appendix C) in a highly competitive society. His advice and counsel deliver a consistent theme that favours cross-cultural communication. He notes at several times in the interview that students need to 'get the heck out of here' (see Appendix C) to acquire more naturalized 'language exposure' (see Appendix C). He values the repetition of lessons because he thinks the culture of EFL in Korea and the potency of cross-linguistic influence between Korean and English do little to help students overcome common errors. This assertion is evident when he exclaims that 'they seem to get stuck on the same *sh*** that students got stuck on 18 years ago' (see Appendix C).

While he values having a textbook, Instructor X does not give the visual discourse a lot of attention and only uses the linguistic content to generate

PowerPoint presentations. Those personally generated PPTs repurpose the material in the textbook with a lot of visual references of his own choosing because they are important to language learning and inspire more robust discussion. He also feels that cultural equality is important, explaining why he mentioned 'in Korea, they have a food pagoda' (see Appendix C). By repurposing the material into his own PPTs, Instructor X is demonstrating his appreciation for what he interprets as *real speech*, noting that the contents in the textbook 'are touch and go because they feel contrived' (see Appendix C). By valuing 'comparative examples of American cities and American food and Korean cities and Korean food' (see Appendix C), Instructor X is demonstrating his beliefs that contextual relevance is important for a student's motivation to learn. Instructor X's beliefs, relating to Korean EFL contexts and the multimodal content in the textbook, will be further explored in the next section.

Stance. As noted in the introduction to these findings, stances are informed by mind and values, to which one applies their experiential interpretation. Instructor X believes he is qualified for his position as a Korean university EFL instructor because he has a degree in international relations and a teaching diploma on which he has built a career teaching EFL. Despite that sufficiency, he believes Korean culture overshadows EFL learning and feels students should try to gain linguistic exposure outside the country.

Instructor X notes that most Korean university EFL students, in addition to completing compulsory credits for their degrees, study English for socio-economic reasons and 'have a strong motivation to learning it at a functional level' (see Appendix C). However, he believes the textbook is not as useful as it could be. He states that visualizations are very important for language learning, but the textbook does not have content that adequately fulfils that requirement, so he designs his own PPTs to supplement the material. 'PPTs are so effective' (see Appendix C), he claims, because they generate more content on their own. He also believes that contextually relevant visualizations in lesson content can assist the handling of multiple levels of English among the students in a class. He notes that visual references can give students something to look at while slower students catch up. Without that, he notes that 'they'll just space out and not pay attention' (see Appendix C). As already noted in Instructor X's mind and values, the right kind of visual content, such as contextually relevant images that reflect some measure of Korean culture, can 'inspire speech and communication and translation of concepts to oral practice' (see Appendix C).

Instructor X admits that the food pyramid featured in Unit 6 (Saslow & Ascher, 2006, p. 62) had the potential to be a good source of class discussion but believes in cultural equivalence in content, so he spoke of it as the food *pagoda*, as it may sometimes be referred by Korean educators in their K-12 education system. When asked about the cultural demographics in the textbook, Instructor X admits he did not give it much thought but immediately claims it should be accountable and must be important to the students. Therefore, Instructor X believes that which may be important to the students should also be important to the teacher, who tempers their lesson in design and in situ.

Instructor Y

Mind. The coded findings of Instructor Y's interview (see Appendix D) regarding his mind, value and stance of Korean EFL and the multimodal content in the textbook are revealed in Figure 4.3. A preference for pedagogically aligned classes in EFL, rather than EFL learning, is evidentiary in his unrestrained and general dislike for ELT textbooks, which extends to the curricular policymakers who make up the milieu of Korean post-secondary EFL programmes. At first, earlier in his career, he ventured to Asia for fun but developed an attitude of respect for the job, noting that 'you can't just come here and screw around and do something to get by everyday' (see Appendix D). That evolving respect for EFL inspired him to research second language acquisition theory. That attitude led to his discovery and implementation of Stephen Krashen's work in his own classes. He also feels that 'the whole reason why we are here' (see Appendix D) is to help Korean students develop a functional use for EFL. As for his regard of the textbook, he only uses it for ideas. He jokingly notes, 'I'll look for things (in the textbook) that are useful that I can use and when I can't find them, I look for grammatical functions that I think I might be able to repurpose' (see Appendix D). In short, his mind towards the multimodal content in the textbook is negative or ambivalent to the extent that he could do without it. He strives to establish a direct line with the students and is concerned about personally meaningful lessons. For those reasons, he feels the multimodal content in ELT textbooks is not worth exploring and only meant to be passed over in class.

   Values. Instructor Y values autonomy and self-chosen resources, which explains why he does not prefer to teach EFL courses where the curriculum is already decided by institutional milieu (see Figure 4.3). He values his role as an EFL educator and the responsibility to be well trained and well prepared in the fulfillment of that job. He repeats several times that his role as an educator is a serious career, evident in an agreeable litany: 'Right, work ethic . . . right . . . work ethic' (see Appendix D). He values Korean culture as a necessary context in EFL

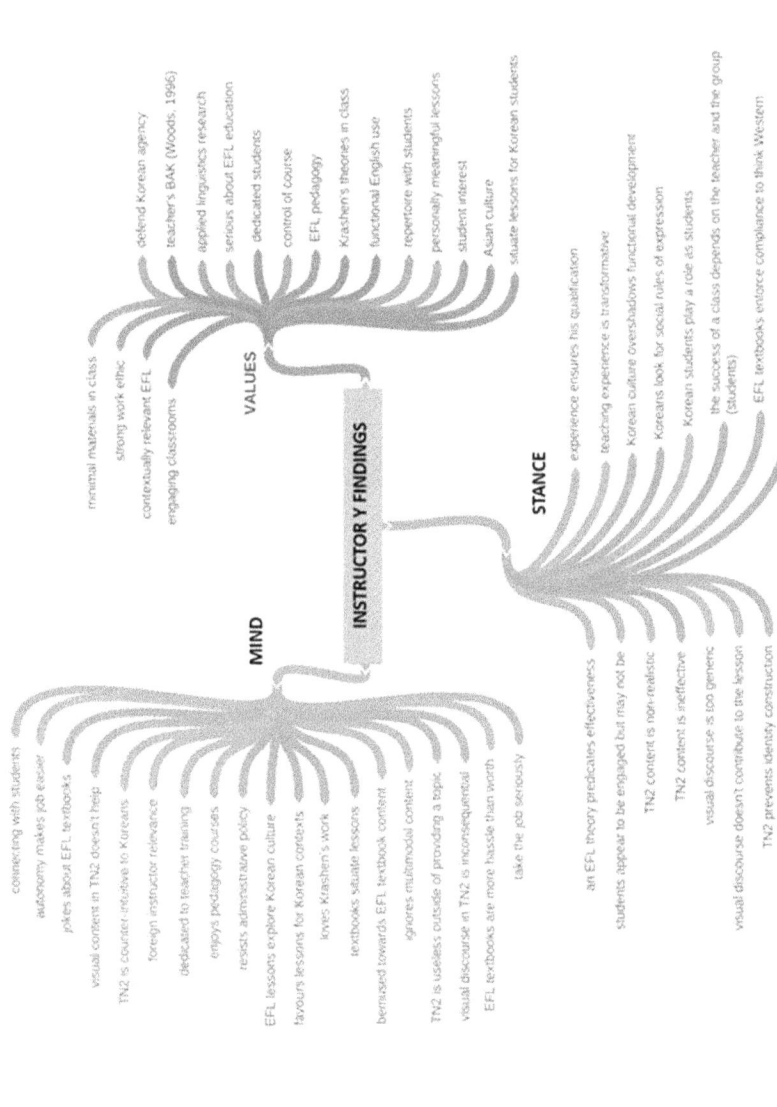

Figure 4.3 Instructor Y findings.

learning to inspire a practicum of live speech. Minimizing material resources but maximizing his repertoire and trust with the students is important for his classroom delivery. Hence, even if the content of the textbook were more Korean-specific in context, it may not be enough for students to feel it is as valuable or intuitive to their language learning investments as it could be if the teacher does not understand Korean culture. For this reason, he emphasizes the value of teacher preparedness by noting learners could benefit from almost anything if you have 'the right teacher using the right approach' (see Appendix D).

Stances. Instructor Y's mind is sourced in his values and stances, reflective of those items featured in Figure 4.3. As already noted, his preference for teaching EFL pedagogy is greater than his desire to teach EFL conversation classes because the textbooks he is often forced to use are 'more of a hassle' (see Appendix D) than they are worth in the classroom. He believes that his experience in the classroom has increased his respect for the role he plays in Korean EFL education. He believes his qualification for that role is sufficiently informed by academic preparedness and experience in the classroom. That belief is extended to a lot of foreign, native English speakers who venture to Korea for work. He believes that culture is a deeply significant factor in EFL learning in Korea and can be a help or hindrance in certain circumstances. For one, Korean culture may play a role in neglecting student use of lessons outside of the class because no one wants to exercise their English in public. Hence, he believes Korean EFL students merely play a role to appear engaged in EFL learning because it is demanded of them. Instructor Y believes that lack of genuine engagement may partially be sourced in textbooks because 'most of the content is counter-intuitive to Korean culture anyways . . . almost all of it' (see Appendix D). Instructor Y believes that his own lessons, designed from the repurposed material he takes from the textbook, better serve Korean university students and inspire them to explore their own *voice* in English communication. He believes that the multimodal content of the textbook should be more inclusive and contextually relevant to Korean students because it would be more personally meaningful. Bearing that in mind, he also believes globally published textbooks impede EFL learning because 'there is almost like a forced compliance to just think in a Western way' (see Appendix D). He believes that the cultural demographics represented in the textbook are non-realistic and may contribute to the lack of genuine engagement that he perceives in class. Instructor Y also believes that Korean students see themselves as separated from the rest of the world and that attitude hinders their practice of functional English communication. By extension, he believes the textbooks contribute to that polarity and diminishes EFL learning, so 'the right teacher using the right approach' (see Appendix D) is required to challenge that diminishment.

Student X1

Mind. The coded findings of student X1's mind, stance and value of the multimodal discourses in their textbook are illustrated in Figure 4.4. She feels Korean EFL education is insufficient because many people seek private instruction. Where she may have felt EFL grammar-translation, largely practised in Korean high schools, was not too hard, she appears to prefer learning more functional approaches to English communication, as it is commonly practised by native-English-speaking instructors in Korean universities. To her, multilingualism is cool and the enjoyment stems from learning about new cultures and having the freedom of expression, where she can 'freely choose the topic' (see Appendix E). For this reason, Student X1 is 'tired of doing enough in high school' (see Appendix E). Although she prefers a variety of visual discourse in textbooks, the content in *Top Notch 2* (Saslow & Ascher, 2006) is not interesting or enjoyable. While it is not hard to imagine more Korean representation in the characters, the content feels contrived and 'out of touch' (see Appendix E). She feels the content is representative of people living in the United States and would prefer a variety of demographic illustration. In general, student X1 feels the book is poorly designed and desires more variety in image but less content in useless text.

Values. Student X1 values EFL learning in Korea and realized, after high school, its importance on a trip to Europe. Whether for civil service exams or for academic progression, EFL is important for international communication and domestic career pursuits. Textbooks are important in that dynamic and so is freedom to explore expression. The textbook activities are not important because they do not have Korean representation. Student X1 feels representation is important because it can ease classroom participation (see Appendix E). However, it is important to represent Korea in comparison to other cultures. To her, multicultural exploration inspires a variety of instruction. To these coded findings, student X1 values this study because she wanted to say this as a 'personal add-on' (see Appendix E). In brief, student X1 values the role of the textbook in EFL learning but does not value the multimodal discourses in their textbook.

Stances. In general, student X1 believes people seek instruction elsewhere in private engagements because EFL education lacks something, to which she

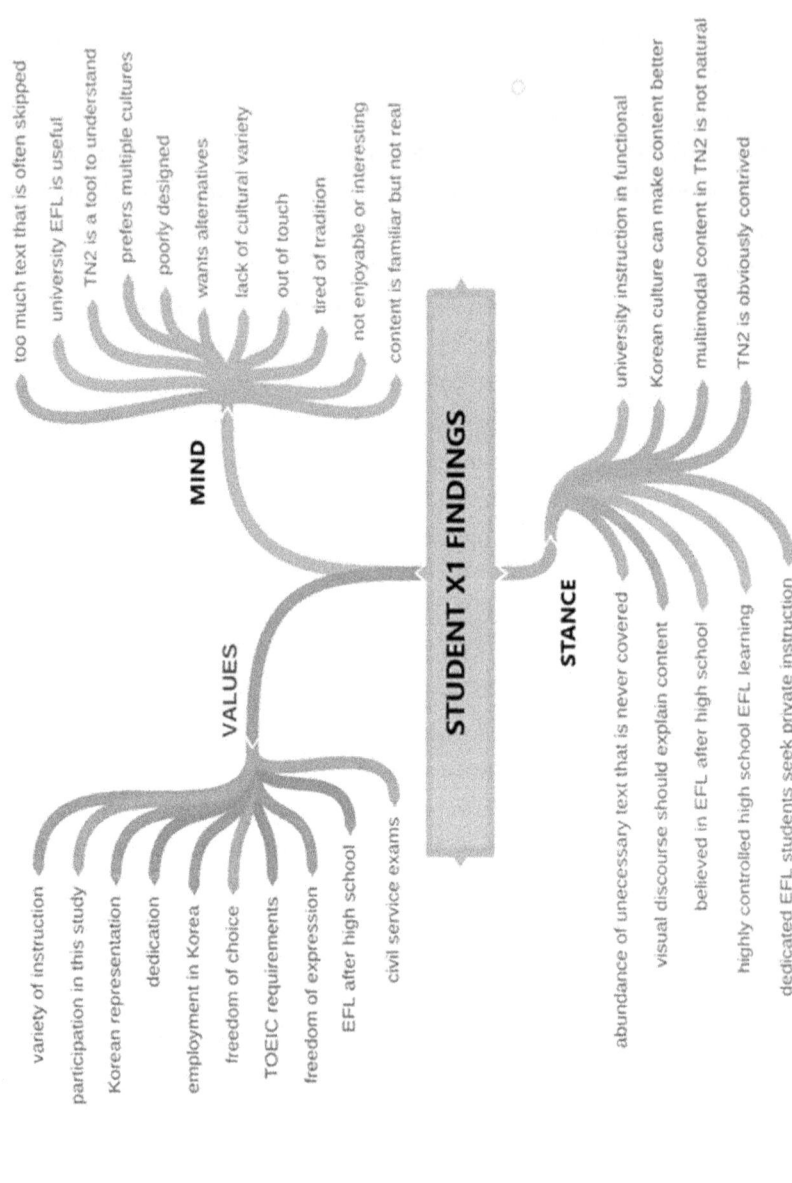

Figure 4.4 Student X1 findings.

has some difficulty specifying. While she believes K-12 EFL lessons contribute towards testing achievements, university is more for communicative practice. When asked about her class with Instructor X, she notes, 'it is a class that learns how to speak English' (see Appendix E). Hence, she believes EFL is important, not only for one's career in Korea but for intercultural communication. Regarding the multimodal discourses in the textbook, she believes textbooks in general are a necessary tool for EFL learning but does not prefer to use the textbook because it does not account for Korean perspectives and appears 'out of touch with Korean life' (see Appendix E). She noticed the lack of Korean representation in the characters and noted more (or even any) of that could inspire students 'without any pressure' (see Appendix E). She feels that textbooks have the potential to inspire dedication to study or help students 'meet TOEIC requirements' (see Appendix E). These stances resonate with student X1's mind and values concerning EFL learning because they generally point to the textbook as unnecessary or not interesting despite her appreciation for the importance of functional EFL learning in Korean society.

Student X2

Mind. Student X2's mind, stance and values of the multimodal discourses in their textbook (see Figure 4.5) are not as expressive as those attitudes revealed in X1's interview but appear to reveal more of the powerlessness students feel within the culture of Korean post-secondary EFL learning. When asked his opinion about the current state of global EFL education, his mind was ambivalent or hesitant and asked, 'Uh, is it essential? . . . to enter a good school? . . . or to get a good job?' (see Appendix F). By seeking verification of the meaning of the question, to which the researcher only nodded, student X2 responded by noting, 'just OK' (see Appendix F). The lack of commitment to fully express opinion regarding the role of global EFL suggests his mind is not completely positive or clear. An air of dissatisfaction surrounds his feeling about EFL learning, whether it is in high school or in university but contradictory. He feels EFL is useless to him but admits in the next sentence 'I think the English is good' (see Appendix F). Considering student X2's English capabilities are not as accomplished as student X1, one might assume the term 'useless' (see Appendix F) may be referring to the *kind* of EFL learning offered in Korean high schools or universities and not that all EFL learning is useless. In any case, *useless* is proximally repeated by student X2 and the repetition resonates emphasis. While the repetition could also be indicative of somewhat limited English proficiency

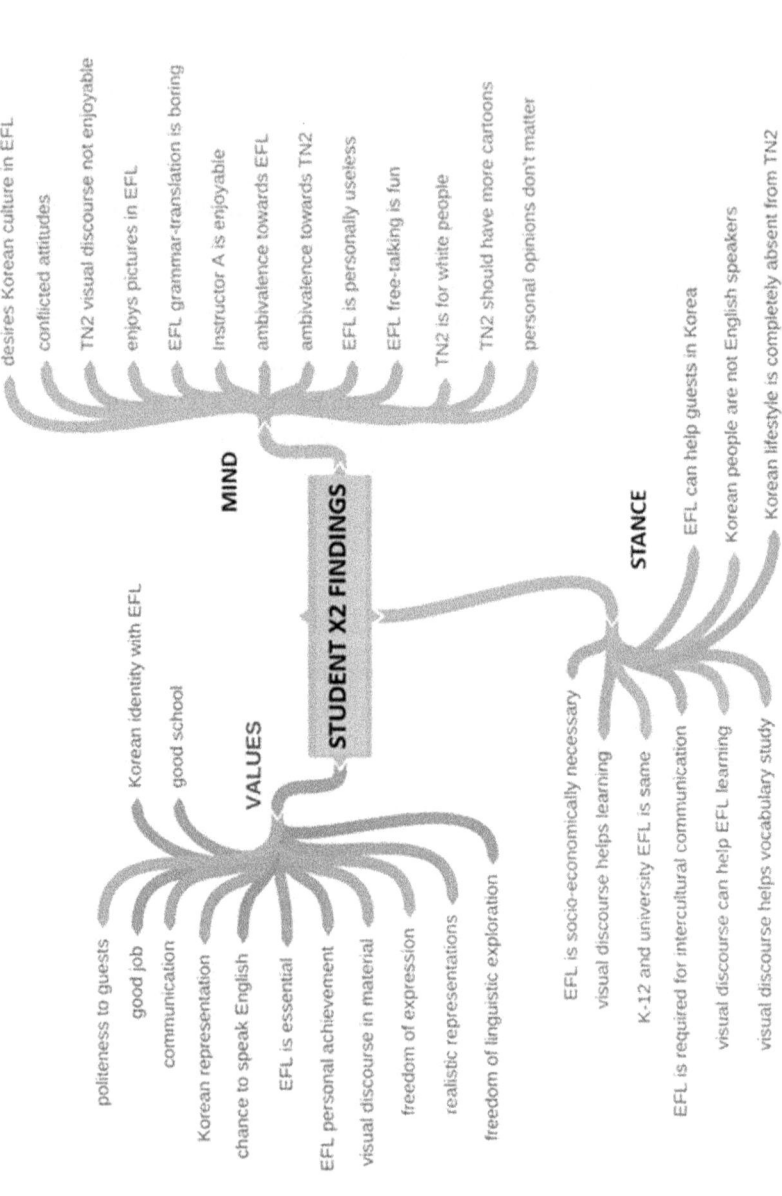

Figure 4.5 Student X2 findings.

(i.e. not having other vocabulary with which to express one's views), it should be noted that the repetition was made in both Korean and English (see note about encouraging participants to feel free to use Korean during the interview in the 'Data and Participants' section), suggesting emphasis rather than a lack of English vocabulary. The exchange is followed by a favourable attitude towards live and free discussion in class and a dislike for grammar-translation approaches, common in Korean K-12 education (Ahn, 2014; Garton, 2014; Huh, 2004). Regarding the textbook, student X2 considers the multimodal discourses in the same way he sees EFL learning – with some measure of ambivalence. The contents of the textbook are considered satisfactory but not clearly expressed. His mind towards the lesson activities is positive and they note the benefit in the *opportunity* to speak English. Student X2's mind towards the multimodal content in the textbook is only favourable in so far as it facilitates a practicum of speech and free expression. When asked about the cultures represented in the textbook, he does not appear to understand or have an opinion but quite expressively gestures to the whole book and indicates the whole book would not be accommodating to Korean people or culture by saying, 'They cannot do these things' (see Appendix F). In this way, student X2 answered an additional question, so in the style of semi-structured navigation, the researcher pressed forward to ask of the X2's thoughts on the instruction of the multimodal discourses in the textbook, to which he replies favourably. Noting that he feels English is for white people, the instruction and respect for Instructor X's efforts appear to outweigh any negative regard for the textbook. He wishes for more realistic depictions to accommodate the linguistic challenges but commits to a reality that his opinion is inconsequential because he states at several points that '. . . I don't know' and his comments are '. . . just my taste' (see Appendix F) as if to diminish or even dismiss his feelings as insignificant contributions to the study.

Values. The values student X2 attributes to EFL learning and the multimodal contents of the textbook appear tied to the usefulness and the worthiness of that investment. 'Essential' and 'good school' and 'good job' (see Appendix F) are inferred important achievements that student X2 associates with EFL learning. He obviously feels EFL is important because of a desire to learn but associates English proficiency as something only gained in live practice. However, the importance he attributes to EFL learning is sourced in what Korean society expects or demands of him, and not one of personal reflection, which appears contradictory to the value he affords English skills. That contradiction indicates two sets of values – one for Korean society and one for himself – and partially explains why the answers to questions in the interview appear confused. He values the importance of having a chance to speak English in class with Instructor X and appears to give further value to that practice noting the importance of accommodating foreign guests in Korea. He values the images in textbooks quite highly and notes their usefulness in learning for assisting in vocabulary study. However, when specifically pressed about the multimodal discourses in the textbook, he avoids discussing the value of the textbook's visual discourse but uplifts his appreciation of the linguistic challenges in the lessons and notes the importance of discussion opportunities with groups of peers. Overall, student X2 appears to value the freedom of expression and exploration in EFL learning, but he feels that is not sufficiently supported in the textbook. He values the efforts of Instructor X to deliver and repurpose realistic sociocultural content that inspires free expression relevant to 'normal (Korean) lifestyle' (see Appendix F).

Stance. Student X2's stances are grounded in his mind and values (see Figure 4.5). He believes that all EFL learning, whether in high school or in university, is good for one's career and international communication. However, he believes English is not useful outside of class. Much like his values, student X2's stances are also split between what Korean society believes and what he personally believes. In either case, he believes that free expression and speaking practice facilitates a strong learning curve in EFL Additionally, he believes that the visual discourse, as found in ELT textbooks, is very important for assisting that learning. He believes the visual content in the lessons inspires free expression or stimulates discussion but then contradicts himself by noting the multimodal discourses in the textbook are not reflective of Korean lifestyle. The lack of Korean representation influences his stances about EFL learning and the content in the textbook because he believes that 'English language textbooks seem to . . . describe by many foreigners for the English' (see Appendix F). It should be noted that in student X2's limited English capability, the word 'foreigner', in the context of EFL learning, often refers to white or Caucasian native English speakers who are in a position of authority in Korean society because they are often assumed to be English educators, in addition to being associated with the value that English capability has as a sociopolitical and economic commodity (i.e. Cho, 2013). Student X2's contradictions suggest he is struggling with his Korean cultural habit of politeness (to his white, professor interviewer – the researcher of this book) and his personal stances because it appears that he condemns the visual content in the textbook for being too *inner circle*. Student X2 appears to be engaged in a power struggle with multiple facets – Korean versus foreigner/ student versus teacher/Korean language versus English language – and he is expressing it by saying there are 'too many foreigners and too much English' in the multimodal contents. While the student's limited English proficiency may appear to be a methodological drawback, the reader is reminded that both the interviewer and the student are exchanging a few utterances to clarify that the researcher has understood what the student was trying to convey (the freedom to use both Korean and English and analyse the English-translated transcriptions was addressed earlier in the 'Data and Participants' section). The condemnation indicates that although student X2 believes the visual discourse of a textbook is important for learning, the multimodal contents do not adequately support that belief. Perhaps most arrestingly, X2 notes that 'Korean people don't speak English' (see Appendix I). In other words, in the multimodal discourses of the textbook, there are no Korean people who are speaking English and so the belief that one might infer from student X2's comment is that were there more Korean representation, either in cultural content or in character participation in the visual discourse, Korean people might speak more English. By conceptual extension, student X2 may have been referring to himself – that if there was more Korean representation in the multimodal content, he believes the textbook might help him speak better and more English. Overall, it appears student X2 believes the textbook is not useful and relies on the trust given to Instructor X to make the multimodal content and EFL learning a worthy, personal investment. Furthermore, it bears repeating that student X2 believes his comments during the interview are insignificant because he repeats 'I don't know' and 'just my taste' as if to remind the researcher that his personal agency in Korean post-secondary EFL learning is inconsequential.

Student Y1

Mind. Student Y1's mind towards EFL and the multimodal discourses in the textbook (see Figure 4.6) present a mixture of begrudging acceptance and criticism. Although she feels EFL grammar-translation is boring, she appreciates and enjoys Instructor Y's lessons for communication practice. She feels there is no difference between K-12 EFL lessons and university but communication lessons with Instructor Y are new and enjoyable. As for the usefulness of EFL lessons outside of the classroom, she simply notes 'never' (see Appendix G) and then laughs. At some points, such as in the interview with student X2, she appears conflicted because EFL is important but follows up with an uncertain 'but . . . I don't know' (see Appendix G). Although textbook visualizations are important to her, she feels the textbook was merely satisfactory and not for adults. She also feels the expressions in the lessons are useful and applicable in a Korean

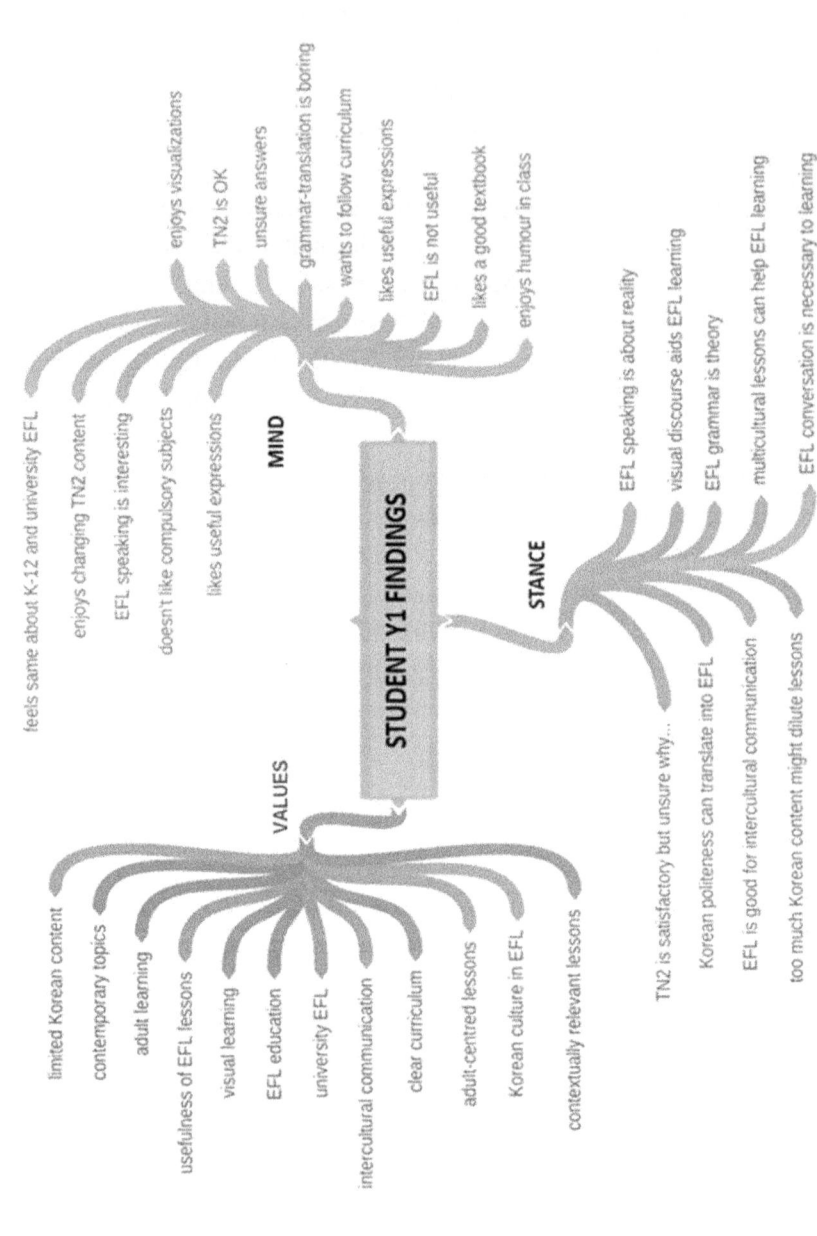

Figure 4.6 Student Y1 findings.

context. However, even that assertion is followed by 'Mmm . . . OK yeah . . .' (see Appendix G), as if to punctuate her continued uncertainty of the textbook. She enjoys Instructor Y's occasional jokes about the content in the textbook and feels he presents the material from the perspective of the students. Although she doesn't feel any of the cultural demographics in the book reflect Korean culture, she doesn't want there to be too much Korean culture either. Although she feels satisfied with the textbook, she follows up with 'I think so . . . but I'm not sure' (see Appendix G), repeating continued uncertainty of her opinions.

Values. The uncertainty of some of student Y1's opinions is, perhaps, contrastive to the values (see Figure 4.6) drawn from her answers. She values her major, English education but does not apply that to grammar-translation as much as university EFL lessons that include communication practice with Instructor Y. She sees visual learning as important to her personal learning curve in EFL values adherence to a well-designed curriculum inclusive of that content. The veiled criticism of Instructor Y's frequent abandonment of the curriculum, such as noting 'I think we are supposed to follow the curriculum' (see Appendix G), is contradicted in her appreciation for his delivery of the content because she appears to value his use of humour in class. She values content that is not anachronistic or counter-intuitive to Korean students but remains multicultural. Despite some contradictions, student Y1 appears to value the multimodal discourses of the textbook but only if presented by Instructor Y.

Stance. Drawn from student Y1's mind and values, her stances about EFL learning in Korea and the content in the textbook (see Appendix G) may present evidence of the internal conflict that student X2 exhibited – that the role of EFL learning in Korean society may differ from an individual's personal account. Student Y1 believes the communication classes with Instructor Y are a necessary complement to the grammar-translation class she must complete with Korean professors. She believes that visual learning is important to EFL acquirement because of personal experience, so she absorbs the multimodal discourses in the textbook as much as possible. Although she feels EFL is a necessary skill in Korean culture, she feels too much Korean content in the textbook might make it less real or contrived. However, her satisfaction with the textbook is confused because she criticizes the content for being too juvenile for her and her classmates and believes the content would be more relevant to adult learning by using current topics. Although she feels the linguistic content is useful in a Korean context, she believes most EFL learning is useless, as noted in her attitudes using English outside of class (see Appendix G). Student Y1's stances give evidence of internal conflict in trying to understand the expectations surrounding EFL education in Korean society and her personal opinion of it. It is important to remember that Korea is an ethno-centric culture (Neuliep, 2020), where 'the group' is prioritized over individual opinion. While Student Y1 appears to regard the content of the textbook as satisfactory, they also feel that only a *good* instructor can make it enjoyable and relevant to her as a Korean citizen and as an English major in university.

Student Y2

Mind. Student Y2's coded mind, values and stances (see Figure 4.7) present some confused statements that imply an inner conflict that these findings have already highlighted in other volunteers. Although student Y2 feels awkward about studying EFL, he is nevertheless interested in acquiring more skills. He feels that watching movies or using other forms of entertainment in EFL learning are more enjoyable than grammar-translation and appears to find Instructor Y's class more inspiring. 'He is excellent' (see Appendix H), he claims more than once, feeling Instructor Y's class is fun for EFL learning. However, Student Y2 feels the textbook is not for him. In other words, he notes 'some people like that' (see Appendix H), indicating that the visual discourse in the book is for other people and not for a Korean student. Although he feels the book is sufficient, that begrudging admission is conflicted with other statements that imply his disfavour of the textbook's lack of Korean cultural content, such as food. That conflict may be situated between Korean society's acceptance of the textbook content (i.e. Song, 2013) and his personal feelings that appear to regard the textbook as insufficient for EFL learning in a Korean context. That confliction of mind is, perhaps, most evident when he is asked if the content might be improved by more Korean cultural representation, to which he replies, 'yes, of course, but . . . I don't know' (see Appendix H). By noting Instructor Y 'only uses the activity' (see Appendix H), student Y2 appears to accept the content of the textbook because it is negotiated between them rather than forced. That acceptance is supported by student Y2's claim at several points in the interview that Instructor Y is excellent and 'makes the lesson' (see Appendix H). Overall, it is obvious student Y2 feels there are significant insufficiencies with the multimodal discourse in the textbook but acceptable because of the way Instructor Y repurposes the content during class.

Values. Considering student Y2's lack of English communication capability, compared to some of the other volunteers, it was difficult to underpin what values he associates with EFL learning in Korea and the multimodal discourses. While

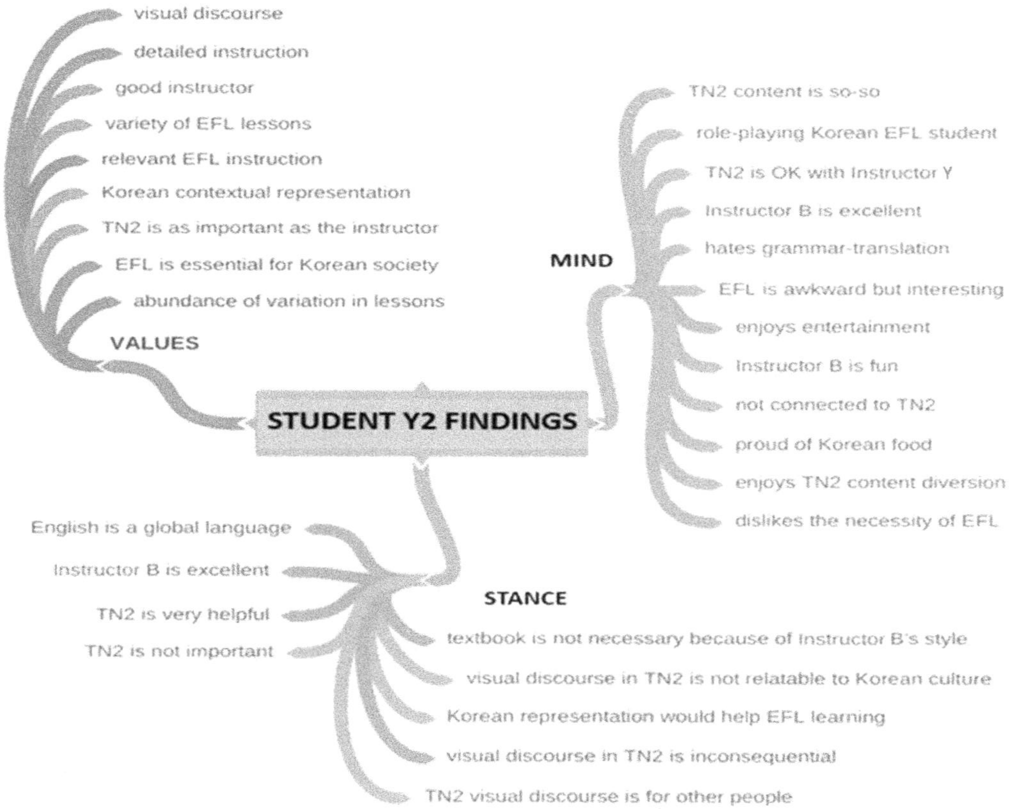

Figure 4.7 Student Y2 findings.

he admits that EFL is a necessity for most Korean post-secondary students, he appears to value the lessons only because Instructor Y is teaching them and not because any of the content in the textbook inspires his motivation to learn. He appears to value Korean content and a variety of detail in the content because he wishes to establish a personal connection with the content in Unit 6 (Saslow & Ascher, 2006, pp. 62–73). In that unit, food is the featured topic and while he values Korea's contributions to global cuisine, which he lists (see Appendix H), he also notes how the textbook would be improved by presenting more variety. That variety is assumed to be more inclusive of Korean contexts, instead of the *one-way logic* that most ELT textbooks present (Curdt-Christiansen & Weninger, 2015).

Stances. Pairing student Y2's values and mind, his stances are more apparent and seem to be an odd combination of *what is expected of him as a Korean student* and *what he personally believes.* He believes that EFL learning is necessary for Korean students because in a global world 'we have to learn' (see Appendix H), but the strong modality, coupled with *we*, indicates an impersonal affirmation. On a personal level, student Y2 believes EFL learning is necessary for travel and business or one's career. He believes that Korean contexts in the visual narratives of the textbook would make the lessons more relevant. He complains that 'there are no Korean food' (see Appendix H) and appears to believe that more personally meaningful discourse would help his EFL studies. In any case, he believes quite strongly that Instructor Y is excellent, noting so more than once, and depends on the latter for helping to understand the textbook because he does not give it much attention until directed to do so. Perhaps the most conflicted belief student Y2 has echoes in his general regard for the textbook, which he notes 'is very helpful . . . but not so important, maybe?' He asked the researcher the last tag-question, as if to confirm his personal commentary that has just contradicted his initial statement, assumed to be his socially acceptable opinion. Whatever the case may be, student Y2 appears to value the linguistic content more than the visual discourse in the textbook and depends on the instructor to make it a worthy investment of time, otherwise it would be useless because he would not engage any of the material without assistance.

Collective SSInC

The findings drawn from the interviews in this chapter were meant to underpin how students and teachers value the materials they negotiated in Chapter 2. More importantly, perhaps, the interviews were meant to offer a *safer* format for students and instructors to share their experiences in a personal way. As Talmy (2010) notes, interviews are a social practice and, in the context of this study, meant to provoke uncensored expression. However, it is important to remember that this section discusses the findings of the coded interviews as they stand alone, not inclusive of insights drawn from findings from analyses in Chapters 2 and 3. The planned synthesis of the triangulated analyses in this book will occur in the following chapter. In more specific contexts, the findings discussed here attempt to amalgamate and account for the commonplace mind, stance and values that the participants have regarding EFL learning and the multimodal discourses in their textbook.

The instructors' mind come from different perspectives, but they each appear to rely on lengthy teaching experience to help build a personal connection or 'repertoire' (see Appendices C and D) with their students. Where Instructor X's self-efficacy is supported in his work ethic and a pressing desire to help his students gain natural English exposure, Instructor Y balanced his frequent digressions from textbook with theoretically informed strategies (i.e. Krashen, 1992) that supplemented lessons, so that they were relevant to Korean sociocultural contexts. They each have an ambivalent regard for anything that provides textual or linguistic reference for their respective courses and actively transform them, visually and linguistically, into Korean contexts at almost every opportunity. While each instructor feels visual discourses are useful for EFL, they each regard the visual content of the textbook as useless or even obstructive to the learning activities because so much of it appears counter-intuitive to Korean culture. Despite their generally negative attitudes towards the textbook, they each try to use the textbook's activities to justify student expenditure in the fulfillment of their respective courses.

Values appear to resonate with each instructor. Where Instructor X uses self-chosen visual references, Instructor Y uses self-chosen linguistic references to augment the visual discourse. They each value situating the multimodal content contextually relevant for Korean culture and believe that motivates their respective students to learn. While Instructor Y favours Krashen's theories (i.e. Krashen, 1992; input hypothesis), Instructor X emphasizes intercultural communication (i.e. Scollon, 1998) as informative to their respective lesson plans. Each instructor puts an implied value on student identity as Korean L1 speakers by drawing attention to cross-linguistic influences in EFL learning. Where Instructor Y appears to value a minimalist approach to classroom materials, choosing instead to emphasize classroom discussion, Instructor X values PowerPoint presentations as a way of repurposing the textbook material.

Each values their own experience in Korea and use their understanding of the curricular commonplaces in Korean university EFL courses to improve their respective classes. Hence, they each appear to value personally meaningful lessons for the students and prioritize reflexivity while delivering the multimodal discourses in the textbook.

Each of the instructor's stances differs somewhat about EFL learning and the multimodal discourses in the textbook, but each arrives at the same conclusion. Where Instructor X believes that naturalized language exposure is the greatest format for learning and acquisition, Instructor Y believes restructured lessons that are personally meaningful for students, in the context of Korean culture, are the most profitable investment he can offer. Instructor Y believes that Koreans look for social rules for expression and try to translate English into their culture, but Instructor Y believes that students do this incorrectly and so chooses to emphasize cross-cultural comparisons by pointing out why students make mistakes, such as noting the use of formal and slang speech in Korean and how that might manifest in English. They each believe that the content in the textbook is non-realistic, ineffective, too generic and, perhaps most importantly, counter-intuitive to Korean culture. For these reasons, the multimodal discourse in the textbook can be more of a hindrance than help in their respective classes. They each believed that by minimizing the use of the textbook and maximizing classroom discussions and supplemental materials, such as PowerPoints provided by Instructor X, they can maximize learning in the short amount of class time that they each are afforded for EFL learning in their respective semesters. In short, each of the instructors feels that they could do without the textbook and find that their multimodal contents are only useful insofar as affording them some topics from which to build. For the most part, the textbook is not a preferable source for EFL learning.

The minds of the students regarding EFL in Korean university programmes and the textbook are, at first, seemingly confused. While some appear to enjoy structure and following content, others do not. While some note satisfaction, they contradict themselves shortly after. However, despite these juxtapositions, which may be resulting from a struggle between what they think Korean society expects and how they truly feel, it was noted by each a displeasure for compulsory nature of EFL learning. That lack of freedom is strongly cautioned by student X2, who feels that his private opinions don't matter (see Appendix F) to the institutional milieu associated with Korean university EFL courses. That explicit lack of agency for student attitudes as meaningful information to policy or curriculum design may partially explain why the students feel conflicting attitudes of the usefulness of EFL in their personal lives. While some perceive English as useful for one's career or intercultural communication, every student interviewee agreed that the textbook was useless for them. A common theme among them, regarding the multimodal discourse in the textbook, was a general ambivalence, likely rooted in their perceptions that the content is familiar but not real, poorly designed, out of touch, anachronistic and counter-intuitive to Korean culture. Despite that disconnection, each student expresses a general interest in free, topic-driven conversation, rather than the grammar-translation methods of the past. While they recognize that visual discourse and cultural representation are important to EFL learning, they all appear to agree that the textbook is not enjoyable and that there is no Korean cultural representation or connection. Generally, student attitudes imply a desire for content diversity, representation of multiple cultures, inclusive of a fair share of *Korean* content. However, their enjoyment of EFL and the textbook is sourced in their appreciation for their respective professors. All students appear to enjoy humour, free discussion and a classroom atmosphere of increased student-agency that each professor gives in their reflexive transformations of textbook content. That effort appears to satiate student needs, entertain their motivations and fulfil their respective investments in language learning.

The values of the students are not as contradictory as their minds. Each of the students appears to value intercultural communication, evident in multiple references to the importance of global or international communication. They appear to value EFL as essential and worthy of dedicated study, likely predicated in Korean cultural norms and rooted in socio-economic reasons, such as achieving high test scores for civil service careers or other realistic investments in learning that increase the potential for gainful employment in their respective futures. For those reasons, the students value the opportunity to speak English rather than have EFL learning directed at them in the form of grammar-translation, to which each of them openly express displeasure. They value a good instructor who can deliver a detailed variety of instruction techniques. In their classes, they value a variety of activities with contemporary topics that include adult issues because they want the lessons to be useful and clearly defined in a curriculum. Regarding the content in the textbook, the students value their Korean identity and wish to see more Korean representation because they want the English that they learn to be contextually relevant in Korean society. For this reason, the visual discourse in the textbook, while recognizably important in EFL learning, is not satisfying to their standards. Perhaps most relevant to the context of this investigation are the values that the students place on their chance to participate in this study and the freedom of expression that they enjoy in the classes with their respective instructors. That narrative of value in *freedom* appears to surface from an undercurrent of silenced-student agency in the curricular milieu surrounding Korean university EFL courses.

Student values and mind, drawn from the coded interviews, give some measure of explanation to their stance on Korean university EFL learning and the multimodal discourses in *Top Notch 2* (Saslow & Ascher, 2006). All interviewees enjoy EFL learning in university and universally regard K-12 English study as high-controlled, test-driven courses of grammar-translation. Their regard for EFL is universally regarded as a global commodity, socio-economically necessary in the context of Korean society and essential for intercultural and international communication. Regarding the multimodal discourse in the textbook, some students believe the visual discourse is almost distracting to the lessons, contrived, unrealistic and only useful if their respective instructors deliver the content in their own way. While they each feel that visual discourse is helpful to EFL learning, the content is inconsequential because it is not relatable to Korean contexts and appears designed for some *other people* (see Appendix H). To the students, some Korean culture could make the content better but not all of it. The prevailing belief is that too much Korean culture in the content would also be *bad* (see Appendix F). Each of the students implies, either explicitly or implicitly, that fair measures of multicultural representation in the multimodal content would be perfectly balanced lessons from which to engage in free discussion. However, all the students agree that their respective instructors' efforts to transform the textbook make any insufficiencies bearable, even enjoyable.

Moving Forward

Collectively, the findings remind us of Richards (2014), who cautioned that teachers should not expect publishers to change anything considering the high profit margins that EFL textbooks generate (Gray, 2010; Harwood, 2014; Littlejohn, 1992; 2012). Hence, if the students and teachers do not have a positive value for their textbook, as has been discovered in the findings presented in this chapter, teachers must inspire their students to participate in the live and active transformation of contents that increases the value of their EFL learning investments.

Chapter Summary

In this chapter, after a discussion of the sociopolitical realities of ELT in global contexts, some attention was given to an unpublished, mixed-methods pilot study by the author, who realized a significant difference between quantitative and qualitative analyses regarding the values placed on ELT textbooks in an expanding-circle EFL programme by students and instructors. The discrepancy of that study inspired the creation of SSInC – the third framework in this book towards understanding negotiated ideologies in the multimodal discourses of globally published ELT textbooks – featuring three points of focus in mind, stances and values. Building from theoretical foundations of qualitative interview design in ELT contexts, the interviews included students and instructors in a sample vignette, using participants from the same course featured in Chapters 3. The findings suggest that students and practitioners have a common measure of ambivalence towards the multimodal discourses in *Top Notch 2* (Saslow & Ascher, 2006). In the following chapter, we synthesize these findings with those from CMAT and MAVREC to corroborate a more robust understanding of the implications that the multimodal discourses in an ELT textbook have for EFL learning.

Discussion Questions

i. This chapter discusses how consumers may not openly share how they value the contents of ELT textbooks. Discuss what social or political reasons, in the contexts of English language education, one might have to be less forthcoming expressing their opinions?

ii. There are plentiful arrays of transcribed interviews available online. Find a short interview sample in educational context, then practice using the SSInC analysis featured in this chapter and discuss your findings.

5

Synthesizing Three Frameworks

Triangulating qualitative analyses that include the perspectives of people involved in the investigation will give the overall research an advantageous and, perhaps more importantly, valid perspective (Duff, 2007). Synthesizing the three analyses proposed in this triangulated framework brings us closer to understanding the multimodal discourses in an ELT textbook. In the convergence of CMAT, MAVREC and SSInC, we look for what pedagogical insights emerge that tell us about EFL learning and textbook consumption in expanding-circle contexts.

In what follows, a brief discussion of critics of critical discourse studies reminds us of the importance of triangulation and how it can be initiated in a procedural synopsis. We decided to include abbreviated versions of the featured analytical procedures in this book so that it can be accessible to non-specialists. The synopsis also includes a brief discussion of the interchangeability of the frameworks with other possibilities of triangulated studies. A discussion of the synthesized findings of the vignettes from Chapters 2, 3 and 4 is followed by deeper discussions towards understanding the multimodal discourses in ELT textbooks and how they might affect EFL learning courses. The deeper discussions are followed by a light exploration of solutions for how one can achieve an effective use of ELT textbooks in a course of study.

Addressing Some Criticisms of CDS

Critics of CDS regard the 'movement' (van Dijk, 2011) and analysts who engage in it as claiming to present an all-inclusive, politically accountable view of social discourse (Hammersley, 1997), raising CDS into a position of superiority over others 'because it is conducted in a spirit of self-reflexive critique' (Breeze, 2011, p. 458). However, Machin and Mayr (2012) contend that the connections between truth and power or language and ideology are not the providence of

CDS but rather a subject of debate for centuries, since the days of Plato and Aristotle, even if some scholars feel that CDS in revealing 'truth' also decides for others what such truths have in society (Pennycook & Candlin, 2017).

For other critics, CDS saturates applied linguistics to such an extent that pure research direction appears diminished next to the abundance of critical investigations into social injustices (Hadley, 2013, Waters, 2009; Widdowson, 2004). In other words, CDS is regarded as a tool for producing measured interpretations masquerading as social science and basically an exercise in political activism where hatched analyses produce interpretation devoid of neutrality (Luke, 2002; Widdowson, 2004). In response to such criticism, Chouliaraki and Fairclough (1999) agree that CDS should include 'insider perspectives', echoed in Duff (2007), yielding a cross-reference of analyses (Machin & Mayr, 2012). Most critics of CDS see interpretations as too selective and too ambitious to effect the change that CDS endeavours to facilitate (Machin & Mayr, 2012). However, despite these criticisms, CDS has illuminated crucial circumstances of power and ideology in discourse, not only contributing to our understanding of the manifestations of racism and sexism, for example, but encouraging people to be critical of the discourses they take for granted on a daily basis (Flowerdew & Richardson, 2017). Whether or not CDS research is seen to balance between social inquiry and political activism, Wodak and Meyer (2016) maintain such criticisms only serve to fuel the engines driving CDS forward, inspiring further questioning, innovation and self-reflection that can only sharpen the lack of social science that Widdowson (2004) bemoans.

Procedural Synopsis of 'In Text, In Class, In Mind'

Certain assumptions are required to describe a procedural synopsis for the triangulated analyses proposed in this book. In the context of EFL learning, we can make some assumptions that may be universally applicable. For example, we have discussed several studies that span multiple decades and global contexts in EFL that textbooks have elements of social inequities in their multimodal discourses (e.g. Canagarajah, 1993; Cortazzi & Jin, 1996; Matsuda, 2002; Mendez and Garcia, 2012; Song, 2013; Smith, 2020; Xiong & Qian, 2012). Even if the term 'multimodal' is not explicitly noted in some studies, they certainly engage the potential for meaning-making in various mechanisms, such as text and image. Therefore, it is reasonable to assume that the multimodal discourses in globally published ELT textbooks are still problematized (i.e. Curdt-Christiansen & Weninger, 2015; Gray, 2010; Smith, 2021).

At the core of the triangulated framework in this book is criticality. While MAVREC or SSInC may not explicitly mention or primarily focus on criticality in those frameworks, as in CMAT, their findings corroborate some of the social unfairness that the CMAT underscores in the power relations and ideologies revealed in the multimodal discourses of an ELT textbook. For this reason, while we keep CMAT at the core of our initial steps in the framework, we need to situate all three analytical procedures in an educational context (see Figure 5.1).

Understanding the educational contexts in a course of study can be achieved in understanding curricular commonplaces (Connelly & Clandinin, 1988; Null, 2016). Establishing curricular commonplaces helps the researcher prioritize and underpin the entities or powerful actors in a pedagogical culture that play a role in choosing the textbook, choosing portions of a textbook or forcing students and practitioners to use textbook material as part of a larger educational policy. Whatever the case may be, the multimodal discourses in a globally published ELT textbook are problematized as a disruptive commonplace in the rhetorical accomplishment of a curriculum (Fox, 2004). If a student or practitioner wishes to understand the multimodal discourses in their ELT textbooks towards a better understanding of their pedagogical value, effectiveness or consequence in a course of study, curricular commonplaces set the contextual stage and positionality of the researcher.

As noted in Table 3.1, establishing the curricular commonplaces in a course of study asks questions that clarify the subject, students, teachers, milieu and

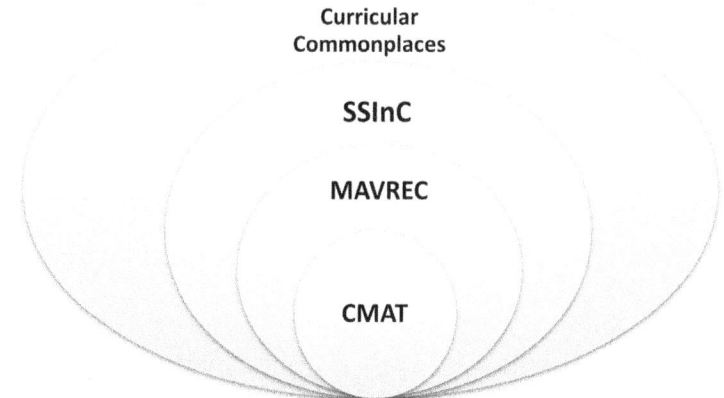

Figure 5.1 Triangulated framework and curricular commonplaces.

textbooks. However, it is important to pay close attention to those points of connection between them, much like a Venn diagram, rather than each component on their own (Figure 5.2).

In the contexts of the vignettes featured in Chapters 2, 3 and 4, where we see an ELT textbook *in action* in an EFL programme at a Korean university, we found that the textbooks play a significant role connecting teachers, students and milieu to the subject. These specific points of connection are given more attention in the following section.

After establishing the curricular commonplaces in a course of study and situating the researcher's positionality among them, a brief application of CMAT can help a researcher understand if a deeper investigation is warranted. While CMAT, detailed in Chapter 2, asks the researcher to find answers to a myriad array of questions that look at specific inventories of multimodal discourses, a simplified version that may be more accessible to non-specialists is CDS.

If the findings of the abbreviated version of CMAT (see Table 5.1) convince the researcher that the matter merits further investigation, they should see the textbook used 'in situ' (i.e. Smith, 2021). In the MAVREC (see Table 3.2), questions regarding the delivery, transformation, neutralization, resistance, appropriation and negotiation of an ELT textbook instruct the collection of detailed information of multimodal interaction during class. However, for non-specialists, a certain measure of MAVREC can be achieved in asking some simple questions related to the items in Figure 5.3.

The items featured in the abbreviated version of MAVREC allow the researcher to form their own set of sub-questions as per their positionality in the commonplaces and the unique contexts of the language learning programme. However, it is important to follow the order from the smallest of

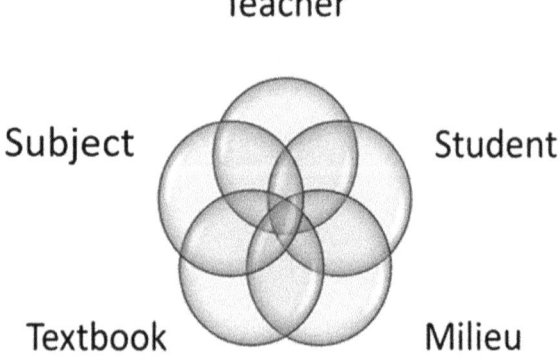

Figure 5.2 Points of connection.

Table 5.1 An Abbreviated Version of CMAT

What are the spatiotemporal and sociocultural contexts of the lesson?

Who or what is afforded agency? Who is doing what to whom in text or in images?

What is the purpose of the lesson? Could it be counter-intuitive to the students?

What is the denotation of the linguistic components?

Do any visual elements emphasize or de-emphasize any aspect of the lesson?

What is the cohesion and coherence between text and image?

Are the structures of social reality relatable to the students' culture?

What symbols, signs or recurring patterns support the social narratives?

What are the connotations in lessons?

What are the multimodal silences? What appears to be missing from the lesson?

How is power supported, challenged or concealed?

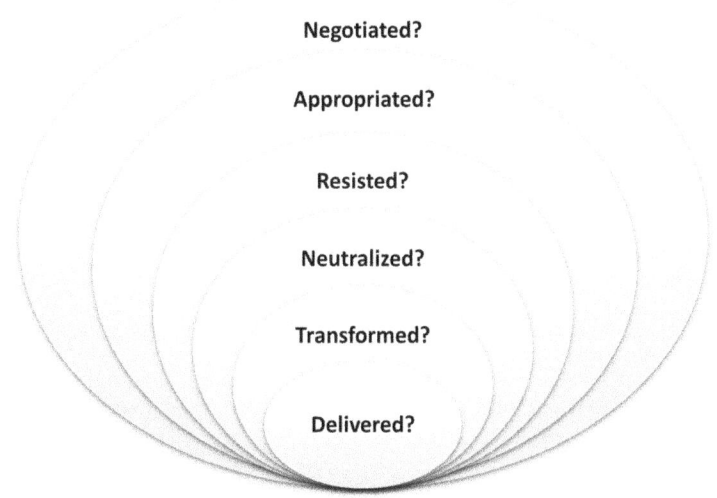

Figure 5.3 Abbreviate MAVREC – items of focus

the concentric circles to the outer, last circle that asks the overarching question: *How are the multimodal discourses in the ELT textbook negotiated in situ?* In other words, the preceding questions inform and build towards the final one, as it is graphically implied in Figure 5.3. Overall, the questions invoked by the items should include questions that require perspectives of students and practitioners – not just one or the other – because they each have a role as curricular commonplaces.

After collecting the findings of CMAT and MAVREC, whether they are abbreviated versions or not, the researcher can gain insider perspectives (i.e. Duff, 2007) by interviewing students and practitioners who are using the ELT textbook. The SSInC framework featured in Chapter 4 is already a simplified analytical toolkit, so it is important to focus on composing semi-structured interview questions (see Appendices I and J) that the researcher feels will inspire the most informative responses. It is also important to invoke discussion that pertains to classwork, so that coded findings may be corroborated with the findings of actual classwork in MAVREC.

Finally, when the findings are collected for each framework, it is time to start synthesizing the findings. There are many excellent, free online resources for idea mapping. The researcher used a variety of these programmes to create idea/concept/theme maps that delineated connected points of interest in the collected findings. However, if you are *old school* (some of us are), get a white board, some markers, print out your findings and have some fun making a conceptual map. Of course, it is a matter of taste, but for some practitioner-researchers, the tactile construction of discovered/revealed narratives that corroborate the finding is a very satisfying achievement. It depends on one's preference. In the next few sections, we will see how our efforts to synthesize the findings of the vignettes featured in Chapters 2, 3 and 4 bring us closer to understanding multimodal discourses in ELT textbooks.

The Ease of Interchangeability – CMAT, MAVREC and SSInC

As Tomlinson and Masuhara (2017) note, a textbook may always have a prime spot in any classroom because it is a focal point from which linguistic reference and activity may spring. Whether it becomes a completely digital interaction or hybrid commonplace, textbooks may always be the centre of attention. If one wishes to achieve a triangulation in methods that corroborate with multimodal critical discourse studies of ELT textbooks, there may be other options. In this book, three analyses construct the triangulation: an analysis of (1) static data, (2) live action data and (3) insider perspectives of the participants.

The CMAT is the core of the analysis featured in this book. However, one may consider other options for *live* and *insider* findings. For example, live analysis of textbooks in situ may be achieved via critical ethnography, where insider perspectives may also be acquired in the approach. Paltridge and Phakiti (2015) offer an excellent treatment, instruction and description of critical research in applied linguistics and ethnographic research in language learning contexts.

Additionally, if the researcher is considering mixed-methods options that include quantitative data to corroborate the findings of CMAT, they might consider surveys, for example, instead of interviews. Creswell (2015) has an excellent chapter on steps in research design for a mixed-methods approach, and Tashakkori and Teddlie (2010) is a rich resource for mixed methods in social and behavioural research. However, if the researcher considers the interchangeability of the frameworks featured in this book and/or chooses mixed methods as part of the triangulation, it is imperative that they heed research designs of Creswell (2015) and Tashakkori and Teddlie (2010). Mixed-methods research is not simply the integration of quantitative and qualitative data because there are specific practices related to the methodology. In other words, 'mixed methods' is 'a method' (Creswell, 2015) from which the findings of well-designed studies yield rich harvests of insights that qualitative or quantitative studies might miss. Creswell's (2015) *A Concise Introduction to Mixed Methods Research* is a lucid and informative introduction to the approach.

Synthesizing the Analyses

In this section, an overall description of the findings connects the three branches of the triangulated framework. Discussion draws conceptual parallels between the analyses towards understanding how findings from static data in a MCDS (CMAT) can be evident in a multimodal interactional analysis (MAVREC) and then be corroborated in interviews (SSInC).

In Chapter 2, the power relations and ideologies that were revealed after applying CMAT (see Table 2.1) examined a far broader array of social injustices in the multimodal contents than were discovered in previous studies of a similar nature (i.e. Giaschi, 2000; Fitzgibbon, 2013; Song, 2013; Xiong & Qian, 2012). The MCDS achieved by CMAT uncovered how language and power worked in tandem to emphasize or de-emphasize, support or delegitimize social realities established by political or commercial interests (Curdt-Christiansen & Weninger, 2015; Fairclough, 1992, 2013; Flowerdew & Richardson, 2017; Machin & Mayr, 2012; van Dijk, 2011; Wodak & Meyer, 2016). The analysis revealed instances of social injustices that resonate with previous studies of ELT textbooks but had only used a non-specific content analysis (i.e. Gungor & Prins, 2010; Healy, 2009; Lee, 2014; Marefat & Marzban,

2014; Nofal & Qawar, 2015). In more specific terms, the research of Wodak and Meyer (2016), Machin and Mayr (2012), and Serafini (2014), served as relevant theoretical frameworks on which to build an analytical procedure for large bodies of data (e.g. in a textbook) because each specifies that their frameworks are malleable sources for others to adjust in a specific analytical context. Serafini (2014) provides a robust framework for looking closer at granular visual elements (shape, texture, perspective, composition, colour, etc.), so that some of those elements that may not be underpinned in Machin and Mayr (2012) or Wodak and Meyer (2016) could be given attention. CMAT contributes to MCDS research by adding a flexible framework in a step-by-step procedure that can only be used by non-specialists, such as EFL students and/ or practitioners, to evaluate textbooks in their respective programmes. CMAT reveals if the multimodal discourses in an ELT textbook could potentially marginalize the consumers. However, despite these insights, CMAT is not able to see or anticipate, in a live situation, how the revealed social injustices in the multimodal discourses are negotiated between students and practitioners. It is important to keep this in mind as this discussion continues to detail the contribution that CMAT gives to the field of MCDS research because it necessitates anchoring the triangulated framework in the analysis of static data before seeing how it performs as live data. In other words, considering the whole focus of this book is about understanding multimodal discourses in ELT textbooks, then the analytical procedure should start and build from there.

As noted in Chapter 1, many critical studies focused on singular, perceived social injustices in ELT textbook content such as cultural marginalization of non-English-speaking communities (i.e. Ahn, 2014; Choi, 2008; Lee, 2009; Lee, 2011; Lee, 2014; Matsuda, 2002; Sherman, 2010; Shin et al., 2011; Song, 2013; Taylor-Mendes, 2009; Yim, 2014), interpellated under the umbrella of education (Apple, 1985; Canagarajah, 1993; 2006; Curdt-Christiansen & Weninger, 2015; Dendrinos, 2015; Fitzgibbon, 2013; Gray, 2010; Harwood, 2014; Littlejohn, 1992; 2012; Smith, 2021; Song, 2013; van Dijk, 2011). For example, much research focused on gender representation, such as male dominance as social actors (Ahour & Zaferani, 2016; Amerian & Esmaili, 2015; Baghdadi, 2012; Giaschi, 2000; Gungor & Prins, 2010; Healy, 2009; Lee, 2014; Marefat & Marzban, 2014; Mustedanagic, 2010; Nofal & Qawar, 2015; Sadeghi & Maleki, 2016; Sahragard & Davatgarzadeh, 2012; Setyono, 2018; Sherman, 2010; Smith & Sheyholislami, 2022; Soylemez, 2010; Stockdale, 2006; Tajeddin & Janebi, 2010; Thomson & Otsuji, 2003) or the perpetual *whiteness* of agency in the multimodal discourse of the textbook lessons (i.e. Gulliver & Thurrell, 2017; Fitzgibbon, 2013; Harper, 2012).

CMAT achieves the discovery of some social injustices in the vignette (i.e. Saslow & Ascher, 2006) by analysing the full complement of a ME on each opened page. The findings (discussed in more detail in the next section) appear more robust than in previous studies because CMAT adheres to a common axiom of multimodal discourse analysis – that the entire field of meaning must be analysed because it is a fabric where all text and image, as interwoven, become, more or less, like the other (Bateman, 2014; Jewitt et al., 2016; Kress, 2010; Machin, 2016; Machin & Mayr, 2012). The full extent of meaning-making, in this sense, cannot be realized if one only focuses on a single thread of that fabric. Therefore, CMAT contributes to the pool of MCDS research of ELT textbooks because it looks at as many meaning-making mechanisms as possible in MEs.

The MAVREC featured in the vignette for Chapter 3 was conducted after the students in each of the university classes had already completed multiple units in *Top Notch 2* (Saslow & Ascher, 2006, pp. 2–61), so the findings are not just a slice of recorded class time but a representation of sentiments, likely influenced by the multimodal discourses that had been simmering under the surface for several months. Among the studies reviewed in this book, where MCDS of an ELT textbook is either implied or explicitly engaged, very few, if any, have attempted to correlate or sequence findings with classroom negotiations, as featured in Chapter 3. For example, Cortez (2008) has research that looked at multimodal content in ELT textbooks and attempted to include instructor and student interactions.

The MAVREC was designed to corroborate the discovered social injustices yielded by CMAT in Chapter 2 with the negotiations of the multimodal discourse in Chapter 3, as they were being reflexively negotiated with their instructors. By following static analysis in CMAT with the analysis of live interaction via MAVREC, we were able to see physical, emotional and interactional reactions to the textbook content, as indicated by student engagement in robust discussion with neighbours, happy facial expressions, active notetaking during lectures and the overall atmospheric sense of accomplishment at the end of each video. In the findings of MAVREC, it is noticeable that students become disinterested or distanced from their textbooks and often choose to stare at the classroom's whiteboard as their instructors delivered the lessons.

MAVREC serves as a bridge on which to connect supporting evidence of the social injustices initially revealed in CMAT, as they manifest in the values that students and practitioners afford the multimodal discourses of the textbook content in their respective, coded interviews. In Chapter 4, the findings of SSInC point to instructors' mind, stance and values of the multimodal discourses in *Top Notch 2* (Saslow & Ascher, 2006) and echo the reactions transcribed in MAVREC: that the textbook discourses are useless for class and only value the active transformation of the content to make the lessons more interesting and more intuitive to their cultural affinities. Students and practitioners believe the textbooks should be used to inspire task-based lessons (Ellis, 2017), relevant to Korean lifestyle. Furthermore, in the critical studies of ELT textbooks reviewed in Chapter 2, none have woven instructor and student values of negotiated textbooks into the findings of an MCDS. The values, mind and stances drawn from the students and practitioners in Chapter 4 play the role of keystones that support the entire heuristic formation of the findings. In other words, we might see the successive phases of this book, in an algorithmic sense, to read: CMAT plus MAVREC explains Values. In turn, the values coded in Chapter 4 explain the findings of MAVREC, each inferred from the power relations and ideologies in the textbook.

Deeper Discussion of the Findings in Three Phases of Analysis

In Chapter 2, the power relations and ideologies that were revealed in CMAT found several instances of othering expanding-circle consumers. For example, looking for interactive or reactive connections to these social injustices in the findings in MAVREC (Chapter 6), we can infer that the instances of othering played a role in the abundance of attention that Instructor Y gives to describing the food pyramid (Saslow & Ascher, 2006, p. 62) to lessen student confusion. Instructor X also tailored activities to augment the textbook's content by providing a completely different food pyramid (or food pagoda), encouraging the students to focus on their own food choices. Each of the instructors responded to the cultural silencing of Korea in kind – by omitting the visual discourse from the lessons unless it was apparently deemed necessary – or in their general reconstruction of some of the lessons. Othering is likely why the students showed expressions of bemused curiosity, especially looking at the food pyramid (Saslow & Ascher, 2006, p. 62) or the curious absence of any kind of Korean dish to which they might find a personal connection. For these reasons, it is not surprising that students afford a stronger measure of value on their respective instructors than in the contents of their textbooks. At several instances in the coded interviews, students responded quite positively to their instructors as 'excellent' (see Appendix H) or 'fun' (see Appendix I), compared to the instructors who expressed concern that students received a value for their investment in language learning or are left with a sense of usefulness in the lessons that they are forced to complete in the compulsory course. In any case, the instructors appear to increase the pedagogical value of lesson content in the ELT textbook by actively transforming the content into Korean contexts for their students.

Diminished female agency, revealed in the depiction of Mieko and Noor in Unit 5 (Saslow & Ascher, 2006, p. 52), was not an easy connection to make in MAVREC or Values. However, cultural silencing in Unit 6 (Saslow & Ascher, 2006, pp. 61–74) resonated quite strongly with the findings from MAVREC and the coded values of the interviews. While the students' reactions to the visual discourse were often reflective of the cultural silencing to which they were being subjected (the atmosphere of the classroom lowered in pitch and discussion was diminished), Instructor X met the visual discourse by ignoring it or by reconstructing it into, for example, a food pagoda, while Instructor Y spoke of 'legumes' (see Appendix D), a relative staple of Korean cuisine that the students did not at first recognize. In these cases, the cultural silencing in the textbook was recognized as deserving of reconstruction or given reasonable attention for the purpose of highlighting the linguistic challenges in the activities, to which the students responded positively after first reacting silently.

The cultural silences revealed in CMAT in Chapter 2 are demonstrable instances of support for inner-circle power and agency in the textbook. Where the food pyramid, filled with inner-circle standards of 'healthy food consumption', endorsed by a medical physician, looms over a smaller, empty pyramid, to which the students are connected because of the expectation to fill it in, the instructors decide to present the images as food pagodas instead of a pyramid or highlight items that may be identifiable to the students (such as rice, underpinned by Instructor Y). By transforming the food pyramid into a food pagoda, Instructor X has lessened inner-circle agency for that visual device, to which student response appeared universally positive because it inspired lively, classroom discussion. The values to which we might connect these causations may be found in some students believing that the visual discourse is almost distracting to the lessons, or contrived, or unrealistic, but useful if their respective instructors deliver the content in their own way.

These connections between CMAT, MAVREC and SSInC are not meant to represent an exhaustive account of all possible connections between the findings in the vignettes but offer demonstrable credence, in a more general sense, that the multimodal discourses in *Top Notch 2* (Saslow & Ascher, 2006) would not be as consequential or impactful on the value of student learning experiences unless it was actively transformed by their instructors – a process that both instructors and students appear to value as a pedagogically relevant, rhetorical accomplishment (Fox, 2004) inside the restrictive curriculum of a typical, Korean university EFL course.

In Chapter 2, the power relations and ideologies revealed by CMAT identified repetitive or collected instances of othering non-inner-circle cultures, presenting culturally neutralized characters into a socio-economic melting pot, strong visual narratives of cultural silencing and a general support for inner-circle or Anglo-centric perspectives, social realities and hegemonic interests. Therefore, it is reasonable to assume that Instructors X and Y transformed the multimodal discourses in those textbook lessons to suit the needs of their students. Those transformations exercise reflexivity in the negotiation of the textbook content while fostering a functional knowledge of English communication (Stoller, 2015). Students enjoyed those transformations, observed in their physical reactions by sitting more perceptively upright, speaking louder, practising dialogues with more enthusiasm and generally exercising keen participation in the activities. On the other hand, the students would often be silent, appear confused or even disinterested if the content was not filtered through the instructor first, suggesting that reflexivity in situ (Smith, 2021) encourages and inspires a more enjoyable negotiation of textbook content, resulting in deeper learning (Stoller, 2015).

From these insights, we can see the mind, values and stance that students and instructors afford EFL learning and the multimodal discourses in their ELT textbook. From the instructor's points of view in Chapter 3, those collected affordances point to a reliance on lengthy teaching experience to help build a personal connection or 'repertoire' (see Appendix D) with their students. However, the research recognizes each of the instructors have a strong understanding of the curricular commonplaces (Connelly & Clandinin, 1988; Null, 2016) that sharpen their BAK (Banes et al., 2016; Woods, 1996) of Korean university EFL classrooms. That heightened state of understanding informs their respective pedagogical mind, values and stance towards EFL learning and the content of the textbook in and out of class. In more specific terms, each instructor appears to value personally meaningful lessons for students, prioritize reflexivity with the content, but ultimately believe they could do without textbook. From the students' perspectives, according to the findings in Chapter 4, all appear to enjoy humour, free discussion and a classroom atmosphere of increased student-agency because those efforts entertain their motivations and provide some measure of fulfilment for student investments in language learning. The students value the opportunity to speak English more than undertaking exercises focused on grammar-translation. 'Opportunity' was a common lexical choice in the coded interviews and likely sourced from an undercurrent of silenced student-agency in their K-12 experiences and education policy driven by the administrative milieu surrounding Korean university education (i.e. KICE, 2001). All students imply a belief that fair representation of multiple cultures would result in balanced lessons for stimulating free discussion. Additionally, all students agree that their instructor's efforts to transform the contents of the textbook are necessary, where otherwise the textbook would be considered a banal artefact of Korean university EFL courses.

The mind, values and stance of the instructors and the students are corroborated by CMAT in Chapter 2 and are evident in the findings of MAVREC in Chapter 6. For example, CMAT revealed the food pyramid in Unit 6 (Saslow and Ascher, 2006, p. 62) was an icon of emphasis, implying, by contrast, the smaller pyramid, empty and associated with expanding-circle cultures, was inferior. In Chapter 3, the instructors avoided it, likely because they perceived it as 'negative', and uplifted Korean cultural agency by talking about Korean foods. In Chapter 4, students appear to appreciate the digression from some of the textbook content. Therefore, it is reasonable to make a linear connection between the qualitative analyses and assume from the synthesis of researcher, learner and instructor perspectives that instances of othering, cultural silencing, socio-economic neutralization and a general preference for all things associated with English-speaking countries play a role in demotivating or diminishing student-agency in EFL classrooms. It is also reasonable to assume that some multimodal discourse in ELT textbooks force instructors to change it so that the mind, values and stance that students harbour for ELT textbooks do not diminish or devalue their respective investments in language learning. In simpler terms, according to the findings of the vignettes in this book, students and instructors do not value their textbook but are forced to buy it and use it as part of a highly structured curriculum in Korean EFL courses. That forced compliance to consume textbook content can demotivate or confuse Korean university students, as noted in the contradictory remarks coded in student volunteer Y2, who appeared to approve of *Top Notch 2* (Saslow & Ascher, 2006) and condemn it the same sentence (see Appendix H). The researcher supports this assertion with personal experience, noting that from a period of seven years between 2005 and 2014 student attitudes towards EFL learning in Korean universities were perceptively negative whenever the textbook was used in class, but ultimately more positive whenever open classroom discussion included the linguistic challenges of the textbook but deviated from its multimodal discourses to allow more agency in classroom discussions.

For students and practitioners of EFL, for example, the implication of this book informs them of potentially harmful multimodal discourse in ELT textbooks. The implication for students is emancipatory – a key fulfilment for critical discourse studies (Wodak & Meyer, 2016) and particularly meaningful to Korean university students, who are forced to take compulsory English communication courses in partial fulfilment of their undergraduate studies. For instructors, the implications are informative because so many rely on ELT textbooks such as a key source for their curricular designs and syllabus (Richards, 2014; Tomlinson & Masuhara, 2017). To that end, critical understanding inspires practitioners to engage in reflexive praxis (i.e. Pennycook, 2008) and to consider the content that they teach might be socially inequitable. For the researcher, the implications of the findings reached in this book satisfy two decades of rising suspicion: that the textbooks used in expanding-circle EFL programmes are consequential artefacts in the language learning ecology of the country's culture, requiring careful, informed selection and considered use in a course of study.

Regarding the findings of the vignettes featured in this book, Korean culture plays a role impeding the honest commentary in interviews, especially one that positions one's personal norms and values in opposition to those of Korean society. In Chapter 4, each student, especially Y2 (see Appendix H), contradicted themselves. While this matter was addressed in Chapter 4, it bears repeating that the students appeared to struggle with answers that are socially acceptable contrasted with answers that reflect personally meaningful affordances, as individual participants. Also, considering that the textbook was chosen for the students and serves as an artefact that connects them to the course of study, they may hesitate to criticize it because that criticism may appear to be reflective of their instructor. Collectivist cultures, such as Korea, usually pressure community members to meet the approval of the common sentiment by performing actions with the group in mind, rather than the individual (Neuliep, 2020). As has already been noted, in the context of Korean culture, those who stand out from the group disrupt the harmony and risk appearing socially objectionable (Neuliep, 2020). In the context of honestly conveying their mind, values and stances about EFL learning and the textbook content, the Korean university students who participated in the interviews may have struggled against their own culture. In other words, a pressure to accept a common Korean sentiment, often cemented in administrative policies formed in upper levels of a curricular milieu (Choi, 2008; Huh, 2004; Smith, 2021), may have weakened the sincerity of their responses.

Sample and Situational Resolutions

It All Depends on the Programme

There are many types of venues for learning English around the world. English language speaking capability is a commodity on the world stage (Cameron, 2012). Therefore, the education of English, whether it is English for specific purposes (ESP), English for academic purposes (EAP), or ESL, or EFL, is reflective of the culture that tunes its worldly positioning on that stage. In Iran, for example, English education is highly regulated and likely some of the processes employed in this book are used by institutional milieu to edit, choose or control narratives in English language learning materials that may be counter-intuitive to the sociocultural visions of the state. In that situation, students or practitioners do not have much ability to control or alter state-sanctioned EFL materials, but there is some measure of flexibility, depending on the situation (Vaezi & Fallah, 2011). In Japan or Korea, on the other hand, EFL programmes in private academies are a multi-billion-dollar industry (Gray, 2010; Harwood, 2014; Littlejohn, 2012), and learning materials chosen for those programmes are usually ones that appear to have the greatest educational affiliations (Cambridge, Oxford, etc.) or the best appearance of prestige despite the contents (Smith, 2020). Students and practitioners in university EFL programmes in Korea and Japan usually have more flexibility in the consumption of their ELT textbook discourses than their counterparts in private academies, where directors normally control all curricular design. Whatever the case may be, it is recommended that students and/or practitioners who want to use some of the analytical procedures in this book first assess their programme to determine how much change or alteration they might be allowed to effect. In a highly regulated system of EFL learning, it is recommended that practitioners use the simplified frameworks illustrated at the beginning of this chapter as a strategy of testing how much they can provoke change. In an open setting, where the students and instructors have more freedom or control over the syllabus and curriculum, such as in a Korean university EFL programme, try the full extent of CMAT, MAVREC and SSInC. From there, one can have a better scope of the potential change or insights that augment your course of study.

Connecting CC with CMAT with MAVREC with Values

Once an understanding of the educational hierarchy is established and the researcher is aware of the approximate measures of change that they can initiate in a course of study, then it is recommended that they create their own curricular commonplace map. In the author's map (see Figure 5.1), points of interest in the crossroads between students, teachers, subject, milieu and the textbook serve as polestars to which the findings from the triangulated analyses in CMAT, MAVREC and SSInC find alignment. After connecting the findings with the points of interest in the curricular commonplaces (see Table 3.1), the researcher can begin to strategize solutions.

As we noted in the procedural synopsis, earlier in this chapter, the synthesized findings of the three frameworks should find some connection in the larger, encompassing realm of the curricular commonplaces so that reasonable strategies of textbook choice or recontextualization can be initiated or recommended for students and practitioners in a course of study. For example, in the vignettes featured in Chapters 2, 3 and 4 it was revealed that a high degree of institutional control forces students and practitioners to use certain, global ELT textbook publications in university EFL programmes. However, there is a lot of freedom to use whatever material inside the ELT textbook that the students and practitioners wish to use. Therefore, once the findings of CMAT, MAVREC and SSInC are gathered, they should be brought to the milieu, whoever those people are (department administration, deans, etc.), with recommendations for training on how to use the textbooks in class or how to change/recontextualize the multimodal discourses to increase the value of EFL learning investments by students and practitioners.

It is also important to be mindful that, especially in EFL contexts, the cultural misalignment of the teacher may play a big role in the misinterpretation of reflexive transformations that they may see as necessary in an ELT textbook. Learning the curricular commonplaces in a particular course of study, especially in those countries or cultures that afford more expertise to native-English-speaking teachers than they may deserve, can help students and practitioners inculcate more critical reflection of the multimodal discourses in their ELT textbooks because they will understand their positionality in a particular course of study and their capabilities as active participants in the learning process.

Chapter Summary

In this chapter, a discussion of criticisms directed at critical discourse studies served as a reminder that triangulated, qualitative analyses can increase validity (i.e. Duff, 2007). By underscoring the importance of triangulation, the corroborated findings from the sample vignettes featured in this book inform a procedural synopsis where alternative combinations or analyses, such as mixed-method approaches, are given consideration. The findings of all three frameworks are given detailed illustration, and a deeper discussion of the findings implies a linear connection, beginning with a MCDS of the textbook. Possible resolutions for textbook use were discussed for students and practitioners and included how a researcher might bring findings to institutional milieu, based on specific points of connection revealed in a researcher's triangulated study with curricular commonplaces. A final word on global EFL learning contexts reminds students and practitioners to be mindful and respectful of the institutional hierarchies in which they are likely invited to be guests.

Discussion Questions

i.   Critics of CDS claim that by contrast to their own research, it is not 'pure research'.

Based on the discussions in this chapter and previous chapters, why do you think CDS draws this criticism? How have CDS scholars responded to this criticism?

ii. Do you subscribe to the author's assertion that ELT textbooks are consequential artefacts in the language learning ecology of a pedagogical culture, requiring careful, informed selection and considered use in a course of study? Why or why not? To what extent do you agree or disagree with the discussions in this chapter or findings in preceding chapters?

6

Summary and Conclusion

This final chapter begins with a reminder of our original purpose and recounts the full extent that the researcher used CMAT, MAVREC and SSInC in the field. The account of research performed to date is followed by a summarization of the chapters and a brief discussion of caveats and limitations as we move forward in more hybrid workplaces, where an understanding of classes in digital learning environments may play a significant role in understanding multimodal discourses in ELT textbooks.

Personal Development of In Text, In Class, In Mind

In this section, we are reminded of purposes driving the triangulated framework forward. The original purpose of this study was inspired by the researcher's personal experience teaching EFL courses at five Korean universities between 1998 and 2014. In that time, numerous fellow expatriate EFL educators collectively criticized the use of globally published ELT textbooks in their respective courses and even made fun of some of the content as ridiculous representations of the world of English (Cortez, 2008). The common sentiment among several of the researcher's colleagues at various Korean universities was that the multimodal content in a typical ELT textbook presented social realities that didn't exist or were as unfamiliar to the instructor as it was to their Korean students. A close colleague of the researcher often remarked, jokingly, each year he would politely accept the chosen textbook for his sections of English communication courses, given to him by administrative staff at his institution, carefully examine the contents, then use it to hold his office window ajar while he designed completely different lessons.

The researcher recognized, over years of classroom use and private critique of several publications, that ELT textbooks, such as *Top Notch 2* (Saslow &

Ascher, 2006), maximize sales by offering generic lessons that are 'usable' in as many expanding-circle countries as possible (Gray, 2010; Littlejohn, 2012), likely to maximize sales. However, by trying to appeal to everyone, meaningful lesson content that is relevant or socioculturally intuitive to any one type of expanding-circle demographic, such as Korean university students, becomes diminished. While many veteran and well-trained instructors can recognize insufficiencies in the multimodal discourses in their ELT textbooks, many more are not capable of seeing or recontextualizing content due to inexperience, so they just push through the content in a bullish way to achieve curricular completion, without thinking that the contents of their lessons could be altered to improve language learning investments. Hence, there is an array of complex, interwoven issues that play a role in the consumption of multimodal discourses in ELT textbooks. This book endeavours to be one kind of solution in that matrix.

In earlier chapters, it was noted that the Korean government had invested in the reformation of EFL education from about 2002 and onward (Garton, 2014; Huh, 2004), much like Japan (Martin, 2004), by means of ensuring only qualified English educators, who were not already experienced in post-secondary contracts, were allowed to teach English. However, the ELT textbooks only changed in appearance and in modes of learning (digital platforms, etc.). As new editions flooded Korean bookstore shelves every year just prior to the spring semester (March is the start of every school year in Korea), students lined up to purchase them as necessary components for their respective post-secondary EFL courses (Fitzgibbon, 2013; Song, 2013). As the years went by, those textbooks invariably increased in price because they expanded into new technologies to accommodate online learning, with endless supplements of multimedia activities, freshly designed covers and the promise of high levels of academic excellence with every purchase (Bell & Gower, 2011). It is not surprising that a culture of textbook reliance increased among lesser trained or inexperienced EFL instructors in Korea at that time because there was always an abundance of multimedia activities for them to draw on and proctor during classroom activity. For many Korean university students, that option to engage in multimedia activities in EFL classrooms may have contributed to the trust that their textbooks gained due to its connection to the course, the institution and their instructor (Ahn, 2014; Choi, 2005; Gray, 2010; Harwood, 2014; Littlejohn, 2012). By conceptual extension, in the context of ELT textbooks, the contents of the lessons are afforded legitimacy because of that promissory connection (Pennycook & Candlin, 2017; Shin & Crookes, 2005; Xiong, 2012).

It is important to keep in mind that even though students and practitioners in expanding-circle countries are often forced to use globally published ELT textbooks, sometimes they are the only choice (Choi, 2008; KICE, 2001; Lee, 2011). The lack of choice and implied institutional endorsement that textbooks carry allow for the consumption of multimodal content that can, for example, construct legitimations of us and them (or others) (Curdt-Christiansen & Weninger, 2015). For many Korean EFL students, their textbooks represent a key component of their curriculum and considered necessary as a material reference for linguistic inquiry and practice via communicative interaction (Cunningsworth, 1995; Lee, 2014; Richards, 2014; Song, 2013; Tomlinson, 2011; Tomlinson & Masuhara, 2017).

Seeking to understand how such blind trust in learning materials might negatively impact English education in Korea, this book looks at the multimodal discourses in ELT textbooks, then sees how the English lessons are negotiated in class and how the consumers privately value the content, post-class. This was accomplished by (a) conducting a novel multimodal critical discourse study of an ELT textbook, outlined in CMAT (see Table 2.1), for the purpose of unveiling power relations and ideologies in its multimodal discourses, (b) observing how that content was negotiated by instructors and students during classroom consumption using MAVREC (see Table 3.2) and (c) extrapolating the value that students and instructors afford that negotiated content from coded interview transcriptions. The triangulated analyses gave credence to the perspectives of three different ELT textbook consumers – the researcher (a former instructor), current instructors and students. A triangulated synthesis of the findings from all three vignettes yielded a richer account of the ELT textbook's multimodal discourse from the consumers than has occurred in other studies (i.e. Ahn, 2014; Choi, 2008; Fitzgibbon, 2013; Lee, 2009, 2011, 2014; Matsuda, 2002; Sherman, 2010; Shin et al., 2011; Song, 2013; Taylor-Mendes, 2009; Yim, 2014).

As we have noted several times, a triangulation of 'insider perspectives' (Duff, 2007, p. 4), inclusive of students and instructors, can be an extremely informative endeavour for education research. The convergence of data harvested from these analyses yields a clearer picture of the multimodal discourses in ELT textbooks and their pedagogical significance in a course of study. Practitioner-researchers embarking on an ELT textbook analysis as prescribed in this book should keep in mind that each of these analyses must occur in successive phases because they are connected, especially MAVREC and SSInC, where the findings are corroborated in succession. To mitigate criticism and increase the validity of one's research, analysts should give generous details for each phase, including what locations were chosen, who the participants will be, what operational procedures will be used, what instruments will be employed, along with justifications for choosing those data and the methods for analysing them.

Limitations

Digital platforms, whether they are learning management systems (LMS) or content management systems (CMS), that integrate textbook material for students to do online activities, where courses are delivered either completely or partially online, may require the researcher to revisit CMAT. Platforms such as modular object-oriented digital learning environment (MOODLE) or Brightspace are popular choices for course content collection and delivery in post-secondary programmes. They present different and more dynamic agencies of meaning-making that may not be as static as the data in a ME of an opened textbook. Therefore, questions regarding these platforms and how they are used to deliver textbook content should be integrated with questions featured in the holistic, compositional and inventory lenses of CMAT.

Additionally, another key consideration that is not sufficiently conclusive in this book is how students develop or establish a style of classroom negotiations and values, with regard to their consumption of the multimodal discourses in their ELT textbooks over time. Although Chapter 2 features a vignette of a MCDS of a few units in *Top Notch 2* (Saslow & Ascher, 2006), up to the time of the video recording for the vignette featured in Chapter 3, it would have been ideal to have recordings for all the textbook content's use in class over a period of several weeks during a course of study to see the evolvement of students and practitioners as they negotiate the multimodal discourses. Therefore, a longitudinal study, complementing qualitative studies in a triangulated analysis, may yield more robust findings.

Summary of Chapters

The journey in this book, from the introduction to the conclusion, includes a review of literature pertaining to the operationalization of three qualitative analyses, followed by a synthesis of sampled findings that serve as blueprints for practitioner-researchers to develop their own studies of multimodal discourses in ELT textbooks.

Chapter 1 highlights how global publishing markets, contrasted against the needs and concerns of students and practitioners, are overshadowed by political interests to maximize sales, perhaps explaining why ELT textbooks receive the most attention in critical studies of textbooks. To meet a lack of research, this book answers the call for a triangulated approach to crisply delineate issues and problems that students and teachers face in ELT textbook use.

Chapter 2 features the first of three frameworks that build from scholarly foundations in multimodal and critical discourse studies. CMAT takes form in design and is demonstrated in a vignette analysing two MEs to reveal power relations and ideologies in the multimodal discourses.

In Chapter 3, a discussion of theoretical foundations of CP explains how students and practitioners share a cooperative engagement in EFL learning and the complex relationships between them and their textbooks in expanding-circle cultures. A framework, the second of three, emerges in these discussions towards analysing ELT textbook use during class time, where the multimodal discourses in lesson contents are actively negotiated between teachers and students. The findings of MAVREC in a sample vignette featured how instructors negotiate, deliver, resist, transform, appropriate or neutralize the multimodal discourses in an ELT textbook in situ.

In Chapter 4, theoretical foundations in CALx help us understand an unpublished, mixed-methods pilot study by the researcher, who realized a significant difference between quantitative and qualitative analyses regarding the value of ELT textbooks in an expanding-circle EFL programme. The discrepancy of that study inspired the creation of SSInC – the third framework towards understanding negotiated ideologies in the multimodal discourse of globally published ELT textbooks. The findings of SSInC featuring interview data collected from participants in Chapter 3 suggest students and practitioners have a common measure of ambivalence towards the multimodal discourses in their ELT textbook.

In Chapter 5, criticisms directed at critical discourse studies serve as a reminder that triangulated, qualitative analyses can increase validity (i.e. Duff, 2007). By underscoring the importance of triangulation, the corroborated findings from the sample vignettes in Chapters 2, 3 and 4 inform a procedural synopsis where alternative combinations or analyses, such as mixed-methods approaches, are given consideration. The synthesized findings of CMAT, MAVREC and SSInC imply a linear alignment of insights that can inform possible resolutions for textbook use or choice for students and practitioners.

Moving Forward and Future Developments

The term 'cash cow' has an historical connection to dairy farming in England, and the idiom roughly refers to the continuous acquirement of profit from an initial investment. *Top Notch 2* (Saslow & Ascher, 2006) is a cash cow for Pearson/Longman Publishing because there have been several editions for more than a decade and while the fiscal specifics are unknown, according to Fitzgibbon (2013), it was the highest grossing sales earner in Asia from 2008 to 2013. As noted earlier, Littlejohn (1992; 2012) reminds us that successful ELT textbook publications can easily exceed sales of one million copies per year. For literally millions of reasons, those textbooks are not going to change much, even if some analysts have found social injustices in their multimodal discourses. Therefore, it behoves students and practitioners to be informed of these lesson materials and, as Richards (2014) notes, own them and reconstruct them for the benefit of one's students. That said, teacher manipulation of textbook content in situ appears to lack literature other than some peripheral studies of classroom ecologies (i.e. Cinkara, 2016; Kramsch, 2008; Sakai & Kikuchi, 2009; Van Lier, 2015).

Additionally, for many of the same reasons that Korean English teachers tend to avoid functional or conversational English and emphasize grammar-translation in their respective classrooms (Ahn, 2014), so have researchers who have investigated ELT textbooks avoided looking at the fine details of the visual discourses in those publications. CMAT offers a more refined approach for looking at the multimodal modes of meaning-making in ELT textbooks, inclusive of some elements which many scholars feel belong to the realm of visual art (such as texture, colour, composition, shape, line, perspective, form). In most of the literature, only some of these items were highlighted but much was overlooked (i.e. Fitzgibbon, 2013; Giaschi, 2000).

Finally, the anachronistic nature of the textbook topics and visual references were challenging to address in this study because it was not a matter of discourse analysis. The eventualities involving language policy and planning richly infiltrate the world of EFL in Korean universities (Garton, 2014), so the question arises as to *who makes textbook choices for university EFL programmes in Korea?* The version of *Top Notch 2* (Saslow & Ascher, 2006) is severely outdated, so some of the topics and visual devices in the book were antiquated remnants of life prior to the widespread use of smartphones. To young university students in 2019, that lifestyle would be a distant memory in their childhood and not even relatable. Perhaps more research into the institutional milieu that make textbook choices would yield richer veins of research that impact EFL learning in expanding-circle contexts.

Conclusion

Partially inspired by personal experience teaching EFL in Korea at the post-secondary level for more than eighteen years, the goal of this book sought to clarify if the multimodal discourses in a popular ELT textbook contained social injustices, then what pedagogical effects would they have on consumers and how would those consumers, in turn, value the textbooks. To accomplish this, research questions reflective of those initial interests guided the operationalization featured in this book: (1) What are the power relations and ideologies in the multimodal discourse of an ELT textbook? (2) How do instructors and students negotiate and account for those multimodal discourses in class? (3) What pedagogical implications emerge from the triangulated findings of a multimodal critical discourse study, on the one hand, and its negotiated discourses and values by the consumers, on the other, about EFL learning and textbook consumption in university EFL programmes? To inform research and methods for answering these questions, a thorough (if not exhaustive) review of literature related to EFL textbook production and consumption on a global scale, followed by a review of critical research of ELT textbooks and finally critical research in expanding-circle contexts, preceded research into theoretical principles of CDS, multimodality, CP and CALx. Inspired by the literature and relevant theoretical frameworks, the operational potential of three frameworks emerged that focused on multimodality, discourse analysis and critical discourse studies. In more specific terms, an amalgamation of Wodak and Meyer (2016), Machin and Mayr (2012), and Serafini (2014) informed the design of CMAT in Chapter 2 to examine the power relations and ideologies in a large body of data, such as in an ELT textbook. Norris (2004, 2019), Wohlwend (2011) and Jewitt et al. (2016) informed the creation of MAVREC for video transcription of university EFL classes in Chapter 3. Finally, Saldana's (2016) Affective/Values coding framework informed the creation of SSInC, used to underscore the mind, values and stance that students and practitioners afford the multimodal discourses in their ELT textbooks. From the vignettes demonstrating the three analyses, the findings show that the power relations and ideologies in the content of *Top Notch 2* (Saslow & Ascher, 2006) contained evidence of social injustices that manifested in MAVREC as poor participatory actions among the students from two separate classes until their professor reconstructed the content. The SSInC featured in Chapter 4 corroborated the findings and pointed to the multimodal discourses in the textbook as something on which the consumers place little pedagogical value because the lessons, particularly the visual discourses that accompany them, are sometimes not appropriate, counter-intuitive to their culture, or generally uninspiring in the language learning engagement of linguistic challenges during class. Without the instructor's effort to reconstruct the material in situ, the value of a student's education suffers. One might infer that if student education suffers because of poor ELT textbook choice and its forcible use in post-secondary EFL programmes, then the other curricular commonplaces (teachers, milieu, subject) must also be misaligned by the social injustices in the consumed content. In other words, a domino effect is seen in the social injustices of the textbook that falls over to impact classroom negotiations of the content, which can then impact curricular commonplaces of EFL in post-secondary programmes. For these reasons, the findings presented in this book are valuable for EFL education, not only in Korean university contexts but for other university EFL programmes in expanding-circle cultures because ELT textbooks serve as the curriculum for poorly trained instructors, whose qualifications and fitness for teaching are often measured in their L1 English-speaking capabilities (Holliday, 2006; Richards, 2014; Tomlinson & Masuhara, 2017). Many young teachers, venturing to expanding-circle nations to teach English, use globally published ELT textbooks as a format for their curriculum (Richards, 2014; Vellenga, 2004). However, as we have seen in the reviewed literature and findings of this research, ELT textbooks contain social injustices in their content that have an impact on language learning and lead to a devaluation of language learning investment. ELT textbooks will never change because the publication industry is far too lucrative (Gray, 2010; Harwood, 2014; Littlejohn, 1992; 2012). Therefore, instructors must repurpose the materials they are often forced to use and make it their own (Richards, 2014). Although many ELT textbooks also serve as the syllabus for EFL programmes in expanding-circle counties (Richards, 2014; Vellenga, 2004), they must be given the distinction of a platform on which to build valued lessons or curriculums for their students so that their investments in language learning do not deter or diminish their motivations to accomplish sufficient test scores or achieve some measure of fluency in functional English.

Between nearly two decades of personal teaching experience in Korea and the qualitative findings that deconstructed *Top Notch 2* (Saslow & Ascher, 2006) in the vignettes, social injustices in the multimodal discourse reverberate in a negative manifestation of performance in the classroom and a pedagogical devaluation of one's instruction from the perspective of one's students. 'In text, in class, in mind', a potential nickname for the triangulated framework featured in this book, demonstrates that multimodal critical discourse studies, textbook reflexivity in situ (i.e. Smith, 2021) and robust attention given to consumer values collectively synthesize a pedagogical stimulus that informs an instructor's capacity to *see* the power relations and ideologies in the multimodal discourses of their ELT textbooks, diminish inner-circle hegemony when those discourses are negotiated in class and raise the value of consumer investment in English language education.

References

Adams, D., & Gottlieb, E. E. (2017). *Education and social change in Korea*. Routledge.

Agiro, C. P. (2012). Comparative critical discourse analysis of student and teacher editions of secondary Christian American literature textbooks. *Journal of Research on Christian Education, 21*(3), 211–234. https://doi.org/10.1080/10656219.2012 .733557.

Ahmadi Darani, P., & Akbari, A. (2016). The ideological import of a second identity: A critical image analysis to global EFL materials. *Multidisciplinary Journal of Educational Research, 6*(3), 231. https://doi.org/10.17583/remie.2016.2174.

Ahn, K. (2011). Conceptualization of American English native speaker norms: A case study of an English classroom in South Korea. *Asia Pacific Education Review, 12*, 691–702.

Ahn, H. (2014). Teachers' attitudes towards Korean English in South Korea. *World Englishes, 33*(2), 195–222. https://doi.org/10.1111/weng.12081.

Ahour, T., & Zaferani, P. (2016). A critical visual analysis of gender representation of ELT materials from a multimodal perspective. *The Journal of Applied Linguistics, 9*(18), 78–98.

Amerian, M., & Esmaili, F. (2015). Language and gender: A critical discourse analysis on gender representation in a series of international ELT textbooks. *International Journal of Research Studies in Education, 4*(2), 3–12. https://doi.org/10.5861/ijrse .2014.963.

Apple, M., & Apple, M. W. (2018). *Ideology and curriculum*. Routledge.

Apple, M. W. (1985). The culture and commerce of the textbook. *Journal of Curriculum Studies, 17*, 147–162.

Apple, M. W. (2001). Comparing neo-liberal projects and inequality in education. *Comparative Education, 37*(4), 409–423. https://doi.org/10.1080 /03050060120091229.

Ascough, R. (2011). Learning (About) outcomes: How the focus on assessment can help overall course design. *Canadian Journal of Higher Education, 41*(2), 44–61.

Auerbach, E. (1995). The politics of the ESL classroom. In J. W. Tollefson (Ed.), *Power and inequality in language education* (pp. 4–17). Cambridge University Press.

Auerbach, E., & Burgess, D. (1985). The hidden curriculum of survival ESL. *TESOL Quarterly, 19*(3), 475–495.

Baghdadi, M. (2012). *A comparison of gender representation in English (EFL) and Arabic (AFL) textbooks in Iran: A critical discourse analysis*. California State University.

Baik, M. J. (1994). *Language, ideology, and power: English textbooks of two Koreas* [PhD Thesis, University of Illinois]. University of Illinois.

Bailey, R. W., Gorlach, M., & Arbor, A. (1986). English as a world language. *RELC Journal, 17*(1), 91–96.

Bakhtin, M. M. (1981). *The dialogic imagination.* University of Texas.

Banes, L. C., Martínez, D. C., Athanases, S. Z., & Wong, J. W. (2016). Self-reflexive inquiry into language use and beliefs: Toward more expansive language ideologies. *International Multilingual Research Journal, 10*(3), 168–187.

Bateman, J. (2014). *Text and image: A critical introduction to the visual/verbal divide.* Kindle ed. Routledge. https://doi.org/10.4324/9781315773971.

Bell, J., & Gower, R. (2011). Writing course materials for the world: A great compromise. In B. Tomlinson (Ed.), *Materials development in language teaching* (pp. 135–150). Cambridge University Press.

Bezemer, J., & Kress, G. (2008). Writing in multimodal texts: A social semiotic account of designs for learning. *Written Communication, 25*(2), 166–195.

Bhatia, V., Flowerdew, J., & Jones, R. H. (Eds.). (2008). *Advances in discourse studies.* Routledge.

Biggs, J., & Tang, C. (2007). *Teaching for quality learning.* McGraw Hill.

Block, D. (2015). Social class in applied linguistics. *Annual Review of Applied Linguistics, 35*, 1–19.

Blyth, C. S., & Thoms, J. J. (Eds.). (2021). *Open education and second language learning and teaching: The rise of a new knowledge ecology.* Multilingual Matters.

Børhaug, K. (2014). Selective critical thinking: A textbook analysis of education for critical thinking in Norwegian social studies. *Policy Futures in Education, 12*(3), 431–444. https://doi.org/10.2304/pfie.2014.12.3.431.

Boriboon, P. (2004). We would rather talk about plaa raa than hamburgers': Voices from low- proficient EFL learners in a rural Thai context. In *11th sociocultural theory and second language learning research conference.* University of Nijmegen, Netherlands.

Bourdieu, P. (1991). *Language and symbolic power.* Harvard University Press.

Breeze, R. (2011). Critical discourse analysis and its critics. *Pragmatics. Quarterly Publication of the International Pragmatics Association (IPrA), 21*(4), 493–525. https://doi.org/10.1075/prag.21.4.01bre.

Brown, D. (2011). What aspects of vocabulary knowledge do textbooks give attention to? *Language Teaching Research, 15*(1), 83–97.

Brumfit, C., & Mitchell, R. (Eds.). (1990). *Research in the language classroom.* Modern English Publications.

Brundage, G. C. (2007). *EFL foreign teacher stress in Korea: Causes and coping mechanisms. Online submission.* ERIC.

Burchfield, R. (Ed.). (1994). *The Cambridge history of the English language.* Cambridge University Press.

Camase, G. (2009). *The ideological construction of a second reality: A critical analysis of a Romanian EFL textbook* [Doctoral dissertation, University of Toronto]. University of Toronto Press. Retrieved from: http://hdl.handle.net/1807/18099.

Cameron, D. (2012). English as a global commodity. In T. Nevalainen & E. C. Traugott (Eds.), *The Oxford handbook of the history of English* (pp. 352–361). Oxford University Press.

Canagarajah, S. (1993). Critical ethnography of a Sri Lankan classroom: Ambiguities in student opposition to reproduction through ESOL. *Tesol Quarterly*, *27*(4), 601–626. https://doi.org/10.2307/3587398.

Canagarajah, S. (1997). Challenges in English literacy for African American and Lankan Tamil learners: Towards a pedagogical paradigm for bidialectal and bilingual minority students. *Language and Education*, *11*(1), 15–37.

Canagarajah, S. (1999). On EFL teachers, awareness, and agency. *ELT Journal*, *53*(3), 207–214. https://doi.org/10.1093/elt/53.3.207.

Canagarajah, S. (2005). Critical pedagogy in L2 learning and teaching. In E. Hinkel (Ed.), *Handbook of research in second language teaching and learning* (pp. 955–974). Routledge.

Canagarajah, S. (2006). TESOL at forty: What are the issues? *Tesol Quarterly*, *40*(1), 9–34. https://doi.org/10.2307/40264509.

Canagarajah, S. (2016). TESOL as a professional community: A half-century of pedagogy, research, and theory. *TESOL Quarterly*, *50*(1), 7–41. https://doi.org/10.1002/tesq.275.

Canale, M., & Swain, M. (1980). Theoretical bases of communicative approaches to second language teaching and testing. *Applied Linguistics*, *I*(I), 1–47. https://doi.org/10.1093/elt/ccm049.

Cha, M. Y. (2002). Koreans learning English in two contrasting situations: EFL in Korea and ESL in Delhi. *Journal of Pan-Pacific Association of Applied Linguistics*, *6*(1), 103–21.

Chang, B. M. (2004). A case study of native English-speaking teachers' understanding of EFL contexts in Korea. *Pan-Pacific Association of Applied Linguistics (PAAL)*, *8*(2), 119–135.

Chao, Tzu-chia. (2011). The hidden curriculum of cultural content in internationally published ELT textbooks: A closer look at new American inside out. *The Journal of Asia TEFL*, *8*(2), 189–210.

Charmaz, K. (2014). *Constructing grounded theory*. Sage.

Charmaz, K. (2017). The power of constructivist grounded theory for critical inquiry. *Qualitative inquiry*, *23*(1), 34–45.

Charmaz, K., & McMullen, L. M. (2011). *Five ways of doing qualitative analysis: Phenomenological psychology, grounded theory, discourse analysis, narrative research, and intuitive inquiry*. Guilford Press.

Chen, Y. (2008). A mixed-method study of EFL teachers' Internet use in language instruction. *Teaching and Teacher Education*, *24*(4), 1015–1028.

Chen, Y. (2010). The semiotic construal of attitudinal curriculum goals: Evidence from EFL textbooks in China. *Linguistics and Education*, *21*(1), 60–74. https://doi.org/10.1016/j.linged.2009.12.005.

Cheng, L., & Fox, J. (2017). *Assessment in the language classroom: Teachers supporting student learning.* Palgrave.

Chiu, L. Y. L. (2011). *The construction of the 'ideal Chinese child': A critical analysis of textbooks for Chinese heritage language learners* [Doctoral dissertation, University of British Columbia]. https://doi.org/10.14288/1.0072083.

Cho, S. (2013). Disciplinary enculturation experiences of three Korean students in U.S.-based MATESOL programs. *Journal of Language, Identity, and Education, 12*(September 2014), 136–151. https://doi.org/10.1080/15348458.2013.775881.

Choi, I. C. (2008). The impact of EFL testing on EFL education in Korea. *Language Testing, 25*(1), 39–62. https://doi.org/10.1177/0265532207083744.

Choi, S. (2005). A critical reflection upon Korean high school English readings: Power relations and orientalism. *English Teaching, 60*(4), 517–532.

Chu, Y. (2015). The power of knowledge: A critical analysis of the depiction of ethnic minorities in China's elementary textbooks. *Race Ethnicity and Education, 18*(4), 469–487. https://doi.org/10.1080/13613324.2015.1013460.

Chun, S., Kim, H., Park, C. K., McDonald, K., Oh, S. H., Kim, D. L., & Lee, S. M. (2017). South Korean students' responses to English-medium instruction courses. *Social Behavior and Personality: An International Journal, 45*(6), 951–965.

Cinkara, E. (2016). An ethnographic investigation of activity modifications in EFL classrooms. *International Online Journal of Educational Sciences, 8*(1), 107–117. https://doi.org/10.15345/iojes.2016.01.010.

Clark, J. S. B., & Dervin, F. (Eds.). (2014). *Reflexivity in language and intercultural education: Rethinking multilingualism and interculturality.* Routledge.

Connelly, F. M., & Clandinin, D. J. (1988). *Teachers as curriculum planners: Narratives of experience.* Teachers College Press.

Cortazzi, M., & Jin, L. (1996). Cultures of learning: Language classrooms in China. *Society and the Language Classroom, 169*(206), 42.

Cortez, N. (2008). *Am I in the book? Imagined communities and language ideologies of English in a global EFL textbook* [Unpublished doctoral dissertation]. University of Arizona.

Cox, M. I. P., & Assis-Peterson, A. A. (1999). Critical pedagogy in ELT: Images of Brazilian teachers of English. *TESOL Quarterly, 33*(3), 433–452.

Creswell, J. W. (2015). *A concise introduction to mixed methods research.* Amazon Kindle ed. Sage.

Creswell, J. W. (2015). *30 essential skills for the qualitative researcher.* Sage.

Creswell, J. W., & Creswell, J. D. (2017). *Research design: Qualitative, quantitative, and mixed methods approaches.* Sage publications.

Crystal, D. (2003). *English as a global language.* Ernst Klett Sprachen.

Cullen, R., & Kuo, I. C. V. (2007). Spoken grammar and ELT course materials: A missing link?. *Tesol Quarterly, 41*(2), 361–386.

Cunliffe, A. L., & Easterby-Smith, M. (2004). From reflection to practical reflexivity: Experiential learning as lived experience. *Organizing Reflection, 2004*, 30–46.

Cunningsworth, A. (1995). *Choosing your coursebook*. Heinemann.

Curdt-Christiansen, X. L., & Weninger, C. (Eds.). (2015). *Language, ideology and education: The politics of textbooks in language education*. Routledge.

Dendrinos, B. (2015). The politics of instructional materials of English for young learners. In X. L. Curdt-Christiansen & C. Weninger (Eds.), *Language, ideology and education* (pp. 43–63). Routledge.

Dörnyei, Z. (2001). New themes and approaches in second language motivation research. *Annual Review of Applied Linguistics, 21*, 43–59.

Dörnyei, Z. (2007). *Research methods in applied linguistics: Quantitative, qualitative, and mixed methodologies*. Oxford University Press.

Duff, P. A. (2007). Second language socialization as sociocultural theory: Insights and issues. *Language Teaching, 40*(4), 309–319.

Duff, P. A., & Van Lier, L. E. O. (1997). Approaches to observation in classroom research: Observation from an ecological perspective. *Tesol Quarterly, 31*(4), 783–787. https://doi.org/10.2307/3587762.

Earl, L., Hargreaves, A., & Schmidt, M. (2002). Perspective on reform. *American Educational Research Journal, 39*(1), 69–95.

Egan, K. (2003). What is curriculum? *Journal of Canadian Association for Curriculum Studies, 1*(1), 9–16.

Ellis, R. (2017). Task-based language teaching. In S. Loewen & M. Sato (Eds.), *The Routledge handbook of instructed second language acquisition* (pp. 124–141). Routledge.

Ellsworth, E. (1989). Why doesn't this feel empowering? Working through the repressive myths of critical pedagogy. *Harvard Educational Review, 59*(3), 297–325.

Eriksen, K. G. (2018). Teaching about the other in primary level social studies: The Sami in Norwegian textbooks. *Journal of Social Science Education, 17*(2), 57–67. https://doi.org/10.4119/jsse-875.

Eun, S. H. (2001). *Contextual autonomy in EFL classrooms: A critical review of English teaching methods in South Korea* [Doctoral dissertation, Ohio State University]. Ohio State University Press.

Fairclough, N. (1989). *Language and power*. Longman Group.

Fairclough, N. (1992). *Discourse and social change*. Cambridge University Press.

Fairclough, N. (2013). *Critical discourse analysis: The critical study of language*. Routledge. https://doi.org/10.4324/9781315834368.

Fairclough, N., & Chouliaraki, L. (1999). *Discourse in late modernity*. Edinburgh University Press.

Fairclough, N., & Wodak, R. (1997). Critical discourse analysis. In T. A. van Dijk (Ed.), *Discourse as social interaction* (pp. 258–284). Sage.

Fitzgibbon, L. A. (2013). *Ideologies and power relations in a global commercial English language textbook used in South Korean universities: A critical image analysis and a critical discourse analysis* [Doctoral dissertation, The University of Queensland]. University of Queensland Press.

Flowerdew, J., & Richardson, J. E. (Eds.). (2017). *The Routledge handbook of critical discourse studies*. Routledge.

Foucault, M. (2003). *Madness and civilization*. Routledge. https://doi.org/10.4324 /9780203164693.

Fowler, R., Hodge, B., Kress, G., & Trew, T. (1979). *Language and control*. Routledge and Kegan Paul.

Fox, J. (2004). Curriculum design: Does it make a difference. *Contact, Special Research Symposium Issue, 30*(2), 1–5.

Fox, J. (2019). Curriculum in language teaching: Overview and introduction [PowerPoint slides]. Retrieved from: https://culearn.carleton.ca/moodle/course/view .php?id=130806.

Franklin, B. (2003). *'McJournalism': The McDonaldization thesis and junk journalism*. Paper delivered to the Politics and Media Specialist Group of the British Political Studies Association.

Franklin, B. (2005). The local press and the McDonaldization thesis. *Journalism: Critical Issues, 1*(1), 137–150.

Fredricks, L. (2007). A rationale for critical pedagogy in EFL: The case of Tajikistan. *The Reading Matrix, 7*(2), 22–37.

Freire, P. (1970). Pedagogy of the Oppressed. *Continuum*, 65–80.

Freire, P. (2018). *Pedagogy of the oppressed*. Bloomsbury.

Fuchs, E., & Bock, A. (Eds.). (2018). *The Palgrave handbook of textbook studies*. Springer.

Garton, S. (2014). Unresolved issues and new challenges in teaching English to young learners: The case of South Korea. *Current Issues in Language Planning, 15*(2), 201–219. https://doi.org/10.1080/14664208.2014.858657.

Gee, J. P. (2004). *An introduction to discourse analysis: Theory and method*. Routledge. https://doi.org/10.4324/9780203005675.

Gee, J. P., & Handford, M. (Eds.). (2013). *The Routledge handbook of discourse analysis*. Routledge.

Giaschi, P. (2000). Gender positioning in education: A critical image analysis of ESL texts. *TESL Canada Journal, 18*(1), 32–46. https://doi.org/10.18806/tesl.v18i1.898.

Gilmore, A. (2011). *'I Prefer Not Text': Developing Japanese learners' communicative competence with authentic materials*. September, 786–819. https://doi.org/10.1111/j .1467-9922.2011.00634.x.

Giroux, H. A. (1983). *Theory and resistance in education: A pedagogy for the oppressed*. Bergin and Garvey. https://doi.org/10.17763/haer.53.3.a67x4u33g7682734.

Giroux, H. A. (1988). *Teachers as intellectuals: Toward a critical pedagogy of learning*. Greenwood Publishing Group.

Giroux, H. A. (2004). Cultural studies, public pedagogy, and the responsibility of intellectuals. *Communication and Critical/Cultural Studies, 1*(1), 59–79.

Giroux, H. A. (2007). Democracy, education, and the politics of critical pedagogy. *Counterpoints, 1*(1), 1–5.

Giroux, H. A. (2017). Paulo Freire and the courage to be political. In A. Darder (Ed.), *Reinventing Paulo Freire: A pedagogy of love* (pp. xii–xvii). Taylor and Francis.

Giroux, H. A., Freire, P., & McLaren, P. (1988). *Teachers as intellectuals: Toward a critical pedagogy of learning*. Greenwood Publishing Group.

Gore, J. (1992). What we can do for you! What can 'we' do for 'you'?: Struggling over empowerment in critical and feminist pedagogy. In C. Luke & J. Gore (Eds.), *Feminisms and critical pedagogy* (pp. 54–73). Routledge.

Graddol, D., Leith, D., Swann, J., Rhys, M., & Gillen, J. (Eds.). (2020). *Changing English*. Routledge.

Grant, A. R., & Lee, I. (2009). The ideal English Speaker: A juxtaposition of globalization and language policy in South Korea and racialized language attitudes in the United States. In R. Kubota & A. M. Lin (Eds.), *Race, culture, and identities in second language education* (pp. 54–73). Routledge.

Gray, J. (2010). *The construction of English: Culture, consumerism and promotion in the ELT global coursebook*. Springer.

Grossman, P., & Thompson, C. (2008). Learning from curriculum materials: Scaffolds for new teachers? *Teaching and Teacher Education, 24*(8), 2014–2026.

Gulliver, T. (2010). Immigrant success stories in ESL textbooks. *Tesol Quarterly, 44*(4), 725–745. https://doi.org/10.5054/tq.2010.235994.

Gulliver, T., & Thurrell, K. (2017). Denials of racism in Canadian English language textbooks. *TESL Canada Journal, 33*, 42–61. https://doi.org/10.18806/tesl.v33i0 .1245.

Gungor, R., & Prins, E. (2010). Reproducing gender inequality: A critical discourse analysis of a Turkish adult literacy textbook. *Adult Education Research Conference*. https://newprairiepress.org/aerc/2010/papers/27.

Hadley, G. (2013). Global textbooks in local contexts: An empirical investigation of effectiveness. In N. Harwood (Ed.), *English language teaching textbooks: Content, consumption, production* (pp.205–238). Palgrave Macmillan.

Haggerty, J. (2011). The validity of consequences: High-stakes language testing and the potential polarization of Young ELLs. *KOTESOL Proceedings, 2010*, 13.

Haggerty, J., & Fox, J. (2016). Test intensity, language testing experience, and the motivation to learn English in South Korea. In V. Arayadoust & J. Fox (Eds.), *Trends in language assessment research and practice: The view from the Middle East and the Pacific Rim* (pp. 486–512). Cambridge Scholars Publishing.

Hall, C. J., Smith, P. H., & Wicaksono, R. (2017). *Mapping applied linguistics: A guide for students and practitioners*. Routledge.

Halliday, M. A. K. (1978). *Language as social semiotics*. Eduard Arnold.

Halliday, M. A. K., & Matthiessen, C. (2014). *An introduction to functional grammar*. Routledge.

Hammersley, M. (1997). On the foundations of critical discourse analysis. *Language & Communication, 17*(3), 237–248.

Harmer, J. (2003). The practice of English language teaching. *ELT Journal, 57*(1), 4.

Harper, K. C. (2012). *Decolonizing education: A critical discourse analysis of post-secondary humanities textbooks* [Doctoral Dissertation, East Carolina University]. East Carolina University Press.

Harris, Z. (1952). Discourse analysis. *Language, 28,* 1–30.

Harwood, N. (Ed.). (2014). *English language teaching textbooks: Content, consumption, production.* Palgrave Macmillan.

Healy, D. (2009). The representation of women and men in a modern EFL textbook: Are popular textbooks gender biased. *Memoirs of the Osaka Institute of Technology, 54*(2), 91–100.

Hodge, R., & Kress, G. (1989). *Language as ideology.* Routledge.

Holliday, A. (2006). Native-speakerism. *ELT Journal, 60*(4), 385–387.

Holliday, A. (2015). Qualitative research and analysis. In B. Paltridge & A. Phakitis (Eds.), *Research methods in applied linguistics: A practical resource* (pp. 49–62). Bloomsbury.

Hong, H., & He, X. (2015). Ideologies of monoculturalism in Confucius Institute textbooks: A corpus-based critical analysis. In X. L. Curdt-Christiansen & C. Weninger (Eds.), *Language, ideology and education* (pp. 104–122). Routledge.

Hruska, B. L. (2004). Constructing gender in an English dominant kindergarten: Implications for second language learners. *TESOL Quarterly, 38,* 450–485.

Hu, G. (2005). Contextual influences on instructional practices: A Chinese case for an ecological approach to ELT. *TESOL Quarterly, 39*(4), 635–660. https://doi.org/10.2307/3588525.

Huckin, T. (1997). Critical discourse analysis. In T. Miller (Ed.), *Functional approaches to written text: Classroom applications* (pp.78–92). USIA.

Huckin, T. (2002). Critical discourse analysis and the discourse of condescension. In E. Barton & G. Stygall (Eds.), *Discourse studies in composition* (pp. 155–176). Hampton.

Huh, S. J. (2004). *Globalization of English teaching practices: When Confucianism meets Vygotskian practices: An ethnography of teaching and learning EFL in a Korean university.* [Unpublished Dissertation]. University of Massachusetts.

Hwang, H. (2003). *The impact of high-stakes exams on teachers and students: A washback study of the university entrance exam at the secondary school level in South Korea.* [Unpublished Master's thesis]. McGill University.

Ihm, H. J. (1996). *A study of the cultural content of illustrations in selected elementary school EFL/ESL textbooks.* [Doctoral Dissertation, University of Georgia]. Proquest Dissertations Publishing.

Iyer, R., Kettle, M., Luke, A., & Mills, K. (2014). Critical applied linguistics. *The Routledge companion to English studies,* 317–332.

Janks, H. (2010). *Literacy and power.* Routledge.

Jewitt, C. (2006). *Technology, literacy and learning: A multimodal approach.* Routledge.

Jewitt, C. (2009). *Different approaches to multimodality.* Routledge.

Jewitt, C., Bezemer, J., & O'Halloran, K. (2016). *Introducing multimodality.* Routledge. https://doi.org/10.4324/9781315638027.

Johnston, B. (1999). Putting critical pedagogy in its place: A personal account. *Tesol Quarterly, 33*(3), 557–565.

Jung, S. K., & Norton, B. (2002). Language planning in Korea: The new elementary English program. *Language Policies in Education: Critical Issues, 245,* 265.

Kachru, B. B. (1992). World Englishes: Approaches, issues and resources. *Language Teaching, 25*(1), 1–14. https://doi.org/10.1017/S0261444800006583.

Kang, D. H. (2000). *Motivation and foreign language learning in Korean EFL context.* ERIC. Republic of Korea.

Kay, S., & Jones, V. (2008). *New American inside out (Elementary).* Macmillan.

Kim, H. (2015). Teachers' opinions on the evaluation of ELT teachers' books. *English Language Teaching, 8*(3), 1–12.

Kim, H. J. (2001). *A case study of curriculum and material evaluation: Elementary English as a foreign language in South Korea* [Doctoral dissertation, McGill University]. McGill University Libraries. https://escholarship.mcgill.ca/concern/theses/fq977w834.

Kim, T. Y., Kim, Y., & Kim, J. Y. (2018). A qualitative inquiry on EFL learning demotivation and resilience: A study of primary and secondary EFL students in South Korea. *The Asia-Pacific Education Researcher, 27*(1), 55–64.

Kohls, L. (2001). *Learning to think Korean: A guide to living and working in Korea.* Nicholas Brealey Publishing.

Korea Institute of Curriculum and Evaluation (KICE). (2001). *Naeyongui Sonjeonggwa.*

Kormos, J., & Nijakowska, J. (2017). Inclusive practices in teaching students with dyslexia: Second language teachers' concerns, attitudes and self-efficacy beliefs on a massive open online learning course. *Teaching and Teacher Education, 68,* 30–41.

Kramsch, C. (1993). Language study as border study: Experiencing difference. *European Journal of Education, 28*(3), 349–358.

Kramsch, C. (2008). Ecological perspectives on foreign language education. *Language Teaching, 41*(3), 389–408.

Kramsch, C. (2020). Educating the global citizen or the global consumer?. *Language Teaching, 53*(4), 462–476.

Kramsch, C., & Vinall, K. (2015). The cultural politics of language textbooks in the era of globalization. In X. L. Curdt-Christiansen & C. Weninger (Eds.), *Language, ideology and education* (pp. 25–42). Routledge.

Kramsch, C., & Zhang, L. (2018). *The multilingual instructor.* Oxford University Press.

Krashen, S. (1992). The input hypothesis: An update. In E. Alatis (Ed.), *Georgetown University Round Table – Linguistics and language pedagogy: The state of the art* (pp. 409–431). Georgetown University Press.

Kress, G. (1993). Against arbitrariness: The social production of the sign as a foundational issue in critical discourse analysis. *Discourse & Society, 4*(2), 169–191. https://doi.org/10.1177/0957926593004002003.

Kress, G. (2010). *Multimodality: A social semiotic approach to contemporary communication.* Kindle ed. Routledge. https://doi.org/10.4324/9780203970034.

Kress, G., Jewitt, C., Bourne, J., Franks, A., Hardcastle, J., Jones, K., & Reid, E. (2004). *English in Urban Classrooms: A multimodal perspective on teaching and learning.* Routledge.

Kress, G., & Van Leeuwen, T. (1996). *Reading images: The grammar of visual design.* Psychology Press.

Kress, G., & Van Leeuwen, T. (2006). *Reading images: The grammar of visual design.* Routledge.

Krulatz, A., & Iversen, J. (2020). Building inclusive language classroom spaces through multilingual writing practices for newly-arrived students in Norway. *Scandinavian Journal of Educational Research, 64*(3), 372–388.

Kubota, R. (1999). Japanese culture constructed by discourses: Implications for applied linguistics research and English language teaching. *TESOL Quarterly, 33*, 9–35.

Kubota, R. (2011). Learning a foreign language as leisure and consumption: Enjoyment, desire, and the business of eikaiwa. *International Journal of Bilingual Education and Bilingualism, 14*(4), 473–488.

Kubota, R., & Lin, A. (2006). Race and TESOL: Introduction to concepts and theories. *TESOL Quarterly, 40*(3), 471–493. https://doi.org/10.2307/40264540.

Kumaravadivelu, B. (1999). Critical classroom discourse analysis. *TESOL Quarterly, 33*(3), 453–484. https://doi.org/10.2307/3587674.

Kumaravadivelu, B. (2006). *Understanding Language Teaching: From Method to Postmethod.* Routledge.

Kuteeva, M. (2020). Revisiting the 'E' in EMI: Students' perceptions of standard English, lingua franca and translingual practices. *International Journal of Bilingual Education and Bilingualism, 23*(3), 287–300.

Lam, P. W. (2010). Discourse particles in corpus data and textbooks: The case of Well. *Applied Linguistics, 31*(2), 260–281.

Ledin, P., & Machin, D. (2020). *Introduction to multimodal analysis.* Bloomsbury Publishing.

Lee, B. (2015). EFL learners' perspectives on ELT materials evaluation relative to learning styles. *RELC Journal, 46*(2), 147–163.

Lee, H., & Lee, K. (2016). An analysis of the failure(s) of South Korea's National English ability test. *The Asia-Pacific Education Researcher, 25*(5–6), 827–834.

Lee, I. (2011). Teaching how to discriminate: Globalization, prejudice, and textbooks. *Instructor Education Quarterly, 38*(1), 47–63.

Lee, J. F. (2014). A hidden curriculum in Japanese EFL textbooks: Gender representation. *Linguistics and Education, 27*, 39–53. https://doi.org/10.1016/j.linged.2014.07.002.

Lee, K. Y. (2009). Treating culture: What 11 high school EFL conversation textbooks in South Korea do. *English Teaching, 8*(1), 76.

Lee, M. Y. (2006). *EFL teacher perspectives on incorporating language learning strategies into their EFL classes in Korea.* New York University.

Lemke, J. L. (1989). *Using language in the classroom.* Oxford University Press.

Lemke, J. L. (2002). Travels in hypermodality. *Visual Communication, 1*(3), 299–325.

Liggett, T. (2009). Unpacking white racial identity in English language teacher education. In R. Kubota & A. Lin (Eds.), *Race, language and identities in English language education: Exploring critically engaged practice* (pp. 27–43). Routledge.

Lin, A. M. (1999). Doing-English-lessons in the reproduction or transformation of social worlds? *Tesol Quarterly, 33*(3), 393–412.

Lin, A. M. Y. (2004). Introducing a critical pedagogical curriculum: A feminist, reflexive account. In B. Norton & K. Toohey (Eds.), *Critical pedagogies and language learning* (pp. 271–290). Cambridge University Press.

Linse, C. (2007). Predictable books in the children's EFL classroom. *ELT Journal, 61*(1), 46–54.

Littlejohn, A. (1992). *Why are English language teaching materials the way they are?* Unpublished PhD thesis, Lancaster University.

Littlejohn, A. (2012). Language teaching materials and the (very) big picture. *Electronic Journal of Foreign Language Teaching, 9*(1), 283–297.

Littlewood, W., & William, L. (1981). *Communicative language teaching: An introduction.* Cambridge university press.

Liu, H. (2020). Ideologies in college EFL textbooks – A content analysis based on critical pedagogy. *Journal of Language Teaching and Research, 11*(6), 937–942.

Luke, A. (2002). Beyond science and ideology critique: Developments in critical discourse analysis. *Annual Review of Applied Linguistics, 22*(1), 96–110.

Luke, A. (2015). Cultural content matters. In X. L. Curdt-Christiansen & C. Weninger (Eds.), *Language, ideology and education: The politics of textbooks in language education* (pp. 207–224). Routledge.

Macgilchrist, F. (2017). Textbooks. In J. Flowerdew & J. E. Richardson (Eds.), *The Routledge handbook of critical discourse studies* (pp. 525–539). Routledge.

Machin, D. (2007). Visual discourses of war: Multimodal analysis of photographs of the Iraq occupation. In A. Hodges & C. Nilep (Eds.), *Discourse, War and Terrorism* (pp. 123–142). John Benjamins Publishing.

Machin, D. (2016). *Introduction to multimodal analysis.* Bloomsbury Publishing.

Machin, D., & Mayr, A. (2012). *How to do critical discourse analysis: A multimodal introduction.* Sage.

Maposa, M. T. (2015). Reflections on applying critical discourse analysis methodologies in analysing South African history textbooks. *Yesterday and Today, 14*, 58–75. https://doi.org/10.17159/2223-0386/2015/nl4a3.

Marefat, F., & Marzban, S. (2014). Multimodal analysis of gender representation in ELT textbooks: Reader's perceptions. *Procedia-Social and Behavioral Sciences, 98*, 1093–1099. https://doi.org/10.1016/j.sbspro.2014.03.521.

Martin, A. (2004). The 'katakana effect' and teaching English in Japan. *English Today, 20*(1), 50–55.

Marx, K., & Engels, F. (1967). *The communist manifesto. 1848.* Trans. Samuel Moore. Penguin.

Masuhara, H. (2011). What do teachers really want from coursebooks? In B. Tomlinson (Ed.), *Materials development in language teaching* (pp. 236–266). Cambridge University Press.

Matsuda, A. (2002). Representation of users and uses of English in beginning Japanese EFL textbooks. *JALT Journal, 24*(2), 182–200.

Matsuda, A. & Friedrich, P. (2012). Selecting an instructional variety for an EIL curriculum In A. Matsuda (Ed.), *Principles and Practices of Teaching English as an International Language* (pp. 17–27). Channel View Publications.

Mauranen, A. (2012). *Exploring ELF: Academic English shaped by non-native speakers.* Cambridge University Press.

McCrum, R. (2011). *Globish: How the English language became the world's language.* Anchor Canada.

McKay, S. L. (2012). 5. Teaching materials for English as an international language. In A. Matsuda (Ed.), *Principles and practices of teaching English as an international language* (pp. 70–83). Multilingual Matters.

McLaren, P. (1988). Culture or canon? *Critical Pedagogy and the Politics of Literacy.* Harvard Educational Review, *58*(2), 213–234.

McLaren, P. (2016). *Life in schools: An introduction to critical pedagogy in the foundations of education.* Amazon Kindle ed. Routledge.

Méndez, T., & García, A. (2012). Exploring elementary students' power and solidarity relations in an EFL classroom. *Profile Issues in Teachers' Professional Development, 14*(1), 173–185.

Meschede, N., Fiebranz, A., Möller, K., & Steffensky, M. (2017). Teachers' professional vision, pedagogical content knowledge and beliefs: On its relation and differences between pre-service and in-service teachers. *Teaching and Teacher Education, 66,* 158–170.

Mesthrie, R. (2006). World Englishes and the multilingual history of English. *World Englishes, 25*(3–4), 381–390.

Meštrović, S. G., & Ahmed, A. S. (Eds.). (1997). *The conceit of innocence: Losing the conscience of the West in the war against Bosnia (No. 4).* Texas A&M University Press.

Mustedanagic, A. (2010). *Gender in English Language and EFL-textbooks.* Halmstad University.

Nam, J. M. (2005). *Perceptions of Korean college students and teachers about communication-based English instruction: Evaluation of a college EFL curriculum in South Korea* [Doctoral dissertation, Ohio State University]. Proquest Dissertations Publishing.

Nelson, M. E., Hull, G. A., & Roche-Smith, J. (2008). Taking, and mistaking, the show on the road: Challenges of multimedia self-presentation. *Written Communication, 25*(4), 415–440.

Neuliep, J. W. (2020). *Intercultural communication: A contextual approach.* SAGE Publications, Incorporated.

Nguyen, M. T. T. (2011). Learning to communicate in a globalized world: To what extent do school textbooks facilitate the development of intercultural pragmatic competence? *RELC Journal, 42*(1), 17–30.

Nofal, M. Y., & Qawar, H. A. (2015). Gender representation in English language textbooks: Action pack 10. *American Journal of Educational, Science, 1*(2), 14–18.

Norris, S. (2004). *Analyzing multimodal interaction: A methodological framework.* Kindle ed. Routledge. https://doi.org/10.4324/9780203379493.

Norris, S. (2019). *Systematically working with multimodal data: Research methods in multimodal discourse analysis.* John Wiley & Sons.

Norton, B., & Toohey, K. (2004). *Critical pedagogies and language learning.* Cambridge University Press.

Null, W. (2016). *Curriculum: From theory to practice.* Rowman & Littlefield.

Nunan, D. (1987). Communicative language teaching: Making it work. *ELT Journal, 41*(2), 136–145.

O'Neill, R., Yeadon, T. and Cornelius, E. T. (1978). *American Kernel Lessons: Intermediate.* Longman.

Ortactepe, D. (2013). 'This is called free-falling theory not culture shock!': A narrative inquiry on second language socialization. *Journal of Language, Identity & Education, 12*(4), 215–229.

Osborn, D. (2017). Constructing Israeli and Palestinian identity: A multimodal critical discourse analysis of world history textbooks and teacher discourse. *Journal of International Social Studies, 7*(1), 4–33.

Paik, K. (2018). The English language in Korea: Its history and vision. *Asian Englishes, 20*(2), 122–133.

Paiz, J. M. (2019). Queering practice: LGBTQ+ diversity and inclusion in English language teaching. *Journal of Language, Identity & Education, 18*(4), 266–275.

Paltridge, B. (2012). *An introduction to discourse analysis.* Bloomsbury.

Paltridge, B., & Phakiti, A. (Eds.). (2015). *Research methods in applied linguistics: A practical resource.* Bloomsbury Publishing.

Park, G. (2009). 'I Listened to Korean Society. I Always Heard that Women Should be this Way . . .': The negotiation and construction of gendered identities in claiming a dominant language and race in the United States. *Journal of Language, Identity & Education, 8*(2–3), 174–190. https://doi.org/10.1080/15348450902848775.

Park, J. S. Y. (2009). *The Local Construction of a Global Language: Ideologies of English in South Korea.* De Gruyter Mouton. https://doi.org/10.1515/9783110214079.

Park, J. K. (2009). 'English fever' in South Korea: Its history and symptoms. *English Today, 25*, 50–57.

Pellegrino, A., Mann, L., & Russell III, W. B. (2013). To lift as we climb: A textbook analysis of the segregated school experience. *The High School Journal*, 209–231.

Pennycook, A. (1994). Incommensurable discourses? *Applied Linguistics, 15*(2), 115–138. https://doi.org/10.1093/applin/15.2.115

Pennycook, A. (2004). Critical moments in a TESOL praxicum. In B. Norton & K. Toohey (Eds.), *Critical pedagogies and language learning,* (pp. 327–345). Ernst Klett Sprachen.

Pennycook, A. (2008). *Critical applied linguistics: A critical introduction.* Taylor & Francis.

Pennycook, A. (2010). Critical and alternative directions in applied linguistics. *Australian Review of Applied Linguistics, 33*(2), 16–1.

Pennycook, A., & Candlin, C. N. (2017). *The cultural politics of English as an international language.* Routledge.

Phillipson, R. (1992). ELT: The native speaker's burden? *ELT Journal, 46*(1), 12–18. https://doi.org/10.1093/elt/46.1.12.

Phillipson, R. (2012). Linguistic imperialism. In C. A. Chapelle (Ed.), *The encyclopedia of applied linguistics* (pp. 1–7). Wiley Online Library. https://doi.org/10.1002 /9781405198431.wbeal0718.pub2.

Phillipson, R., & Skutnabb-Kangas, T. (2017). Linguistic imperialism and the consequences for language ecology. In A. F. Fill & H. Penz (Eds.), *The Routledge handbook of ecolinguistics* (pp. 121–134). Routledge.

Popson, N. (2001). The Ukrainian history textbook: Introducing children to the 'Ukrainian nation'. *Nationalities Papers, 29*(2), 325–350. https://doi.org/10.1080 /00905990120053764.

Rahimi, M., & Hassani, M. (2012). Attitude towards EFL textbooks as a predictor of attitude towards learning English as a foreign language. *Procedia – Social and Behavioral Sciences, 31*(2011), 66–72. https://doi.org/10.1016/j.sbspro.2011.12.018.

Ramanathan, V. (1999). 'English is here to stay': A critical look at institutional and educational practices in India. *TESOL Quarterly, 33*(2) 211–232.

Ramanathan, V., & Morgan, B. (2009). Global warning? West-based TESOL, class blindness, and the challenge for critical pedagogies. In F. Sharifan (Ed.), *English as an international language: Perspectives and pedagogical issues* (pp. 153–168). De Gruyter.

Rashidi, N., & Safari, F. (2011). A model for EFL materials development within the framework of critical pedagogy (CP). *English Language Teaching, 4*(2), 250. https:// doi.org/10.5539/elt.v4n2p250.

Richards, J. C. (2001). *The role of textbooks in a language program.* Cambridge University Press.

Richards, J. C. (2014). The ELT textbook. In S. Garton & K. Graves (Eds.), *International perspectives on materials in ELT* (pp. 19–36). Palgrave Macmillan.

Richards, J. C., Hull, J., & Proctor, S. (1994). *Interchange. English for International Communication: Students Book. Dl. I.* Cambridge University Press.

Ritzer, G. (1993). *The McDonaldization of Society.* Pine Forge.

Rogers, R., Malancharuvil-Berkes, E., Mosley, M., Hui, D., & Joseph, G. O. G. (2005). Critical discourse analysis in education: A review of the literature. *Review of Educational Research, 75*(3), 365–416.

Roulston, K. (2010). Considering quality in qualitative interviewing. *Qualitative Research, 10*(2), 199–228. https://doi.org/10.1177/1468794109356739.

Rubdy, R., & Tan, P. (2008). *Language as commodity: Global structures, local marketplaces*. Bloomsbury Publishing.

Ryu, J., & Boggs, G. (2016). Teachers' perceptions about teaching multimodal composition: The case study of Korean English teachers at secondary schools. *English Language Teaching, 9*(6), 52–60.

Sadeghi, B., & Maleki, G. (2016). The representation of male and female social actors in the ILI English series. *Journal of Language Teaching and Research, 7*(2), 307–317. https://doi.org/10.17507/jltr.0702.09.

Sahragard, R., & Davatgarzadeh, G. (2012). The representation of social actors in interchange third edition series: A critical discourse analysis. *Journal of Teaching Language Skills, 29*(1), 67–89. https://doi.org/10.22099/JTLS.2012.401.

Sakai, H., & Kikuchi, K. (2009). An analysis of demotivators in the EFL classroom. *System, 37*(1), 57–69. https://doi.org/10.1016/j.system.2008.09.005.

Sakui, K. (2007). Classroom management in Japanese EFL classrooms. *JALT, 29*(1), 41.

Saldaña, J. (2016). *The Coding manual for qualitative researchers*. Sage.

Saslow, J. M., & Ascher, A. (2006). *Top Notch 2: Student Book*. Pearson Longman.

Savignon, S. J. (1987). Communicative language teaching. *Theory into Practice, 26*(4), 235–242.

Savignon, S. (2002). *Interpreting communicative language teaching: Contexts and concerns in teacher education*. Yale University Press.

Sayer, P., & Meadows, B. (2012). Teaching culture beyond nationalist boundaries: National identities, stereotyping, and culture in language education. *Intercultural Education, 23*(3), 265–279.

Schwab, J. (1969). The practical: A language for curriculum. *School Review, 78*(1), 1–23.

Scollon, R. (1998). *Mediated discourse as social interaction*. Longman.

Scollon, R., Scollon, S. W., & Jones, R. H. (2011). *Intercultural communication: A discourse approach*. John Wiley & Sons.

Serafini, F. (2014). *Reading the visual: An introduction to teaching multimodal literacy*. Teachers College Press, Columbia University.

Setyono, B. (2018). The portrayal of women in nationally endorsed English as a Foreign Language (EFL) textbooks for senior high school students in Indonesia. *Sexuality & Culture*, 1–17. https://doi.org/10.1007/s12119-018-9526-2.

Shapiro, S. (2015). Towards a critical pedagogy of peace education. *Kultura- Społeczeństwo- Edukacja, 7*(1), 7–20.

Sharifan, F. (2009). *English as an international language: Perspectives and pedagogical issues*. De Gruyter.

Sharma, A., & Buxton, C. A. (2015). Human–nature relationships in school science: A critical discourse analysis of a middle-grade science textbook. *Science Education, 99*(2), 260–281. https://doi.org/10.1002/sce.21147.

Sheldon, L. E. (1988). Evaluating ELT textbooks and materials. *ELT Journal, 42*(4), 237–246.

Sherman, J. E. (2010). Multiple levels of cultural bias in TESOL course books. *RELC, 41*(3), 267–281. https://doi.org/10.1177/0033688210380576.

Shin, D. M. (2003). *Social and Economic Policies in Korea: Ideas, networks and linkages.* Routledge.

Shin, H., & Crookes, G. (2005). Exploring the possibilities for EFL critical pedagogy in Korea: A two-part case study. *Critical Inquiry in Language Studies: An International Journal, 2*(2), 113–136.

Shin, J., Eslami, Z. R., & Chen, W. C. (2011). Presentation of local and international culture in current international English-language teaching textbooks. *Language, Culture and Curriculum, 24*(3), 253–268. https://doi.org/10.1080/07908318.2011 .614694.

Shor, I. (1992). *Empowering education.* University of Chicago Press.

Shor, I. (2014). *When students have power: Negotiating authority in a critical pedagogy.* University of Chicago Press.

Sinclair, J., & Coulthard, M. (1992). Towards an analysis of discourse. In Coulthard, M. (Ed.), *Advances in spoken discourse analysis* (pp.1–34). Routledge.

Sleeter, C. E., & Grant, C. A. (2017). Race, class, gender, and disability in current textbooks. In M. W. Apple & L. K. Christian-Smith (Eds.), *The politics of the textbook* (pp. 78–110). Routledge.

Smith, C. A. (2020). Establishing a zone of prioritized curricularivity: Exploring a critical approach to negotiating multimodal discourses in EFL textbooks. *Journal of Language and Cultural Education, 8*(2). https://doi.org/10.2478/jolace-2020 -0011.

Smith, C. A. (2021). Mapping reflexivity in situ: A multimodal exploration of negotiated textbook discourses in Korean university EFL classrooms. *Language Teaching Research,* 10.1177/13621688211024932.

Smith, C. A., & Sheyholislami, J. (2022). Current trends in critical discourse analyses of textbooks: A look at selected literature. *The Canadian Journal of Applied Linguistics, 25*(1). https://www.researchgate.net/deref/https%3A%2F%2Fjournals.lib.unb.ca %2Findex.php%2FCJAL%2FlibraryFiles%2FdownloadPublic%2F41.

Soars, J., Soars, L., Falla, T., & Cassette, W. (2015). American headway: Starter: Student book. Oxford University Press. *Society, 4* (2), 249–283. https://doi.org/10.1177 /0957926593004002006.

Song, H. (2013). Deconstruction of cultural dominance in Korean EFL textbooks. *Intercultural Education, 24*(4), 382–390. https://doi.org/10.1080/14675986.2013 .809248.

Song, J. J. (2011). English as an official language in South Korea: Global English or social malady? *Language Problems and Language Planning, 35*(1), 35–55. https://doi .org/10.1075/lplp.35.1.03son.

Söylemez, A. S. (2010). A study on how social gender identity is constructed in EFL coursebooks. *Procedia-Social and Behavioral Sciences, 9,* 747–752. https://doi.org/10 .1016/j.sbspro.2010.12.228.

Steffensen, S. V., & Kramsch, C. (2017). The ecology of second language acquisition and socialization. *Language Socialization*, 17–32. DOI 10.1007/978-3-319-02327-4_2-1.

Stockdale, A. D. (2006). *Gender representation in an EFL textbook*. [Unpublished Master's thesis]. University of Birmingham.

Stoller, A. (2015). Taylorism and the logic of learning outcomes. *Journal of Curriculum Studies*, *47*(3), 317–333, https://doi.org/10.1080/00220272.2015.1018328.

Strauss, A. L., & Corbin, J. (1994). Grounded theory methodology – an overview. In. Y. S. Lincoln & N. K. Denzin (Eds.), *The Sage handbook of qualitative research* (pp. 273–285). Sage.

Sung, K. (2008). A study on culture teaching and learning through the analysis of ELT materials and survey. *English Language Teaching*, *20*(4), 209–235.

Svendsen, A. M., & Svendsen, J. T. (2017). Contesting discourses about physical education . . . *European Physical Education Review*, *23*(4), 480–498. https://doi.org /10.1177/1356336X16657279.

Syrbe, M., & Rose, H. (2018). An evaluation of the global orientation of English textbooks in Germany. *Innovation in Language Learning and Teaching*, *12*(2), 152–163.

Tajeddin, Z., & Janebi Enayat, M. (2010). Gender representation and stereotyping in ELT textbooks: A critical image analysis. *TELL*, *4*(2), 51–79. https://doi.org/10.22132 /TEL.2010.66107.

Talmy, S. (2010). Qualitative interviews in applied linguistics: From research instrument to social practice. *Annual Review of Applied Linguistics*, *30*, 128–148. https://doi.org /10.1017/S0267190510000085.

Tashakkori, A., & Teddlie, C. (2010). *Sage handbook of mixed methods in social and behavioral research*. SAGE publications.

Taylor, F. W. (2004). *The principles of scientific management*. Routledge.

Taylor-Mendes, C. (2009). Construction of racial stereotypes in English as a foreign language (EFL) textbooks: Images as discourse. In R. Kubota and A. Lin (Eds.), *Race, culture, and identities in second language education: Exploring critically engaged practice* (pp. 64–80). Routledge.

Thoma, M. (2017). Critical analysis of textbooks: Knowledge-generating logics and the emerging image of 'global economic contexts'. *Critical Studies in Education*, *58*(1), 19–35. https://doi.org/10.1080/17508487.2015.1111248.

Thompson, A. S., & Lee, J. (2018). The motivational factors questionnaire in the Korean EFL context: Predicting group membership according to English proficiency and multilingual status. *The Language Learning Journal*, *46*(4), 398–414.

Thompson, K. D. (2013). Representing language, culture, and language users in textbooks: A critical approach to Swahili multiculturalism. *The Modern Language Journal*, *97*(4), 947–964. https://doi.org/10.1111/j.1540-4781.2013.12047.x.

Thomson, C. K., & Otsuji, E. (2003). Evaluation of business Japanese textbooks: Issues of gender. *Japanese Studies*, *23*(2), 185–203. https://doi.org/10.1080 /1037139032000129711.

Timmis, I. (2010). 'Tails' of linguistic survival. *Applied Linguistics, 31*(3), 325–345.

Tomlinson, B. (Ed.). (2011). *Materials development in language teaching.* Cambridge University Press.

Tomlinson, B., & Masuhara, H. (2017). *The complete guide to the theory and practice of materials development for language learning.* John Wiley & Sons.

Turner, D. W. (2010). Qualitative interview design: A practical guide for novice investigators. *The Qualitative Report, 15*(3), 754–760. https://doi.org/http://www.nova.edu/ssss/QR/QR15-3/qid.pdf.

Ushioda, E. (2011). Language learning motivation, self and identity: Current theoretical perspectives. *Computer Assisted Language Learning, 24*(3), 199–210. https://doi.org/10.1080/09588221.2010.538701.

Vaezi, S., & Fallah, N. (2011). The relationship between self-efficacy and stress among Iranian EFL teachers. *Journal of Language Teaching and Research, 2*(5), 1168.

van Dijk, T. A. (1993). Principles of critical discourse analysis. *Discourse & Society, 4*(2), 249–283.

van Dijk, T. A. (Ed.). (2011). *Discourse studies: A multidisciplinary introduction.* Sage.

Van Dijk, T. A. (2016). Critical discourse studies: A sociocognitive approach. In R. Wodak & M. Meyer (Eds.), *Methods of critical discourse studies* (pp. 62–85). Sage.

van Dijk, T. A., & Atienza, E. (2011). Knowledge and discourse in secondary school social science textbooks. *Discourse Studies, 13*(1), 93–118. https://doi.org/10.1177/1461445610387738.

van Leeuwen, T. (1996). The representation of social actors in discourse. In Caldas-Coulthard, C. R., & Coulthard, M. (Eds.), *Texts and practices: Readings in critical discourse analysis* (pp. 32–70). Routledge.

van Leeuwen, T. (2005). *Introducing social semiotics.* Psychology Press.

van Leeuwen, T. (2008). *Discourse and practice: New tools for critical discourse analysis.* Oxford University Press.

van Lier, L. (1997). Observation from an ecological perspective. *TESOL Quarterly, 22,* 783–87.

van Lier, L. (2004). The ecology of language learning. In *Conference proceedings UC Language Consortium Conference on Theoretical and Pedagogical Perspectives*, March 26–28.

van Lier, L. (2015). Approaches to observation in classroom research from an ecological observation. *TESOL Quarterly, 31*(4), 783–787. https://doi.org/10.2307/3587762.

Vasilopoulos, G. (2015). Language learner investment and identity negotiation in the Korean EFL context. *Journal of Language, Identity & Education, 14*(2), 61–79.

Vellenga, H. (2004). Learning pragmatics from ESL & EFL textbooks: How likely? *Tesl-Ej, 8*(2), n2.

Ververi, O. (2017). The council of Europe's citizenship conception . . . a CDA of two textbooks. *Globalisation, Societies and Education, 15*(4), 518–530. https://doi.org/10.1080/14767724.2017.1335594.

Vinall, K., & Shin, J. (2018). The construction of the tourist gaze in English textbooks in South Korea: Exploring the tensions between internationalisation and nationalisation. *Language, Culture and Curriculum*, 1–18.

Wang, W. C., Lin, C. H., & Lee, C. C. (2011). Thinking of the textbook in the ESL/EFL classroom. *English Language Teaching*, 4(2), 91–96.

Waters, A. (2009). Ideology in applied linguistics for language teaching. *Applied Linguistics*, 30(1), 138–143. https://doi.org/10.1093/applin/amp005.

Weninger, C. (2018). Textbook analysis. In C. A. Chapelle (Ed.), *The encyclopedia of applied linguistics* (pp. 1–8). Wiley Blackwell. https://doi.org/10.1002/9781405198431 .wbeal1489.

Weninger, C., & Kiss, T. (2013). Culture in English as a foreign language (EFL) textbooks: A semiotic approach. *TESOL Quarterly*, 47(4), 694–716. https://doi.org/10.1002/tesq.87.

Wertz, F. J. (2011). *Five ways of doing qualitative analysis: Phenomenological psychology, grounded theory, discourse analysis, narrative research, and intuitive inquiry*. Guilford Press.

Widdowson, H. G. (2004). *Text, context, pretext. Critical issues in discourse analysis*. Blackwell.

Wiggins, G., & McTighe, J. (2005). *Understanding by design*. ASCD.

Wodak, R., & Meyer, M. (2001). *Methods of critical discourse analysis*. Sage.

Wodak, R., & Meyer, M. (2016). *Methods of critical discourse studies*. Sage.

Wohlwend, K. E. (2011). Mapping modes in children's play and design: An action-oriented approach to critical multimodal analysis. In R. Rogers (Ed.), *An introduction to critical discourse analysis in education* (pp. 242–266). Routledge.

Woods, D. (1996). *Teacher cognition in language teaching*. Cambridge University Press.

World Health Organization. (2020). *Obesity*. January 14. Retrieved from: https://www .who.int/health-topics/obesity#tab=tab_1.

Wu, J. (2010). A content analysis of the cultural content in the EFL textbooks. *Canadian Social Science*, 6(5), 137–144. https://doi.org/10.3968/g1128.

Wyatt, M. (2016). 'Are they becoming more reflective and/or efficacious?' A conceptual model mapping how teachers' self-efficacy beliefs might grow. *Educational Review*, 68(1), 114–137.

Wyatt, M. (2018). Language teachers' self-efficacy beliefs: A review of the literature (2005–2016). *Australian Journal of Teacher Education (Online)*, 43(4), 92.

Xiang, R., & Yenika-Agbaw, V. (2021). EFL textbooks, culture and power: A critical content analysis of EFL textbooks for ethnic Mongols in China. *Journal of Multilingual and Multicultural Development*, 42(4), 327–341.

Xiong, T. (2012). Essence or practice? Conflicting cultural values in Chinese EFL textbooks: A discourse approach. *Discourse*, 33(4), 499–516. https://doi.org/10.1080 /01596306.2012.692958.

Xiong, T., & Qian, Y. (2012). Ideologies of English in a Chinese high school EFL textbook: A critical discourse analysis. *Asia Pacific Journal of Education*, 32(1), 75–92. https://doi.org/10.1080/02188791.2012.655239.

Yim, S. (2007). Globalization and language policy in South Korea. In A. B. M. Tsui & J. W. Tollefson (Eds.), *Language policy, culture, and identity in Asian contexts* (pp. 37–54). Routledge.

Yim, S. Y. (2014). An anxiety model for EFL young learners: A path analysis. *System, 42,* 344–354. https://doi.org/10.1016/j.system.2013.12.022.

Yin, R. K. (1994). Discovering the future of the case study. Method in evaluation research. *Evaluation Practice, 15*(3), 283–290.

Young, L., & Fitzgerald, B. (2017). *The power of language: How discourse influences society.* Equinox Publishing.

Zamir, S. (1995). *Dark voices: WEB Du Bois and American thought, 1888–1903.* University of Chicago Press.

Zappa-Hollman, S., & Duff, P. A. (2019). Qualitative approaches to classroom research on English-medium instruction. In X. Gao (Ed.), *Second handbook of English language teaching* (pp. 1029–1051). Springer.

Appendix A

Recorded Transcripts – Class X

Instructor X = X; Students = S

X: So! Everyone looking at Unit 6 . . . this is our study material for today. So! The topic is *Eating well*. So! First thing we are going to talk about is *habits*. . . . Alright, we are going to talk about *habits* to begin with . . . do you know what a habit is?

S: It's a routine?

X: A routine! Yes, a habit is a kind of routine – very good! <*A begins writing on the white board*> And . . . like we just studied, in the daily activities thing that we do on a regular basis, so they are habits that you do as part of a routine, again and again and again and again . . . and . . . also, we have good habits. . . . We have good habits, and we have bad habits . . . we have good and we have bad. So! There are different kinds of habits that we can have – healthy and unhealthy habits – OK some volunteers? What would be some examples of some good healthy habits?

S: Exercise?

X: Excellent – Exercising! Ex . . . er . . . ci . . . sing <*writing on the board*> Ok! Anyone else?

S: sleep early?

X: sleeping earlier . . . anyone else?

S: Have breakfast

X: Having breakfast. Ok. So! what are some bad or unhealthy habits?

S: eat junk food

X: <*nodding and writing*> eating junk food . . . I love junk food . . . what else . . .

S: drink alcohol <*student laughter*>

X: Drinking too much alcohol. One glass of wine is maybe ok for a healthy diet but 20 glasses of wine . . . <*student laughter*> . . . that's not a very good or healthy diet. Uh, over-drinking . . . bad habit . . . or drinking alcohol in excess <*writing on board*> Excess . . . excess . . . everyone understand 'Excess'?

Too much . . . or eating junk food in excess too . . . like, eating one potato chip won't hurt you but two bags *<shaking his head>* . . . is excessive! OK, one more unhealthy habit?

S: Smoking?

X: Yes! Smoking! It doesn't matter if you have only one or a whole pack . . . it doesn't matter because even one is unhealthy. So! Let's think about another kind of habit such as *study habits*. What are some examples of good study habits?

S: Review?

X: OK! Reviewing . . . reviewing your notes. That's a good study habit.

S: Focus on class?

X: OK focusing on class. That's good . . . and when you sit down to do homework, what is a good study habit? *<silent consideration among the students>* Like . . . think about when you sit down to do homework. A lot of people have a method or regularly do something to save time or to focus better or to relax so that they can study harder.

S: write down?

X: OK! Writing down everything . . . but I'm talking about . . . like, when you do your homework, when you sit down, you do some things that you think are necessary for you to study better.

S: drink coffee?

X: OK! Drinking coffee . . . yeah, that can be a good habit.

S: Typing?

A: Huh? . . . Oh typing! Yes. *<student mumbling>* Ok. cleaning the table . . . Having a neat area or how about making sure there is enough light? . . . I like that . . . 5:40

S: Making deadline?

X: Oh! Making a deadline, yep . . . And having a quiet atmosphere like that . . . those are some good study habits *<student mumbling>* Frustration? What's that? Frustration, you said? Ah, . . . procrastination! Procrastinating . . . didn't we learn that already in this class? OK, procrastination is a bad habit. *<many students nod and mumble agreement>*

X: others? *<student holds up a hand to mimic speaking on a cell phone>* Ok! phones . . . having your smart phone in easy reach? Any more . . . *<Students mumbling>* Watching TV . . . OK . . . watching TV . . . having the TV on . . . OK! let's look at . . . other than study habits, there are many other kinds of habits . . . so, do you like to travel? What are some are some traveling habits?

What's a good traveling habit if you go to travel internationally . . . what are some good traveling habits to make sure you are having a good time and are safe and so on?

S: plan?

X: Planning! OK planning ahead is good . . . I never do that though, I just go *<student laughter and mumbling>* SIM cards? Yep . . . Being on time? Ok . . . Now! What are some bad traveling habits that keep you from being on time or having a good time?

S: Going around at night?

X: OK! going around at night it depends where you are in Korea it's not too bad but in America no . . . in certain areas at least. Other bad traveling habits?

S: unsafe area?

X: Going to unsafe areas. Yeah, that's a good habit. Find out where the unsafe areas are . . . bad is going there, unless you are a thrill seeker or . . . if you have drunk too much alcohol.

S: Bring too much carrier?

X: Yeah! Bringing too much luggage. That's a bad one because it can be an issue. So! The next thing we're going to talk about is . . . *<pointing to the whiteboard>* So! we have eating habits as the last one and we're going to talk about them, so let's look at the first page of the handouts . . . *<Instructor X is holding up the book and pointing to the page so the students can see>* and here we have the food pyramid . . . what about here in Korea? Do you have a food pyramid?

S: Yeah . . .

X: It's called *the* food pyramid? I remember at the high school I used to teach that they used to have the food pagoda . . . anyway . . . anyway, everyone . . . look at this healthy eating pyramid and . . . Let's look at the foods in here and let's think about some of the foods that you never eat? That you see here . . . that some of these things you never eat or see your friends eat or is everyone healthy . . . especially, the vegetables, look at the vegetables. Some people don't like certain kinds of vegetables.

S: Carrots!

X: You don't like carrots why not?

S: I don't like the texture.

X: OK what about broccoli? Anyone here like broccoli?

S: I like broccoli . . .

X: The only food I hate is eggplant does anyone here know eggplant?. . . (Korean) 'gachi'? *<Student Laughter>*

X: I've hated that ever since I was young . . . So! Next, we're going to do partner work. So! This is your *diet*. . . . Now, this word here – Diet – a lot of people think that diet means only losing weight but if I ask you: 'What is your diet?' I'm not talking about losing weight. I'm talking about what food you eat regularly. You can have a good – healthy – diet and you can have a bad – unhealthy – diet. You can have an unhealthy diet, or you can have a healthy diet. So! Let's get together and look at the bottom <*A is holding up the book again and pointing to the content*> Under this food pyramid . . . You have a blank pyramid. So, with your partner, I want you to discuss the different foods that you rarely eat and the foods that you eat at least one to five portions per day and something you eat almost every meal and this can include drinks too so if you want to talk about alcohol or Cola, these liquids are part of your diet because you can have like green tea which is healthy but then you can have something else that is not healthy so with your team everyone talked together and help each other filling the pyramids together and help each other

S: what is poultry?

X: *poultry* is a bird, like chicken or turkey, etc. . . .

S: Ahh . . . <*Students are discussing 12:25–19:50*>

<*Instructor X is walking around the classroom and paying attention to each table*>

X: Also, compare and contrast too . . . discuss why you eat *this* or why you don't eat *this* 12.40

<*Students continue discussion and Instructor X speaks with one group*>

X: Remember liquids can be part of a diet too . . . soju and beer, coca cola, juice . . . <*enthusiastic student discussion*> I'm going to give you around two more minutes . . . then we are going to move on . . . (18:13) <*student discussion as Instructor X walks around the classroom*> Alright everyone, it is time to move on . . . everyone please turn to the next page (19:50)

<*Students turning page*>

X: All right on the next page if you look at the top there is a conversation model . . . we're going to practice reading this. <*A is holding up the book and pointing to the speaking exercise*>

So, there is a A, B & C but B only speaks once so if you have 3 people in your team everyone reads through 3 times so that everyone is ABC so that everybody can get a chance . . . so everyone take a couple of minutes to read through this and practice the conversation read through it as a team together <*student ask a muffled question*> Oops! Sorry I don't know what happened . . . I was on the wrong page OK there we go *<Student discussion/ practising dialogue>* 21:34

X: OK! We're gonna skip the next . . . everyone turn to the next page . . . Ok we're gonna skip the conversation model . . . look at this one *<A is holding up the textbook and pointing to a page>* Everyone look at Part A for the new vocabulary . . . so vocabulary! We're going to be talking about excuses. Everyone understand what excuse is? What's an excuse? *<Students mumbling>* OK an excuse is . . . it can be a reason why you don't do something or it can be a reason for why you are unable to do something . . . so if I ask you 'Do you want to go bungee jumping?' OK who does not want to go bungee jumping? *<some students put up their hands>*

So, you don't like it . . . you don't want to, so usually you give an excuse. So why don't you want to go bungee jumping? *<student mumbling>* You have agoraphobia? You let your Achilles heel show! OK, so do you want to drink soju right now hopefully you should say 'no'. Hopefully, you wouldn't say yes but if you do say no what is your excuse? *<student mumbling>* A: Right now, I am in class! *<student laughter>* A: That's a bad study habit! *<Student laughter>* OK if I am unable to do something like 'Have you ever gotten a bad score on a test?' *<student mumbling>* In your whole life. Yeah, so you get a bad score. You've never done that in your life but how did you get a bad score? . . . and so you can say 'Well, I didn't sleep well' or something 'I didn't study' or 'the test was too difficult' and so on, so we have excuses for things we can't do or unable to do up to your expectations. So here you have a vocabulary for excuses for not being able to eat something . . . *<student mumbling – holding up the book and asking Instructor X to explain>* So sure, you have an excuse for, I don't care, for something, or I hate something . . . so if someone offers you – I don't know – a hamburger, you can say 'I don't care for hamburgers.' That means you don't like it. This one, um, 'does not agree with' – some people say this – but it's kind of old fashioned. It's possible you could say it, but you can say why it doesn't agree with you. For example, you could say it gives me a headache or it gives me a stomachache, or it makes me sick. Next one, so if someone offered you a hamburger . . . so you could say, as an excuse, I'm . . . I'm a vegetarian. *<Instructor X addresses the classroom at large because many nearby students are listening>* Is anyone here a vegetarian? *<student laughter>*

A: I'm not a vegetarian . . . and there are many different levels of vegetarians . . . what's the name of that one . . . completely 100 per cent vegetables – no eggs, no milk . . .

S: vegan

X: Yeah, vegan! Vegan is just 100 per cent . . . then, some of you can use an excuse like 'I'm on a diet' and 'this one, I'm avoiding' . . . because it is something, normally, you wouldn't drink or eat this . . . like if I'm on a diet, I'm avoiding hamburgers. I'm avoiding alcohol and cigarettes if I'm trying to be healthy. Also, allergies – some people cannot eat the food because it can kill you! Like, some people are allergic to shellfish, you know clams, crabs, and things like that . . . some people are allergic to shellfish, some people are allergic to other things. Anyone here allergic to anything? <*Student laughter*> OK, what I want you to do next if you want to just run on the back of this I want you to write 5 foods or 5 drinks that you don't eat or don't drink . . . you don't need to write the reason just 5 things you don't need or 5 things you don't drink or it can be 5 things you don't eat or drink at this time but you did in the past

<*Students writing and in quiet discussion*> 29:20~

S: Professor, when I say 'I work out to lose weight' or 'I work out to lose my weight'

X: try to stay away from possessive in the second sentence. 'Your' is implied when you say '. . . to lose weight' . . . the first is fine <*student nodding and writing*>

X: Alright, so after you write your five things, with your partners, I want to ask you why do drink, why don't you drink and I want to give an excuse for each one . . . with your partners go ahead and ask about each of these things and give an excuse <*student discussion*>31:02 ~ 35:01

X: Alright, ladies and gentlemen, we have to move on because we're running out of time so let's skip ahead to page 66 . . . OK, the last thing we're gonna do here is talk about food passions, so we just did excuses for foods we don't normally eat or foods that we don't normally eat at the moment. Now, we're going to talk about other reasons why you like something or why you don't care for it, so these are good expressions you can use. So, 'I am crazy about something' . . . 'I am crazy about doing something' . . . so 'crazy'? Does it mean stupid or anything like that? <*Students mumble, looking at textbook*> Crazy means really, really, really like something . . . so if somebody says 'I'm crazy about you' – what does that mean? <*student laughter*> I love you; I can't be away from you; Yeah, so, I'm crazy about you would be like that but for food and for drinks these are the things you like . . . 'Oh my God, I'm crazy about chocolate!' So, there are foods that you will eat if someone gives it to you and it doesn't matter when you will eat it or want to eat it, so same thing . . . So, you can also use a restaurant too. If you're a big, fat person you can say 'I'm a big Domino's eater' 'I'm a big McDonald's eater' or drinks, 'I'm a big beer drinker' . . . and you could ask people too, when you sit down for dinner, are you a big *sam-gyeop-sal* (Korean BBQ bacon) eater? <*student laughter*>

X: OK! 'Addiction' – everyone knows 'addiction' right? Now, with this conversation it doesn't mean you are literally shaking . . . it's like saying you really love this thing and with alcohol, you shouldn't . . . I would avoid using this one with alcohol *<student laughter>* I would avoid using this one because if you say you're addicted to soju or something some people might think you're addicted . . . don't say *Coke* because that means something completely different in western culture! *<student laughter>* OK, how about wine lovers? There's a club of people or clubs of people from around the world who drink wine or collecting wine or beer lovers from around the world . . . pizza lovers you just like consuming all these things . . . just be careful to use these expressions carefully. So! All these things are good just be sure to be careful using them. OK, now, the bad things – I can't stand – usually you're going give some emphasis on *stand* so . . . 'I can't stand' is something you absolutely positively hate, something . . . so again, if someone says 'I can't stand her' 'I don't like her' or 'I don't speak to her' or 'I can't stand doing something' . . . So, food you know, I can't stand eating eggplant, so I can stand it, I can't stand you, or can't stand weekends, crazy about, it's the same over here *<A is holding up the book and pointing to a page>* . . . *not crazy about* is somewhat opposite . . . it just means 'I don't really like it' . . . 'I can't eat it but if I have to, I will' So, it's not really the opposite, like, if someone invites me for dinner, I'll eat it but let's go ahead and have this kind of food . . . I'm not crazy about it, but I'll eat it . . . and the same here, 'I don't care for something', that means the same . . . 'I'll do it but it's not my first choice' and we already studied this one anyway 'I'm not much of a something eater' . . . I will drink this but it's not my first choice, so really, I can't stand means 'I hate it' or 'I absolutely will not eat it' *<student discussion>* OK how 'bout this real fast with your partners . . . let's talk about some things from this column. *<A is holding up the book and pointing>* Some things from this column . . . you and your partners talk about these perspectives.

<Student discussion>

41:23

X: Alright everyone. We have to call the day because you have to go to your next class . . . thank you very much for everyone for participating in this classroom audit . . . thank you very much and everyone think about your teams for next week. . . . Everyone says goodbye *<students waving at camera>* 'Bye' (43:44)

Appendix B

Recorded Transcripts – Class Y

Instructor = Y; Student(s) = S

<students talking loudly together>

Y: Are you ready?

S: yes

Y: OK . . . let me talk . . . Did you have breakfast this morning?

S: Yes.

Y: What did you eat? How about you? Did you have breakfast this morning?

S: I forgot

Y: I forgot?!? It's not homework! *<student laughter>*

Y: Young-Ju *<student name>* What did you eat?

S: I had rice.

Y: Okay . . . good . . . this topic is about eating well . . . if you look at the top-right order of this unit, these are the goals that we are trying to achieve so some of the material will cover making an excuse to decline food *<Instructor Y is writing the word 'decline' on the WB and repeating the word to the students while nodding his head>* got that? decline? Decline?

S: nodding and quietly reading unit page and handout

Y: let's talk . . . talk about food passions . . . so things you really, really like . . . so food passions can also include things that you dislike something or you really, really hate so, if you think about it, 'passion' – this word passion *<Instructor Y is writing the word next to decline on the WB>* This word can mean very strongly in favour of something . . . passion can be a very strong emotion with something . . . so it can mean food that you really, really love or food that you really, really hate and then, later, we'll look at discussing lifestyle changes and then, if we have time . . . describing unique foods *<Instructor Y is holding up TB>* . . . so these are the unit goals if you look at the topic preview. We're talking about a healthy eating pyramid that suggests eating habits to avoid heart disease . . . that's a key expression 'heart disease' . . . so we're not just thinking about something that we enjoy, we are talking about health. If you look at the top of the pyramid and then we go down, what is the organizing principle?

S: pyramid . . . ?

Y: Yeah okay that's a pyramid but if you look at the foods at the Top and then you look at the foods at the bottom why is this at the Top?

S: essential?

Y: essential? <*shrugging his shoulders, writing essential on the WB*>

S: frequency?

Y: ok frequency . . . that's it, OK I'll accept that . . . frequency . . . <*Instructor Y writes 'frequency' on the whiteboard*> OK, let's look at the book . . . <*holding up the book; students are looking down at their books with expressions of bemused curiosity*> if you look at the top We have meat and butter rarely but on the right side white rice and white bread and then we get to the bottom which is almost every meal alright so like . . . vegetables, etc., frequency is the word and the organizing principle describes this let's look at the second one 'Dairy' and it says one to two portions per day . . . what are portions?

S: Amount?

Y: Amount. OK, so how much is a portion?

S: Portion is . . .

Y: How much is one portion?

S: one meal?

Y: one meal. Right so the amount you have in one meal is one portion. . . . Have you ever heard the word serving?

S: serving is portion?

Y: right so the amount that you have in one meal is one portion or one serving. . . . So if you have this amount of rice that is one serving or that is one portion. . . . This is for one person that is one serving Alight so <*pointing to the book*> dairy, one to two portions per day and seafood and poultry what is poultry?

S: chicken?

Y: yeah, so chicken or things like birds and poultry it also includes eggs; so, eating chicken and eggs . . . nuts and legumes? what are legumes?

S: Legumes?

Y: yeah, legumes . . . but in British English 'Leh-gyumes'

S: <*laughter*> beans?

Y: Right so beans that come in a pod . . . you know pod? Like soybeans come in a pod, they come in a pod, you have to take them out of the pod? Those are legumes.

S: <*students collectively*> 'ahh' <*understanding*>

Y: Alright, fruits two or three portions/day, vegetables 5 times/day, and then whole grain foods . . . what are whole grain?

S: '(Korean) grains'?

Y: so like (Korean) 'grains' Okay up here you have white rice . . . .but here you have whole grain foods This whole grain also includes rice . . . see the picture of that white rice so here you have white rice and then you have whole grain rice so what's the difference here ?

S: colour?

Y: colour? Ok that's true but why is that colour different?

S: Because of polishing the process polishers rice

Y: okay so polished rice means you take off the outside part and then there's only the inside part so the nutrition in that outer part is taken away so you're just left with the inside what's on the inside of that white part

S: carbo . . . carbo . . . carbo . . . carbohydrate

Y: right carbohydrate carbohydrates in Korean are 'tan-su-hwa-mul'

S: ahh! <*students collectively*>

Y: Right so if you think there is only the carbohydrate . . . there is no protein . . . which one is better?

S: whole grain?

Y: right the whole grain is much better . . . you get much more out of it . . . okay, alright, so this is the ideal . . . and below this here you have your own ideas And your own pyramid <*holding up the book*> go ahead and write what you actually eat put your real life diet in here <*students quietly speaking with each other and writing*> 9:50~12:50

Y: All right after you finish writing your pyramid please compare that to your partner's <*students continue discussion*> 12:55~16:40 students are engaging in very lively discussion and appear to be thoroughly enjoying the chance to discuss their eating habits with neighbours in the classroom <*Instructor Y is walking around the class answering questions and speaking of eating habits*>

Y: ok, let's move on to the next page. All right it says town bites about a bite is a small part of something alright so it says read along silently and listen however we do not have the sound file so I am going to be your sound file . . . there are 2 people Iris and Terri. . . . So I will be Iris and UB Terri okay?

S: <*student nodding*> Instructor Y and students role-play Terri and Iris (Saslow & Ascher, 2006, p. 62).

Y: good! Alright in the first line she says what in the world are you eating what is that what is what in the world?

S: How can you do that?

Y: yeah ok that's OK . . . OK in the 4th line 'I used to be' 'I used to be' what does that mean; In the past it was my habit And I quit so we usually see those 2 things together I used to be and not anymore on the right side on the second line well I would what does that mean what is well I would ?

S: I am glad too?

S: I want too?

S: I would like to eat that, but I will not?

Y: OK, very similar to that, on the page, Terri was on a diet . . . Right? . . . But now she's not on a diet anymore so she's eating chocolate and so on but Iris, in the past, was not on a diet, but now she is on a diet, so their situation has switched . . . alright, so Iris says I would but now I'm on a diet, so in the past before she was on a diet she would have eaten that cake . . . would have . . . would have. . . . So, in the past, I would have eaten that cake, but now I'm on a diet and so now I'm not going to do it . . . so in the past I would not have done it *<Instructor Y is using a physical reference to indicate past present and future [See Figure 1]>* 21:00 Okay, below you can see that repeated . . . I *used to* but not anymore . . . I *used to* be but not anymore Okay? *<students mumbling in agreement>*

Y: Collocations? *<asking the class while pointing to the dialogue>* Collocations?

S: *<students collectively>* used to and but not anymore

Y: good yes, please write these down . . . Alright let's take a look at these questions here . . . alright check the statements that are true according to the conversation and explain your answers . . . so Iris doesn't need sweets now . . . Yes?

S: Yes

Y: check that?

S: yes

Y: #2 Terri doesn't eat sweets now?

S: No.

Y: alright do not check that. That's not true. OK #3 Iris doesn't want any cake . . . no this is a little bit ambiguous *<writing on the board>* do you know ambiguous? It's a little bit ambiguous because she's actually ambiguous when she said I would but I'm on a diet so In other words she saying I want to but I'm not going to do it so the question I was doesn't want any cake . . . that's kind of strange because she wants it but she's not going to eat it so it's an ambiguous statement

S: yes < *many students nodding in agreement*>

Y: All right #4 Terri doesn't want any cake?

S: No.

Y: right, she is eating cake . . . Alright # 5, Iris changed her eating habits?

S: Yes.

Y: Yes. Number 6, did Terri change her eating habits?

S: Yes

Y: Yes, they both changed their eating habits . . . okay so one last time make a list of foods you are trying to eat if you're trying to lose weight or gain weight . . . gaining weight or losing weight . . . <*Student discussion in pairs looking at the book*>24:00

Y: Alright, if you are trying to lose weight, what do you want to eat?

S: vegetables?

Y: yes vegetables . . .

S: Eggs

Y: eggs

S: whole grain foods

Y: Whole grain foods, OK, you're not trying to gain weight, are you? <*Instructor Y points to a student; students laugh*> How do we gain weight?

S: Chicken?

Y: OK chicken . . . perhaps

S: pasta

Y: Yes, pasta. Alright, so those things have a lot of carbohydrates . . . so if you eat a lot of carbohydrates you're going to gain weight . . . so if you are trying to lose weight, you want to eat more fiber and less carbohydrates <*students nodding*> . . . Alright to the next page next page please . . . <*students turning page*> Alright, at the top of the page it says *make an excuse* to decline food . . . Alright? So, someone is offering you some food, but you don't want to eat it and this helps you give a reason why you don't want to eat it . . . this has to do with something we call *white lies*? . . . little white lies? <*walking towards the students to seek their opinion*> Does anybody know what that means? Little white lies?

S: <*shaking heads . . . confused*>

Y: Alright so imagine you go over to somebody's house and they cook something for you and they say let's have dinner and you look at it and it looks really bad and this person can't really cook you don't know what to say 'You suck!'

S: <*students laugh*>

Y: You don't want to say that directly so instead you say, Oh I have a bit of a stomach-ache, so I'll pass for now . . . so, sometimes it's true but sometimes it's just a *white lie* out of politeness . . . polite? Polite? Understand? Alright, so listen while I read this conversation to you so you can hear so I'm pronouncing everything <*Instructor Y reads conversation model on p. 64; students listen and read textbook page quietly*> Alright, so now we're talking about specific language you can use to reject some food that somebody is offering to you . . . the first one says I don't care for broccoli . . . I don't care for broccoli . . . alright so people in Korea think that English doesn't have honorifics like *jon-daet-mal*. But we do have something like it and this is a good example of that . . . so maybe you are sitting at the table with your boss or your manager or somebody use a higher social standing so you want to be careful how you say things so if you say 'broccoli sucks!' that's really strong kind of a strong, rude 'banmal' (friend speech) sound . . . so you might want to say I don't care for broccoli it sounds nicer and is less harsh <*Students collectively saying*> Ahh! <*mumbling together in realization*> Alright let's look at the second one – coffee doesn't agree with me . . . So if you look at that picture in the cloud she is thinking what is she doing <*holding up the textbook and pointing*> she says coffee doesn't agree with me . . . what do you think? what is she saying? <*Instructor Y is holding his hands to his stomach in a display of discomfort*>

S: can't take it? Don't like it?

Y: what about a physical discomfort?

S: sick?

Y: If you want to be really direct and kind of rude, you could say it gives me diarrhea, but being so specific can make other people feel uncomfortable, so you want to say it doesn't agree with me it is applied more agreeable way of refusing it . . . My body is a bad reaction to coffee . . . OK, the next one – I'm a vegetarian . . . this is pretty simple . . . everybody knows that? <*students nod*> OK, the next one – I'm on a diet? I'm trying to lose weight . . . I use this one a lot I'm always a little bit fat here <*grabbing his stomach and spare tire*> so if somebody invites me to dinner and I don't want to go I usually say: Oh, I'm on a diet! Sorry! The other thing that you can say is: I'm trying to lose weight so this is a good way to reviews and the opposite is I'm trying to gain weight . . . <*writing on the board*> Alright, in Korean some of you are translating directly from Korean so you might say I'm trying to lose my weight but in English we don't use that we don't say I'm trying to lose my weight or I'm trying to gain my weight or you are trying to lose your weight . . . OK, next time avoiding sugar that's pretty easy an I'm allergic to chocolate . . . do you understand these words avoiding an allergic I'm allergic to seafood you understand that *<students nod>* Alright, in the next page *<students turning the page>* OK, here at the top it says 'grammar' – grammar! Alright, before the mid-term exam, you remember we talked about the difference between *acquisition* and *learning?* so if you were the teacher of this class, a class about practising English communication, would you spend a lot of time on this?

S: No . . .

Y: I'm not going to but let's be fair that grammar is not 100 per cent useless in these language communication classes in fact it is extremely important but I would normally focus on this as homework rather than put it in class time because our time together can be more profitable another stuff *<students nodding and some taking notes>*29:00

Y: Alright, pass, pass, let's move on to the next page *<students turning the page>* So, talking about food passions so just before you were talking about rejecting food but now you're going to talk about something you really, really like . . . *<students and instructor practice the dialogue together; instructor is so much in control at this point that he doesn't require to inform the students, he merely gestures for everyone to collectively play the other speaker in the model dialogue on p. 66 (see Figure 2)>* . . . And the last sentence is well I couldn't live without it . . . and that's pretty much true for myself too! Alright, let's talk about things that you're passionate about . . . so I'm crazy about seafood . . . look at the picture . . . I'm crazy about . . . Something

S: really like

Y: Yeah, so if you say something like mania . . . a maniac is somebody who's like crazy about something . . .

S: Ah

Y: OK the next one I'm a big meat eater a big coffee drinker a chocolate addict a pizza lover So that means I eat a lot me that drink a lot of coffee so when do you see the words an emphasis here it means pay attention to those . . . for me, I'm a big *Gamjatang* (Korean – pork rib stew) eater . . . *<students laughing>* I had Stew last night i had stew last week I think I'm going to have stew tomorrow! *<students are pleased and suddenly more attentive>* So, you know addicted to something? Like alcohol or drugs? So, we're talking about this word *<writes hyperbole>* So, if you see your chocolate addict it's not like you're shaking because you need chocolate but you are speaking hyperbole . . . and these ones focusing on food people speak this way . . . but you can use these expressions for anything really so for example . . . I can't stand country music, I can't stand traffic jams, I'm not crazy about chocolate, so it means I can eat it if offered but I don't really seek it, I don't care for steak and I'm not much of a pizza eater and I'm not much of a coffee drinker . . . alright so does everybody understand these? <*students nodding taking notes*> Alright, let's move on to the next page because we're running at a time And I want to focus on this next part <*students turning the page*> 33:00

Y: this page is something different . . . Please get a partner and practice . . . this should only take you a little while <*the students appeared to know what to do because the instructor has not given them any instructions . . . this suggests that the students are used to a particular routine. The instructor walks around the room to help and/or participate in the conversations that are being created by the class. This portion of the class is concluded with students passing the created and recorded dialogues to the instructor*>

   <*Students actively talking among themselves and with Instructor Y*> 45:00

Y: OK, let me get your attention please, we're just about out of time . . . Alright, so during this class, our goals were to make excuses declining food, talk about food passions, discuss lifestyle changes alright so in this discussion topic we didn't have a lot of chance to talk about everything if we had more time we would talk about more topics but that's good enough for today well done everyone and thank you very much for participating. Any questions?

   <*Students shaking heads*>

Y: Alright thank you! <*Student applause*>

Appendix C

Instructor X – Interview Transcript

C = Researcher

A = Instructor X

C: So, how long have you been teaching university EFL classes?

X: about 18 years . . . I came here in 2000

C: What kinds of EFL classes do you commonly teach or have taught in Korea?

X: I've taught extra English classes on multiple levels including high school. . . . I have also taught US cultural studies class and this year I started doing English composition for journalism majors.

C: So, from those, what kinds of classes you prefer and why?

X: I think my favorite one was US cultural class . . . that was my favorite one and that was a graduate class too . . . so the students were fairly high level . . . also I like basic conversation classes because the discussions are fun to do . . . stimulating . . .

X: So, what is your education and training, then, for this job at the university? Do you feel qualified?

X: I have a bachelor's degree in international relations and I also double majored in history with an education degree in each. . . . International relations is probably one of the best side or peripheral degrees one could have as an ESL or EFL educator . . . yeah it definitely helped with my conversation and composition classes . . . do I feel qualified? Yeah I guess so . . . I don't have the know-how of a lot of theory but I've been learning as I work . . . developing style in class, watching other professors and so on . . . I think the time spent here has made me qualified . . . so yeah . . .

C: Right . . . So, what do you think of global English education and your role in it . . . do you feel you are adequately contributing to Korean university education? Do you think of those things, especially when you're teaching the class? Do you think about what you do and how it affects the students?

X: Yeah sure I definitely think about all of that . . . I think my role helps the students . . . especially in Korea when students are working really hard to make something of themselves . . . and I think the majority of university students I think the best thing for them to do is get the heck out of the country . . . I generally advise them to get into some international engagements. . . . Find something that involves English in some way to get their exposure for the language . . .

C: I think getting out of the country is just generally opens your stubborn mind because I've seen so many close minded people in my world back home in Canada, where people think that nobody is racist and where people haven't left their hometown in 40 years, suddenly their whole personality changes with that kind of international exposure

X: Koreans in general are pretty well travelled now so that's a good thing for their exposure but they need more

C: So, how do you perceive your students with respect to their EFL capabilities? And . . . how do you think Korean culture contributes to your assessment of their capabilities in EFL learning?

X: most of my students are Korean English speakers . . . you know what I mean? . . . their culture is really strong so it overshadows their grasp of some stuff we cover . . . I repeat lessons and they seem to get stuck on all the same sh** that students got stuck on 18 years ago . . . it's all the same issues . . . and when I try to interview them or test their speaking abilities they're all shy and giggle in class . . . it is like nothing has changed in two decades . . .

C: What practical situations do you think your students use the English that you are teaching in class?

X: Well, in terms of English . . . most of my students who actively study it . . . maybe they wanna have friends or improve their social life political life and economic life and there are a lot of international students here who spend a lot of time outside of class communicating in English for those reasons and a lot of students get jobs where they have to speak English quite a bit with foreigners who come to Korea or in foreign locations so I think they really need a strong motivation for learning

C: OK so in a typical class describe how you use the textbook or any textbook? Do you use the visual content a lot? Is it useful?

X: I actually do use a textbook in all of my classes because it gives me a base from which to work from . . . and often I have students who are super low level and if I don't have something for them to look at . . . then they'll just space out and not pay attention or not fix their attention to . . . the visual content helps in that way I guess but I don't give it a lot of attention . . . and the class is useless for them, the low level students, so the textbook is a base from which to build for the variety of the levels of English among my students

C: So, do your students ever comment or talk about the visual content or the multimodal content in the textbook at all?

X: What do you mean by multimodal?

C: Multimodality in discourse refers to multiple modes of meaning making or the assumption that meaning in discourse is from the combined meaning that is generated from text or image . . . all things together . . . colour, shape, composition, font . . . how all those things emphasize or de-emphasize stuff in the book . . . including the text . . .

X: ahh ok . . . well, most of the books I use, like this one don't really have any useful pictures . . . but I do use PPT presentations that are designed by myself and a lot of my classes are visual but its generic visualizations for these students . . . they give examples for certain vocabularies and so on . . . PPTs are so effective so I do you use a lot of visual stuff in those . . . yeah I use a lot of visuals because visualizations really draw their attention and forced them to think . . . there's a lot of information that goes into visualization that is useful for the classes and class participation . . . it generates more content on its own . . .

C: So, what is your opinion of the visual content in the book?

X: Well, like I said, not very useful but . . . well . . . it's very colourful and well-designed I suppose . . . and eye catching . . . you can tell that the designers want to use advertising or design techniques to make everything balanced . . . that's about all I feel about that . . . I haven't really given it much thought because most of the material I use are black and white excerpts from books like these . . . I like the food pyramid though because when i told them to discuss or having a discussion about it they have pictures to look at and they can talk about it, but I feel it's not enough . . . I feel like if it were different pictures it might be better

C: So, do you think the visual content is helpful to you or is it inconsequential?

X: Well I don't know it depends on the situation but if the books have it . . . I'll use that but if the books don't have it . . . I'll just use my own in PowerPoint presentations because I think visualizations have a place in conversation classes because they inspire speech and communication and translation of concepts to verbal oral practice

C: So, how do you relate to the visual content in the textbooks is it familiar to you? Is it intuitive or counterintuitive to your culture?

X: It's definitely in tune with our culture because . . . meaning western culture . . . for example, in Unit 6, the food pyramid is something we use in the United States . . . So yeah that's pretty normal

C: yeah me too as soon as I saw it, I instantly knew what it was . . . do you feel the students felt that way as well?

X: Well, sort of because in Korea they have a food pagoda . . . so they may have translated that as such . . . but I'm not really too sure if they felt the kind of familiarity that we might feel, looking at the book . . . which is ironic because they're the ones that should come to learn some of the images . . . so I'm wondering if the textbook publishers got it the wrong way around?

C: Good! Yeah, I ask the same . . . okay, so, last 2 questions . . . what cultural demographics did you notice in the multimodal content?

X: You know, I didn't really notice any, to be honest, I didn't really pay attention . . . I didn't really look at what nationality or race they may have been . . . I'm sure there were some . . . in fact, I now that I recall, there were but I didn't really pay attention to any of that stuff . . . and I bet it would be important to the students, you know, because to me it's not important but I have to be aware of what the students want or require . . . but, as you know, there is that weird Korean thing . . . where white equals good and brown equals bad

C: Yeah that's called whiteness theory . . . that's a very real area of research with some literature associated with that . . . especially in critical research of textbooks . . . and you can see how it appears in a lot of textbooks . . .

X: that's right . . . then the Let's Go series of books in Korea have a lot of that . . . all of the kids are roughly the same colour and even the kids that are roughly depicted as darker skinned are not really darker skinned, they are only slightly tanned . . .

C: Would you change anything in the book? Did you think any of it is not useful?

X: Um, I don't know . . . the conversations, most of the times, are touch-and-go because they feel contrived or not real speech . . . but I guess they're kind of useful for students to initiate back and forth banter in class to practice speaking so they can develop their own voice . . . However, if something appears anachronistic like an older expression, I'll see a lot of that in the books and bring it to the attention of the students. . . . Like if I say 'I don't know it doesn't agree with me' I'll tell the students that's an old way of saying it like coffee doesn't agree with me . . .

C: Yeah, I would never discourage teaching that . . . yeah some of the text appears older but the nuances of the expression is presented as an alternative to being rude in a social situation . . . so some students appeared to like that. . . . Do you agree?

X: Yeah, that's right it's an old expression but some people like to say that . . . and for Koreans, these are good lessons because they connect with their culture . . . because it's not polite be rude!

<Laughter>

C: Indeed, being rude is rather impolite! Ok . . . So, generally speaking, do you think if the visual content were Korean specific would it make your jobs easier or would it be better for the students?

X: Nope, A lot of my PowerPoint examples I do a lot of comparative examples of American cities American food and Korean cities in Korean food and also for international students i used their cities and their cultures and their food . . . relevance is also subjective to their particular motivation to learn for most of the students they want to learn because of a socio economic reasons but some students are only in class because mom told them to be there.

C: OK, OK that's great! Thanks a lot, I appreciate your time today.

Appendix D

Instructor Y – Interview Transcript

C = Researcher
Y = Instructor Y

C: Alright, how long have you been teaching Korean university EFL classes?

Y: About 20 years, except for a small hiatus to Thailand for a year.

C: Right, right . . . and what particular EFL classes do you commonly teach?

Y: Well, apart from the academy where we met, I've been at the one university for more than two decades. Also, the odd side gig teaching executive programmes with government training programmes for the summer vacation . . . government officers English training . . . that kind of work . . . in my department at the university, it is English Education so, in addition to communication course, I do English language learning pedagogy . . . then for students of other departments, I'll just teach whatever basic English classes they need which is just required freshmen education . . .

C: Right, so which ones do you prefer? The communication or the pedagogy?

Y: Well it depends on the group, but I tend to enjoy the pedagogy more than the communication because I often have to explain why I don't always follow the curriculum the administration makes.

C: So, you prefer pedagogy because its . . .

Y: Yeah, it's my class . . . I choose the books and class resources and design the curriculum . . . that autonomy makes life a lot easier . . . the crap they usually make us use in conversation classes is more of a hassle than its worth . . .

C: right . . . ok let's come back to that . . . so, your education and training is . . . an MA in general? And do you feel that qualifies you for this position at the university?

Y: It an MA in humanities from Cal-state . . . and yeah, I think I'm qualified requirements are met . . . my experience helps me . . .

C: OK, describe what you think about global EFL learning and your role in that like . . . so its kind of a big question . . . like is it just a job for you or is there something more to that? And whatever the case may be, do you feel like you make a difference in Korean EFL education?

Y: Oh yeah, in the beginning it was just a . . . a way to explore Asia . . . just a foothold in Asia . . . in my second year in Korea I stepped up to university and I started understanding you know this is a career . . . you need to take it seriously . . . you can't just come in here and screw around and do something to get by the day everyday . . . and they gave me these pedagogy classes and . . . I didn't know anything at all about English as a foreign language pedagogy . . . I did take the teachers exam in the USA and I did take some specialty area in English education . . . but I didn't have any special or higher academic training in theory, I just used my general knowledge to pass the tests . . . so, after I got into university here, I started realizing they really expected me to know what I'm talking about . . . so, I went around buying all these pedagogy textbooks and burying myself in them over a couple of years . . . in fact I researched applied linguistics programmes in American schools and tried to teach myself some of the courses . . . and that's how I discovered a love for Krashen's work . . . first, I did this broad overview of English pedagogy and then I figured, like, 'how can I use this improve my effectiveness in class or in my classes?' and so that's when I started to figure out the practical application of Krashen's theories and hypotheses and applying them in the classroom . . . I started implementing them in all of the classrooms, actually . . . so, I teach some of the basic writing classes and some of the basic conversation classes, but I also teach pedagogy classes . . . so when I teach the pedagogy classes most of the foundations are like a spinner of other people's work on Krashen . . . so I teach them with amendments . . .

C: Very interesting . . . I think I had a similar evolution . . .

Y: Yeah, It's really interesting . . . because I've been here for a couple of decades and I watched myself evolve from someone just doing a job to someone who actually cared about my work and I think a lot of us actually went through that transformation . . . I'm not sure . . . like, I'm speaking for Dale but I don't think he had a teachers degree . . . he didn't really plan on coming here . . .

C: Yeah, that's right. He's got a great work ethic though and does his best with international relations background . . .

Y: Right, work ethic . . . Right . . . work ethic.

C: Alright, so, how do you perceive your students with respect to their EFL capabilities? How do you think Korean culture contributes to your assessment of their capabilities in EFL learning?

Y: Culture is everything here and where sometimes it is helpful, in terms of a Korean's dedication to learning form, it also mitigates their grasp of function.

Like, if one foreigner like us stands on the street corner eating an ice cream cone, then they must think that all foreigners like to eat ice cream beside roads. That's how they think of English . . . they're constantly looking for all the rules of social behaviour and etiquette that they have ingrained in Korean upbringing . . . but sometimes they can't grasp speaking . . . I kind of think, like, that's the whole reason why we are here. Korean teachers teach grammar and we are here to help them use that stuff naturally...

C: Great . . . ok then how do you think they use the English we teach them?

Y: *<shrugs>* Nothing? Online? Who knows . . . I certainly don't see or hear anyone using English outside other than to say hello to me or chat online in video games or something . . . but maybe people like Seung Joon (a common friend) use it as a lingua franca when he goes to Brazil on business.

C: Yeah, I hear ya' . . . So, you actually answered several questions . . . so, that's what I wanted. . . . To get to the heart of the matter . . . did the visual content of the textbook help you effectively in negotiating the content and teaching a lesson that day . . .

Y: It helps somewhat . . . you know the first page with the food pyramid visually help the student situate the context of the lesson and put together their ideas. . . . As far as the graphics . . . I can only think of one image . . . so that's all I recall

C: OK, so . . . in a typical class, describe how you use the textbook. Do you prepare lessons then teach them?

Y: Usually, if I'm going through a textbook that I have to use, like in the basic conversation classes here on campus, I'll look for things that are useful that I can use and when I can't find them . . .

<laughter>

. . . I look for grammatical functions that I think I might be able to repurpose into my own activities . . . you know, make them relevant in live speech . . .

C: Alright, so what about the visual material then, is the inconsequential? Do you repurpose, as you say, any of that?

Y: So far, I haven't . . . but the visuals are usually there to just make the material seem more meaningful or relevant in a communicative situation . . . like a picture of two people in a café or something . . . but I've never given 'em much attention unless, like, an aside to emphasize when or where some of the language might be used . . .

C: So, how did the students react to the lessons you use from those books?

Y: They're doing what I expected them to do . . . it's hard to know their true feelings because I think, sometimes, they're just playing a role . . .

C: Yeah, I felt the same, like, they will make good efforts in class but outside class they probably don't give two thoughts to my class until they have to show up again . . .

Y: Yeah, as far as the lesson really being personally meaningful and engaging . . . I don't think it was happening very much . . . most of the content is counter intuitive to Korean culture anyways . . . almost all of it, I'd say . . . but at the end I started the discussion . . . we were talking about saturated fat bombs like instant pizza and stuff like that and they appeared to be a little more engaged and interested . . . but I also think and feel that they were playing a role to appear to be engaged rather than actually being engaged.

C: Okay then, you answered another question so . . . then, back to my other question, did you find any of the visual content to be affective towards the lesson? Like in class, I mean . . . could you have done without it?

Y: Definitely could've done without it, yeah.

C: Would that be a marker of your style then? To use material as little as possible then let the class guide itself or something?

Y: Yeah, for conversation? Yep, yep . . . using minimal materials and pretty much use my memory and repertoire with the students . . . I might use the board . . . and establishing a direct line of communication with the students without using a book or anything like that

C: Are there any cultural demographics that appeared more prevalent in the textbook than any other?

Y: Oh yeah . . . from what I could see they didn't try to represent every culture . . . generally speaking, like Asia . . . but there appeared to be regional cultures or ambiguous types of cultures that were non-stereotypic but in doing so they were not affective . . . or appeared to be non-realistic . . . I think I tried to cover it all but I don't think it really made a difference . . . it did not feel effective . . . like I don't think any of the Asian images in the book contributed to students' interest in the lesson . . .

C: Do you think a lack of Asian imagery in the book or a lack of culture to which the students could identify is an issue?

Y: Alright, when I think it would've been more personally meaningful and engaging to the students if they were giving something specific about Korea vs. another culture . . . I think the book is trying to pander to a global audience and it so watered-down potatoes really mean anything to anyone

C: Do you think if the visual content were Korean specific would it make your jobs easier or would it be better for the students? Would you change anything to make it better for you?

Y: When I'm making my own materials for my classes, I used the Korean local newspapers usually or if there's like a CNN or BBC story related to Korea or something like that, you know, they are embedded in this culture . . . where it is like, them against the rest of the world . . . and their kind of isolated here in this little peninsula and that's the way they are thinking about the themselves . . . Korea vs. the world. . . . So, I think it's really important if you're going to engage them . . . it's very, very helpful, and very, very relevant to situate them . . . situate their lessons and keep each in perspective . . .

C: So, you read my proposal for this research . . . you know I'm drawing attention to the visuals these kinds of books publish . . . can you share anything else?

Y: well, in roundabout way, it sounds like the visual content of the book is sort of a non-issue . . . which can be a benefit to the students . . . because if it were an issue, in other words, if they were concentrating on it, because it is so western . . . there is almost like a forced compliance just think in a western way preventing them from developing a new identity with the language to which they're learning

C: Yeah, that's the inspiration for this research . . . are these books impactful? So, it sounds to me that even though we feel the books are terrible . . . it doesn't matter because of the way we would teach them . . . and the way I saw you were negotiating its contents in the video . . . mitigates any marginalization the students might feel . . . do you agree with all of that?

Y: Yep, so you know something that the learners could benefit from . . . almost anything, if you have the right teacher using the right approach . . . can achieve that . . . I don't really think the images and the other modes are significant . . . they're just something to look at, blow by, and turn the page . . .

C: Thanks.

Appendix E
Student X1 Interview

C = Chris

X1 = Instructor X's first volunteer student

C: Describe what do you think about English learning in Korean society?

X1: I've seen a lot of people around who do just as much as the TOEIC requires. People who are greedy for foreign languages seem to go to private academies or study on the Internet.

C: What is the difference between high school English and university English classes? How you feel about English learning in Korean university?

X1: High school English is a lot of studying to read short passages quickly and to pick the answer from one of the five. For the testing. It's not a very difficult grammar to ask for, so it's less burdensome than reading questions. Most of the English classes I learned in college were active through direct participation. There was a time when I freely chose the topic and presented it in English, and I had a lot of time to talk about it through team play. It's a class that learns how to speak English, so I think I can use it more effectively when I go abroad or meet foreigners.

C: Is English important to you? Why or why not?

X1: I didn't really feel that English was important until high school, but when I became a college student, I actually went on a trip to Europe during vacation and felt that English was useful. And I feel important because there are so many places in Korea that ask for TOEIC scores when Koreans get a job. And I feel cool when I see people who are good at foreign languages such as English.

C: Describe what kinds of English learning are interesting and/or boring for you?

It's fun to have a class that introduces Western culture or brings out a free story. It's really fun to get to know a new culture, and I can freely think about it even if I'm not good at it! A class that lists and explains grammar all the time, or a class that reads short passages . . . I'm tired of doing enough in high school.

C: Explain how and when you might use English in your daily life?

X: I usually use English when I study for civil service exams or do homework for English conversation classes. I rarely use English when talking in real life.

C: In your English class in university, how often do you use the textbook?

X: I write it almost every time. I use scripts a lot. I have to go home and read a separate textbook after watching the quiz every time.

C: Do you think the pictures in the textbook lessons are good? Informative? Why or why not?

X: I prefer books with a proper mix of pictures to hard textbooks with only letters.

C: How helpful are the pictures of the textbook lesson for helping you understand the lesson?

X1: It's a tool to help you understand the situation when you look at a script. Other pictures help you become more immersed in your book.

C: Do you enjoy the textbook's lesson activity? Why or why not?

X1: I don't enjoy it that much. Textbook activities are also textbooks anyway. It's not that interesting to me that I have to do something set.

C: How do you relate to the cultures portrayed in the textbook? Are any Korean people represented in the visual representations? Can you imagine any Korean person in any of the situations presented in the lessons?

X1: It is not very strange because there are many Western cultures in Korea, too. Few people in the textbook seem to look like Koreans. It is possible to imagine Koreans in any of the situations. However, it does not seem natural to enter a culture that is out of touch with Korean life.

C: Describe how Instructor X used the pictures in the textbook.

X1: When the professor describes the situation, he explains it with words, but I can understand it better by using the picture in the textbook.

C: What cultural groups appear to be most represented in the textbook lesson? (For example: Asian people, white people, etc.). Are there any Korean characters? If not, do you think Korean characters would make the lesson more approachable/enjoyable? Why or why not?

X1: It's a cultural group living in the U.S. I don't think it's a Korean character. If there are Korean characters, it will be more accessible to the culture, so it will be a good idea to understand the class without any pressure.

C: Regarding the pictures in the textbook, how would you change the content to be more enjoyable or satisfying for learning English?

X1: I think I'll select and add images of both Korean and Western cultures. I think I'll use pastel colours that will give me more stability than original colours.

C: Do you have any general comments about pictures in your English textbook?

X1: That's the same as 13 answers. This is a personal add-on, and I'd like to reduce the amount of extra information in the textbook in too small a print. It doesn't seem necessary. I hope these answers will help. Thank you!

Appendix F
Student X2 Interview

C = Chris

X2 = Instructor X's second volunteer student

C: Describe what do you think about English learning in Korean society?

X2: Uh, it is essential? . . . to enter a good school? . . . or get a good job? OK, but . . .

C: . . . but?

X2: No. just OK . . .

<laughter>

C: Ok, don't be nervous. It's OK . . . you are helping me a lot . . . so, what's the difference between high school English and university English classes? And . . . how you feel about English learning in Korean university?

X2: Yeah, OK. Uh, in high school, learning English usually focuses on the grammar and the reading comprehension, and in college, learning English seems to be focused on conversation.

C: So . . . how do you feel about that . . .

X2: Yeah, it's good for the communication and the job . . . but it is not really useful to me.

C: Why do you say that?

X2: Um, I think the English class is good and I want to know . . . but after school I'm not useful . . . sorry, it is not useful

C: OK, so you said 'you want to know' . . . why? Is English important to you?

X2: Yes, I think it is very important. Especially, Korean society requires high English skills in any area.

C: OK good. So, describe what kinds of English learning are interesting and/or boring for you?

X2: I like the English class that talk and discuss various topics. On the other hand, I do not like classes that teach grammar or reading skills throughout class without giving me a chance to speak English. OK?

C: Good . . . OK that is clear. Umm . . . explain how and when you might use English in your daily life?

X2: I usually use English when I attend English conversation class and when I meet a foreigner on the street.

C: Really? OK, so how often does that happen? Meet a foreigner . . .

X2: Well, never actually!

<laughter>

C: Why did you say that then?

X2: I don't know . . . just, it is nice to do that . . . for the foreigner . . . to meet or help

C: OK, well that's a good reason, I guess. OK, OK . . . So, in your English class in university, how often do you use the textbook?

X2: I use the textbook every class.

C: Do you think the pictures in the textbook lessons are good? Are they informative or helpful to you?

X2: I think having pictures inserted is a way to help the learner. It helps learners memorize better.

C: OK, but are they informative or helpful?

X2: Umm . . . yes, sometimes, I think so . . . yes.

C: OK, yes . . . So, then . . . do the pictures help you understand the lesson?

X2: Umm, OK, for example, when memorizing words, I think the picture is the most important to help. Pictures help to remind me of English words.

C: Do you enjoy the textbook's lessons or activities? Why or why not?

X2: I like the textbook's lesson activity. It creates an opportunity to speak English.

C: How do you relate to the cultures portrayed in the textbook? Are any Korean people represented in the visual representations?

X2: I'm sorry but I don't know about that . . . Um, no I don't know . . .

C: OK . . . Can you imagine any Korean person in any of the situations presented in the lessons?

X2: No, never. They cannot do these things.

C: You mean travel or eat food at a buffet?

X2: I mean it is not normal lifestyle. These things . . .

<student indicates the book in general>

C: OK, good. So, describe how Instructor X uses the pictures in the textbook.

X2: OK, so he likes discussion . . . it creates discussion opportunities with groups while using pictures.

C: OK, so . . . what kind of people appear in the lessons? For example, Asian people or white people, black people . . . ? Are there any Korean characters? If not, Why or why not?

X2: Umm, I think mostly white . . . but . . . I don't know . . .

C: Do you think Korean characters would make the lesson better?

X2: Yeah, I think but usually English language textbooks seem to . . . describe by many foreigners for the English . . . Korean people don't speak the English so maybe the textbook would not be good . . . but . . . you know, popular? I don't know . . .

C: Regarding the pictures in the textbook, how would you change the content to be more enjoyable or satisfying for learning English?

X2: Umm, I think it would be more fun and good if you put in the short cartoons as well as pictures.

C: Do you have any general comments about pictures in your English textbook?

X2: I don't really know but I hope a more realistic picture will be inserted. I don't like pictures now but just my taste . . . maybe OK but . . . I don't know . . .

C: OK thank you for your time today.

X2: OK, thank you for coffee!

Appendix G

Student Y1 Interview

C = Chris

Y1 = Instructor Y's first volunteer student

C: So, can I ask you some questions about your English class?

Y1: Sure.

C: So, yesterday, did you have an English class?

Y1: Yes, with Instructor Y.

Chris: So, can you tell me, how do you feel about English classes in general and in your university?

Y1: Every class about English?

C: Yeah. Just generally. Describe what do you think about global EFL learning then . . . How you feel about EFL learning in Korean universities?

Y1: Actually, my major is English education . . . but we have to take English conversation . . .

C: OK . . .

Y1: Actually, I think some lectures provided by the Korean professors are not that interesting because they all deal with some theories about something hard . . . but I think some lectures provided by the foreign professors are quite interesting and it helps us with the acquisition of language – I think.

C: Ok, how do you feel about the difference between high school English classes and current English classes? Are they the same or different?

Y1: It is almost exactly the same. Yeah. the same. I feel no difference from high school to this situation.

C: In that case, how do you feel about learning styles that are interesting or boring for you? What is something that is interesting and fun about learning English?

Y1: a few days ago, I got a test about checking my learning style. I was determined to be a visual learner. So, I think I need something to see. Like, to see something . . . actually, I don't know about that . . .

C: Do you use any of the English you learn in either high school or university, outside, in the real world?

Y1: Never.

<laughter>

Y1: . . . but, umm, OK sometimes I have friend in USA, and we might talk a bit, you know on Kakao . . . do you know Kakao?

C: Yes, sure . . . I have that.

Y1: ah yes . . . but . . . OK for online game, English is good and help with friends . . . I think I use before . . . but . . . I don't know . . .

C: OK. So, what about the textbook . . . how often do you use it for Instructor Y's class?

Y1: Almost never . . . but he uses the topics and some of the lessons but then we make other activity . . . I think we are supposed to follow the curriculum but Professor change that . . .

C: I see, so, today you used the textbook . . . so what about that? What about the textbook colours and pages? The content? The pics? Generally, what do you think about all the pictures and activities?

Y1: Mmm . . . I don't know . . . but it was a little bit interesting for me . . . but I think . . . for about . . . but I think for elementary and high school students, I think the textbook would be really interesting for them . . . as an adult . . . just yeah . . .

C: So, you think the textbook might be more useful for a younger audience?

Y1: Yes, but not that young because the words are a little bit difficult, I think . . . like portion, for example . . . I think elementary school students don't know portion . . . this word . . .

C: So, the content does not match adult style?

Y1: Content is about middle or high school . . . content is really interesting for them . . . Also, I like 'I don't care for . .' and some things like that . . . that is really useful to me.

C: So, were the visual parts, like the pictures, were they helpful to your learning of English?

Y1: the pictures? Yes. Mmm . . . OK yeah.

C: Alright, well . . . describe how the instructor uses the book . . . does he ever include the visual parts?

Y1: Sure, sometimes . . . but sometimes he makes fun of it . . .

C: How so?

Y1: So, he jokes about the phone . . . in another unit . . . he jokes about how old something is . . . and the book is not up to date . . . like old things in there . . .

C: I see, OK . . . like anachronistic?

Y1: what is this?

C: anachronistic . . . a-n-a-c-h-r-o-n-i-s-

Y1: Ahh yes thank you . . .

<student checking phone>

C: . . . not the right time . . . the image of the phone in the textbook is old so it's not in the right time, that's how we might say anachronistic . . .

Y1: OK thank you . . .

C: Sure . . . OK, so then, are you satisfied with the instructor's attention to the visual parts of the book?

Y1: yes, he explains very clearly but something not exact to the lesson or something, he skips that . . .

C: Oh, I see . . . OK, so, how do you relate to the cultures portrayed in the textbook? Can you imagine any Korean person in any of the situations presented in the lessons?

Y1: OK, yes . . . because reject politely? We learn how to reject politely . . . that is similar. For example: how about go ahead without me . . . rather than 'I don't like drinking coffee.'

C: Yeah, that's the Korean style isn't it?

Y1: Mm . . . yes, so some is good.

C: Ok, so, are there any Koreans in the textbook? Do you see any there?

Y1: Well, there are some Asian people, but I don't think they are Korean.

C: OK, would you like to see more Korean representation in the textbooks?

Y1: No. I think this is enough.

C: Why so?

Y1: Mm . . . I'm not sure but Korean is enough . . . because English book maybe not the right place . . .

C: I see . . . Ok, so, would you change any of the content? If you were a book publisher? Would you change it to be better for Korean students?

Y1: Mm . . . well its good . . . I think . . . but I don't know . . . because I don't know about publishing.

<laughter>

C: OK then, um, did you learn anything fun today? Anything interesting about this lesson?

Y1: I learned portion is the same meaning with serving in this lesson . . . so I like that . . . and . . . I really like the expressions like, 'are you sure?' or 'I'm avoiding sugar' and like 'something doesn't agree with me' . . . this expression is really good. I like that . . . and 'I don't care for broccoli' etc . . . it's good . . .

C: Right, right. They are very helpful . . . OK good. OK then, so did the professor ask you to do some activity related to but not in the book today? Did he do that?

Y1: Ah yes, yes. He did.

C: OK then, so, over all today, were you satisfied with the textbook content?

Y1: Yes, I was.

C: So, would you like to see anything different?

Y1: I think so but not sure . . . any way satisfied . . . for now . . .

C: OK then, thank for everything today.

Y1: Your welcome.

Appendix H

Student Y2 Interview

C = Chris

Y2 = Instructor Y's second volunteer student

C: So, describe what do you think about English learning? How you feel about EFL learning in Korean universities?

Y2: English in Korea?

C: Yes, and generally around the world . . . ?

Y2: Usually I feel something awkward, but it is interesting

C: What about universities? What do you think about English in university?

Y2: because English is global world and we have to learn . . . we usually use in real life or for going abroad so we need that . . .

C: What kind of English learning do you like?

Y2: Anything?

C: Yeah

Y2: Watching the English movie . . .

C: Ahh, why do you like movies?

Y2: just funny and not grammar so interesting . . .

C: OK, so, in your EFL class in university, how often do you use the textbook?

Y2: Almost every class but not too much . . .

C: Would you like to use it more than you do?

Y2: No, Instructor Y is excellent so . . . just follow him . . .

C: Do you think the visual elements of the textbook are helpful or informative to the lesson?

Y2: It's funny but I hope there are more examples

C: . . . more examples?

Y2: Uh . . . for example, there are only a kind of meat or seafood that covers . . . something that some people like that . . . I hope that more detail . . . I hope there is more detail in there . . .

C: OK, more detail . . . so are some of the pictures helpful to you? How helpful are the visual parts of the textbook . . . to the kind of English you want to learn?

Y2: . . . yeah there are not some seafood or cucumber or some food of Korean . . .

C: What kind of Korean foods would you like to talk about, in particular Korean culture?

Y2: Uh, famous food . . . kimchi, bulgogi, white rice . . .

C: So, do you enjoy the exercises and their accompanying illustrations or visual aids?

Y2: sure, enjoy . . . I'm sure that it is very good.

C: How do you do you relate to the cultures portrayed in the textbook?

Y2: Culture? I think not Korean . . . yeah there are no Korean food or other Korean thing

C: Are any Korean people represented in the visual representations?

Y2: yeah no in the picture . . . there is only picture not Korean

C: Can you describe how the instructor addresses the visual elements of the textbook?

Y2: He only uses the activity . . . we only look at . . . pictures but it is not in lesson.

C: Are you satisfied with the instructor's delivery of the textbook visual content?

Y2: Yeah, he is excellent.

C: Of the people visually represented in the textbook, what cultural groups appear to be most represented?

Y2: Mm, maybe western people? . . . I'm not sure because I don't look at that . . .

C: So, you want more Korean food, how about people? Would you like to see Korean people in the book?

Y2: Yes, of course but . . . I don't know . . .

C: Do you think the textbook is necessary?

Y2: maybe not . . .

C: So, do you think the instructor can do without the textbook?

Y2: Textbook is very helpful but not so important maybe? Instructor is the . . . make the class . . .

C: Regarding the visual elements in the textbook, how would you change the content to be more enjoyable or satisfying in the learning process?

Y2: Just, uh, so-so . . . I think . . . I did not think about that before . . .

C: So, overall are you satisfied with Instructor Y's presentation today?

Y2: Yes, of course he's really excellent . . .

C: If you were to make a book for Korean students how would you change it or make it?

Y2: Uh, I would make a . . . many pictures and many more examples to help the students understand . . .

Appendix I
Student Interview Questions

1. Describe what do you think about global EFL learning? How do those opinions compare to Korea? How you feel about EFL learning in Korean universities?
2. Describe why you need to learn EFL in university? How does this compare to EFL learning in secondary education?
3. Is EFL important to you? Why or why not?
4. Describe what kinds of EFL learning are interesting and boring for you?
5. Explain how and when you might use EFL outside of the classroom or after university?
6. In your EFL class in university, how often do you use the textbook?
7. Do you think the visual elements of the textbook are helpful? Informative? A good reference? Adequately assist the lesson? Why or why not?
8. How helpful are the visual elements of the textbook to the kind of English you want to learn?
9. Do you enjoy the exercises and their accompanying illustrations or visual aids? Why or why not?
10. How do you relate to the cultures portrayed in the textbook? Are any Korean people represented in the visual representations? Can you imagine any Korean person in any of the situations presented in the lessons?
11. Describe how the instructor addresses the visual elements of the textbook? Do you feel that the instructor adequately integrates or presents the visual elements into the lessons? Are you satisfied with the instructor's delivery of the textbook visual content? Why or why not?
12. Of the people visually represented in the textbook, what cultural groups appear to be most represented? Are there any apparent Korean characters? If not, do you think Korean characters would make the lesson more approachable/enjoyable? Why or why not?

13. What ethnic or demographic groups/communities appear to be least represented in the visual elements of the textbook?
14. Regarding the visual elements in the textbook, how would you change the content to be more enjoyable or satisfying in the learning process?
15. Do you have any general comments about the visual content in your EFL textbook?

Appendix J
Instructor Interview Questions

1. How long have you been teaching Korean university EFL classes?
2. What kinds of EFL classes do you commonly teach?
3. Describe what kinds of classes you prefer? Why so?
4. What is your education and/or training, conventional or otherwise, to teach EFL in Korean universities? Do you feel qualified to teach EFL in a Korean university?
5. Describe what you think about global EFL learning and your role as an educator? Do you feel you are adequately contributing to Korean university education? Why or why not?
6. How do you perceive your students with respect to their EFL capabilities? How do you think Korean culture contributes to your assessment of their capabilities in EFL learning?
7. In what practical situations do you think your students use the EFL you teach in class?
8. Does the visual content in the textbook help you prepare for a class? Why or why not?
9. In a typical class, describe how you use the textbook. How do you present the visual content with the lesson? Do you ever alter the representations or comment on them in the classroom discourse?
10. Can you recollect how the students normally react to the lessons? Do they ever comment or remark on the visual content?
11. What is your opinion of the visual content in the textbook? Does it assist the delivery of the lesson? Is it helpful or not helpful to the lesson? Why or why not?
12. How intuitive or counter-intuitive does the visual content appear to be to your Korean students? Do they appear accepting of the visual representations or dismissive of them?
13. How do you relate to the visual content of the textbook? Is it familiar or unfamiliar to you?

14. What cultural demographic groups appear most and least represented in the visual representations?

15. Regarding the visual elements in the textbook, would you change the content to improve the lessons? How? Why or why not?

Index

Milton Keynes UK
Ingram Content Group UK Ltd.
UKHW030741040324
438872UK00004B/116

9 781350 256996